A GRIM ALMANAC OF
BRISTOL

A GRIM ALMANAC OF
BRISTOL

NICOLA SLY

ALSO BY THE AUTHOR

A Ghostly Almanac of Devon & Cornwall
A Grim Almanac of Dorset
A Grim Almanac of Somerset
Bristol Murders
Cornish Murders (with John Van der Kiste)
Dorset Murders
Hampshire Murders
Herefordshire Murders
More Bristol Murders
More Cornish Murders (with John Van der Kiste)
More Hampshire Murders
More Somerset Murders (with John Van der Kiste)
Murder by Poison: A Casebook of Historic British Murders
Oxfordshire Murders
Shropshire Murders
Somerset Murders (with John Van der Kiste)
West Country Murders (with John Van der Kiste)
Wiltshire Murders
Worcestershire Murders

First published 2011

The History Press
The Mill, Brimscombe Port
Stroud, Gloucestershire, GL5 2QG
www.thehistorypress.co.uk

British Library Cataloguing in Publication Data.
A catalogue record for this book is available from the British Library.

ISBN 978 0 7524 5934 9

Typesetting and origination by The History Press
Printed in Great Britain

CONTENTS

INTRODUCTION & ACKNOWLEDGEMENTS

While researching my books *Bristol Murders* and *More Bristol Murders*, I came across dozens of dark deeds from Bristol's history, which I kept on file for such a book as this. The true stories within are sourced entirely from the contemporary newspapers listed in the bibliography at the end of the book. However, much as today, not all of the events were reported accurately and there were frequent discrepancies between publications, with differing dates and variations in names and spelling.

As always, there are a number of people to be thanked for their assistance. Jan Oakes of The Web Childhood Museum and Roy Winkleman of the Florida Center for Instructional Technology were particularly helpful and kindly gave me permission to use some of their pictures as illustrations. My husband Richard provided constructive criticism (as well as endless cups of tea) and I would also like to thank Matilda Richards and Anna O'Loughlin, my editors at The History Press, for their help and encouragement in bringing the book to print.

Every effort has been made to clear copyright; however my apologies to anyone I may have inadvertently missed. I can assure you it was not deliberate, but an oversight on my part.

Nicola Sly, 2011

BIBLIOGRAPHY

Bath Herald
Bristol Journal
Bristol Mercury
Illustrated Police News
Ipswich Journal
The Guardian / Manchester Guardian
The Times
Western Mail

JANUARY

A group of Bristol children. (Author's collection)

1 JANUARY

1830 Six-year-old Hannah Jones stayed with her mother's friends, Sarah and John Webb, in the parish of All Saints. While Sarah celebrated the New Year, fifty-five-year-old John raped his young guest, threatening to call a watchman if she made any noise. Sarah Jones had no idea of the outrage perpetrated on her daughter until Hannah became ill and was taken to a doctor, who diagnosed gonorrhoea.

By that time, the visible injuries of a violent sexual assault had long since healed and when Webb was tried for rape at the Bristol Assizes in October 1830, the jury were unable to agree on a verdict. Matters were further complicated by the fact that Sarah Webb (aka Sarah Horwood) had married John bigamously, in the mistaken belief that her first husband was dead. As Webb's wife, Sarah could not testify against him but, if their union was not legal, she could be called as a witness, in which case she should also have been charged with bigamy.

Although the jury eventually found Webb guilty, sentencing was deferred while the legal queries were resolved. Webb appeared at the next Bristol Assizes in April 1831, where he was sentenced to death. His sentence was commuted to transportation for life and he sailed for New South Wales on the convict ship *Isabella*, on 22 November 1831.

2 JANUARY

1861 Coroner Mr J.B. Grindon held an inquest on the deaths of William and Caroline Saunders, who were found dead in bed at their marital home in Hamilton Court. A post-mortem examination conducted on William by surgeon Mr Gardiner showed that he died from 'suffocation by poisonous air'.

A broken gas main was found beneath the pavement, directly outside the couple's two-roomed home. Their bedroom had no chimney but it did have a drain, which ran directly beneath the bed and, probably bothered by draughts, Mr and Mrs Saunders had carefully sealed the window with cork and canvas.

The inquest jury found that, 'the deceased died from suffocation caused by an escape of gas from the public pipe.' Although they attributed no blame to Bristol United Gas Company, the jury voiced their opinion that the dwelling on Hamilton Court was unfit for human habitation and should be condemned.

3 JANUARY

1820 *The Times* printed an account of a highway robbery, taken from *The Bath Herald*. An unnamed labourer was returning to Redland when he was accosted by two men demanding his money or his life. The victim had just purchased a new jacket and had only 7s remaining from his weekly wages, which he refused to hand over. The robbers knocked him down and took his new jacket as well as his money but, since it was a very cold day, they humanely left one of their own jackets in exchange.

When the victim got home, he found a £10 Bank of England note in the pocket of the old jacket, almost certainly the proceeds of another robbery.

4 JANUARY

1873 Brothers Henry and Jabez Holbrook were drinking in The Rose, Thistle and Shamrock on West Street. Henry seemed determined to start a fight with Jabez, who continually asked him to 'sit down and be quiet.' When the brothers' uncle George joined them, Henry began arguing with him too, accusing both men of neglecting their (Jabez and Henry's) father and of not assisting him with money while he was ill.

Eventually, Henry threw a punch at Jabez. George defended his nephew and soon the three were fighting in earnest, until Henry fell onto the fire grate and died within minutes.

Dr R.S. Smith conducted a post-mortem examination and found no marks of violence on Henry, who, having eaten a very large supper, had choked on his own vomit. Since the blows and kicks to Henry's distended stomach caused the vomiting, George and Jabez were charged with his manslaughter.

At their trial on 1 April 1873, the jury decided that Henry had been quarrelsome and aggravating, as he had instigated the fight and struck the first blow. Although they returned a guilty verdict, they recommended mercy, believing the defendants to have acted in self-defence. George and Jabez were each sentenced to three months' imprisonment, with hard labour.

5 JANUARY

1894 As people skated on Duchess Pond, Stapleton, the ice gave way, plunging a young man into the freezing water. James Joseph Verschoyle and his brother Theodore went to his rescue but the ice cracked and James fell into the water, along with another would-be rescuer. Theodore got clear, but the following day the bodies of James Verschoyle (20), William Edward Long (19) and Henry James Pollard (24) were recovered.

At an inquest held at the Barton Regis Workhouse by coroner Mr Grace, the jury tried to establish the order of events. It was dark at the time and nobody could be sure whether Long or Pollard was first to get into difficulty, although, after learning that the first man to fall through the ice had dark hair, the jury surmised that it was William Long. They returned a verdict that Long was accidentally drowned and Pollard and Verschoyle perished while trying to save him. There was much dispute about whether or not the privately-owned pond was open to the public for skating since, if this were the case, the jury felt that there should have been warning signs displayed and

Duchess Pond, Stapleton. (Author's collection)

life saving equipment available. As there was an adjacent public footpath, the coroner took the view that those who ventured onto the ice did so at their own risk, although he agreed that it was unfortunate that there had been no life saving equipment to hand at the time of the tragedy.

6 JANUARY   **1865** At the Bristol Quarter Sessions, twenty-two-year-old dressmaker Elizabeth Wilcox was found guilty of stealing nearly 50 yards of mohair from a shop owned by Messrs Philips and Wearing.

Since Elizabeth already had a previous conviction, she was harshly sentenced to seven years' penal servitude. Addressing the Recorder, Elizabeth expressed her displeasure, saying, 'Thank God, may you break both your legs and your arms. May the Lord paralyse you in all your limbs, you hard-hearted old bastard.'

7 JANUARY   **1924** Twenty-five-year-old Frederick George Noel appeared at Bristol Police Court charged with assaulting Mr Crump, the referee of a football match between Bristol Rovers and Boscombe.

As players and officials returned to the pitch for the second half, Noel leaped out of the crowd and hit Crump, knocking him to the ground. Crump, who suffered a cut to his hand, a grazed knee and a bruised shoulder, generously said that the blow wasn't overly violent and, had he been expecting it, he would probably not have been knocked over.

Noel explained that he was drunk at the time and could recall nothing about the incident. Magistrates fined him £5 or one months' imprisonment.

8 JANUARY   **1879** Coroner Mr H.S. Wasbrough held an inquest at The Dock Hotel, Cumberland Basin, on the death of nineteen-year-old Henry Gunney.

Henry spent the previous evening in the Nova Scotia Inn, with around twenty other men. The men were drinking 'whisky bullings' – water placed in an empty whisky cask – and, according to Henry's fellow drinkers, the water was barely coloured with whisky.

Hotwells and Cumberland Basin, 1928. (Author's collection)

Gunney drank only three or four glasses but was unaccustomed to alcohol and quickly became intoxicated. He was not a troublesome drunk, but by closing time he was asleep in the corner of the bar and nobody could rouse him. Eventually stable boy George Salmon and another of the pub's servants carried him home and laid him on the sofa to sleep off his excesses. Gunney's parents checked on him regularly throughout the night and at four o'clock in the morning, he was sleeping like a baby. At five o'clock, he was dead.

Surgeon Mr L.M. Griffiths carried out a post-mortem examination and found signs that the otherwise healthy young man had consumed a narcotic poison. Yet the only 'poison' in his system seemed to be alcohol, of which there were only slight traces found in his stomach.

Since none of the other drinkers – all of whom had consumed far more bullings than the deceased – seemed to have suffered any ill effects, the coroner suggested that there was something peculiar in Gunney's constitution that made him more susceptible to alcohol than most. The inquest jury returned a verdict of 'found dead', adding that the probable cause of death was alcoholic poisoning.

1869   Twelve-year-old baker's daughter Susan Brown of Stokes Croft was helping her father's employee clean windows. While they were upstairs, twenty-nine-year-old Solomon James Male raped her, holding his hand over her mouth to prevent her from crying out.   **9 JANUARY**

As soon as she could escape, Susan ran downstairs and told her stepmother what had happened and, although Solomon begged Sarah Ann Brown to overlook it 'just this once', Mrs Brown called a surgeon and the police. When Dr Henry Robertson examined Susan and found that she was telling the truth, Male was arrested.

He appeared at the Bristol Assizes in April 1870, where his defence was that Susan had told him that she was older than her actual years and had flirted with him and led him on. Male alleged that Susan had seduced him,

Stokes Croft. (Author's collection)

but the jury didn't believe a word of his explanation and found him guilty, leaving Mr Justice Hannen to sentence him to seven years' penal servitude.

10 JANUARY   1867 Coroner Mr H.S. Wasbrough held an inquest on the death of sixty-three-year-old John Hill, late of Lawrence Hill.

John, a diabetic, lived in abject poverty. Although he had several children, only his youngest, George, made any effort to care for him. John rarely had enough to eat and neighbours believed that he was half-starved. He had no proper furniture and nor fuel for a fire, yet the neighbours' appeals to his children were ignored.

James Barrett heard Hill groaning on the morning of 9 January and found him lying on the floor. With the help of another neighbour, Barrett put Hill to bed. He had no mattress or blankets, just a bed frame with sacking stretched over it, despite the freezing temperature. Barrett made hot tea for Hill, who could barely swallow it. He believed Hill was dying and so went to his children.

George tried to get medical help but doctors wouldn't visit, since John could not afford to pay. John's eldest son earned £3 a week, but refused to pay the doctor and wouldn't permit his wife to give Barrett a blanket for the old man.

A second son dismissed Barrett, saying that he would visit his father 'some time or another'. Hill's daughter refused to provide a blanket on the grounds that she needed all of hers for her children.

George Hill finally found a doctor, but it was too late. John's children promptly descended on the house, taking anything of value, cleaning up the filthy room and even buying a decent bed for the corpse.

The inquest jury wanted to prosecute Hill's children for 'gross neglect'. However, when the coroner pointed out that George had done his best for his father and that nothing could be proved against the other children that would make them answerable in law for their father's death, the jury reluctantly decided that Hill 'died suddenly of an internal illness accelerated by want and the inclemency of the weather.'

11 JANUARY   1863 Mary Welsh appeared before magistrates charged with being drunk and disorderly and for damaging windows at The White Lion. At ten o'clock at night on 9 January, Mary Welsh staggered into the pub on Gloucester Lane. The other drinkers were disgusted to see that she was not only very drunk, but was also practically naked and urged landlord Mr Pollard to throw her out.

Pollard complied, but no sooner had he ejected Mary than she was back in the pub. Pollard tried again and this time she struggled so much to avoid eviction that she punched her arm through a window, smashing five panes of glass and cutting herself badly. Mary ran off, but was losing so much blood that she swooned and was apprehended by a policeman, who took her to the Infirmary.

Her injuries were so severe that Mr Pollard decided she had been punished enough and didn't want to press for damages at the magistrates' court, even though replacing the windows had cost him 2s 6d. Thus Mary was merely cautioned about the effects of constant drinking and then discharged.

1872 Coroner Mr Gaisford held an inquest on the death of policeman George Phillips, who died near Sea Mills Station.

On 9 January, Phillips and Acting Sergeant Stevens were walking back to Shirehampton from Fishponds. When they got to Coombe Dingle, Phillips stopped and Stevens walked on, expecting Phillips to catch up with him very shortly. However, Stevens reached Shirehampton alone and, after three hours waiting, went back to look for his colleague. Although he searched until three o'clock that morning, he couldn't find Phillips.

Two hours later, three men heard groans coming from a ditch at the side of the railway line and found Phillips lying there, covered in mud and blood. They carried him to Sea Mills Station, where Dr Ormerod found that he had a fracture at the base of his skull, exposing his brain. Too ill to be transported to hospital, a bed was brought to the station waiting room and Phillips was treated by Ormerod and a colleague, Mr Alexander, but died without regaining consciousness on 11 January.

Coombe Dingle, 1904. (Author's collection)

Sea Mills Station. (Author's collection)

The coroner surmised that twenty-three-year-old Phillips was hurrying to catch the 7.30 p.m. train from Sea Mills to Clifton, when he tripped on the signal wires that ran next to the railway line and hit his head. Blood, hair and brain matter were found on the front of the train, which had obviously hit Phillips, knocking him into the ditch where he lay all night in the bitter cold.

The inquest jury returned a verdict of 'accidental death'. Uncannily, on the night of 9 January, before Phillips's fate was known, his wife dreamt that he came home covered in mud and blood, unable to speak to her.

13 JANUARY   **1898** A fire broke out on board the steamer *Xema*, which was moored in Bristol Docks, and cabin boy William Hawkins was trapped by the flames. The crew tried to get to him through a porthole and then cut a hole in the deck, but Hawkins had roasted in the furnace-like heat by the time his rescuers reached him. Once the fire was extinguished, the body of another crew member, Daniel Kidney, was found in the steering gear house.

The fire originated in a paraffin storage locker, which was located very close to a steam pipe. At the subsequent inquest, the jury returned two verdicts of 'accidental death', recommending that flammable substances should be stored away from steam pipes and commending all those who battled in vain to save sixteen-year-old Hawkins.

Bristol Docks, 1905. (Author's collection)

14 JANUARY   **1863** Habitual criminal Ellen Shute, described in the contemporary newspapers as 'a passionate woman', appeared at the Council House charged with wilfully breaking windows and with assaulting the police constable who was called to deal with her.

Magistrates sentenced her to fourteen days' imprisonment with hard labour. On hearing this she put up her fists and challenged anyone to try and remove her from the dock. PC 163, the constable whom she had assaulted, was first to try but Ellen flew at him like a woman possessed, screaming, cursing, scratching and kicking.

It eventually took four policemen to overpower her and remove her to the Bridewell.

1859 The *Porto Novo* returned from Africa with a cargo of palm oil, bar wood, ebony, coconuts and beeswax.

As the ship was being unloaded in Bristol Harbour, labourers James Quick and Robert Muffin accidentally dropped a candle, which ignited some spilled gunpowder in the hold. Both badly burned, they were taken to the General Hospital, while their colleagues set about dealing with the fire resulting from the explosion.

At first it was only a small blaze and the men were confident of extinguishing it. However, as the flames made contact with the highly flammable cargo, the fire burned out of control, defying their efforts to douse it with water. Eventually a message was sent to the fire brigade for assistance.

By the time the fire brigade arrived, there was little hope of controlling the conflagration, which was now threatening other ships. Consequently the harbour master gave orders for all surrounding ships to be moved and decided to scuttle the *Porto Novo*, in the hope of saving some of her cargo.

Holes were cut in the side of the ship but, as well as being highly flammable, her cargo was also very buoyant and she refused to sink. Fed by the palm oil and beeswax, the fire burned so furiously that the entire city was illuminated. Eventually, the fire waned sufficiently for men to cut off the ship's masts in the hope that this would sink her.

The fire burned for more than twelve hours before it was finally brought under control and the ship was completely destroyed. Although the cargo was insured, the ship itself was only partially covered, resulting in huge financial losses for its African owners.

1863 Maria Harvey and her friend walked from Fishponds to Bristol, but the girls got separated and Maria was unable to find her way home. She approached a police constable for directions, who advised her to spend the night at the police station and walk home in the morning.

John Devereux overheard their conversation. He told the constable that he was going to Fishponds, offering to escort Maria home and, against the advice of the policeman, Maria accepted.

They got as far as Tower Lane, when Devereux suddenly knocked her down, covered her mouth with his hand and began to pull up her skirts. Maria screamed and was fortunately within earshot of another policeman, who arrived to find Devereux on top of her and promptly arrested him.

At the Council House, magistrates sentenced Devereux to three months' imprisonment with hard labour and advised Maria to be more careful with her 'nocturnal ramblings' in future.

1863 William Jones (aka Adams) was enlisted in the Royal Artillery by Sergeant Holloway. Later that day, Sergeant Richard Fair enlisted him in the Enniskillen Dragoons.

Having received money on both occasions, Jones then disappeared until he was arrested by chance two days later, having deserted from the 9th Lancers. Brought before magistrates at the Council House on charges of desertion and obtaining money under a false pretence, it was discovered that he had already been dishonourably discharged from the Army.

Jones was found guilty of both charges and sentenced to one month's imprisonment with hard labour.

18 JANUARY

1862 Almost the entire Lovelace family from Kingswood had been confined to bed for several days with fever and diarrhoea. The only person to avoid the illness was two-year-old Ellen.

By 18 January, Lovelace, his wife and their five children were much better, thanks to surgeon Dr Henry Grace, who had prescribed medicine for them all. Grace advised Lovelace that, since he was unable to pay, he should consult the parish doctor if there was any recurrence of their symptoms. As three of the children were not completely recovered, Grace wrote out an order for them to see the parish doctor, noting their complaint as 'fever'.

That evening, the oldest daughter purchased 1lb of fresh butter and 1lb of salt butter from the local grocer. The next morning, everyone but Mrs Lovelace had bread and fresh butter for breakfast and quickly developed stomach ache. For the rest of the day, the family ate salt butter but the next morning, Ellen had bread and fresh butter again and her intense stomach pains developed into sickness and diarrhoea.

Mr Lovelace went to Dr Grace, who gave him a bottle of medicine for Ellen and promised to call in later. Ellen was unable to keep the medicine down and began convulsing. By the time Grace arrived, she was dead. Then precisely the same sequence of events occurred with five-year-old Hepzibah, who ate fresh butter for breakfast and died two days later.

Dr Grace and his son, Dr Henry Grace junior, performed post-mortem examinations on both girls but could find no natural cause for their deaths, so sent the children's stomach contents and viscera to analyst William Herapath for testing.

Herapath found no traces of animal or vegetable poison, but suggested that the butter might have been stored in a zinc vessel and dissolved some of the metal. However, grocer Joseph Hale told the subsequent inquest that the butter had been kept in stoneware or tin vessels, thus this theory was quickly discounted.

With no apparent explanation for the deaths of the two children, the inquest jury eventually recorded that they 'died from excessive purging and vomiting but how that was occasioned there is no satisfactory evidence to show.'

19 JANUARY

1869 The schooner, *Mary Nixon*, was moored in the Floating Harbour and her Captain, Geoffrey Rimmer and his wife, Mary, left the ship in the evening to buy provisions. Afterwards, the Rimmers went to The Royal George Inn, where they enjoyed refreshments. The couple left to return to the ship and nothing more was seen or heard of them until daybreak the next morning, when their bodies were found in the Floating Harbour.

Floating Harbour
and tramway
centre, Bristol,
1920s. (Author's
collection)

At an inquest held later that day by coroner Mr H.S. Wasbrough, it was surmised that Mary Rimmer had stumbled while walking up the gangplank to the ship in the dark and that her husband may have died in an attempt to rescue her. The landlord of The Royal George Inn testified that, while the couple were sober when he last saw them, Mary was rather chatty and merry and he guessed she may have had a glass or two of wine.

With no definitive explanation for the two deaths, the inquest jury returned an open verdict of 'found drowned'.

1897 Thomas Cole was a former landlord of The Glasshouse Tavern in St Philip's, who fell foul of the police over allegations that he was permitting betting on the premises. In 1895, Superintendent Wookey of the Bristol Police organised a raid on the pub during a big race and found that the allegations were true.

20 JANUARY

Seventeen people were arrested and, although most were later discharged, Cole was fined £50, the bookmaker £25 and his clerk £10. As a consequence, Cole lost the tenancy of the pub and took a job as a sugar boiler in a confectionery business owned by Mr and Mrs Withey, who also became his landlord and landlady. However, he soon quarrelled with the Witheys and was dismissed from both his job and his lodgings.

On 20 January, Cole went into the Witheys' shop and asked for some nuts. He then went into the back room and, pulling out a revolver, fired at Mr Withey, who bolted through the back door. Mrs Withey dived under a table and was shot in the back, then, before anyone could stop him, Cole ran into the yard and shot himself in the head. He died instantly and a post-mortem examination revealed that he had also drunk at least half a bottle of laudanum.

Cole had frequently talked about his grievances with the Witheys and had also threatened to shoot Superintendent Wookey for his part in the raid that lost Cole his pub. At the inquest into his death, the jury returned a verdict of 'suicide while temporarily insane'. Fortunately, Mrs Withey survived the attempt on her life.

21 JANUARY **1908** American Arthur Hyne appeared before magistrates charged with bigamy. From his dental practice in Clifton, Hyne advertised for a wife, stressing 'no triflers need apply.' On promising to marry a woman from Weston-Super-Mare, he defrauded her of £100 and absconded.

He then married widow Alethea Margaret Stevens, who responded to his advertisements, ignoring the fact that he was already married to Alice Esther Maria Bell of New Cross, London, by whom he had two children. She also overlooked that he had also bigamously married another woman in Dublin during 1906. (Alice, who was in court, knew her errant husband as Albert Charles Weston.) Hyne then left Alethea, taking another Bristol woman away with him. He went to Paris, then to Aberdeen, by which time he had left his lover stranded and had yet another woman in tow.

When arrested, he told police that he was wanted everywhere, claiming to have sired five unborn children in Bristol and adding that he was also sought in Manchester and Aberdeen. However, the Bristol police had him in custody and it was there that he faced magistrates on 21 January. He made a second appearance on 30 January, when the charges against him included obtaining £100 by deception from Bristol woman Kate Matthews, £74 from Miss Collins (who was too ill to come to court) and £400 from Thomas Dack, the father of Alethea Stevens. He was committed to appear at the next Bristol Assizes, where he was found guilty of bigamy and fraud and sentenced to seven years' penal servitude.

After the trial, the Chief Constable of Bristol received a letter from the Chief of the New York Detective Bureau, to whom he had sent details of the case. The American officer named Hyne as George A. Witzhoff, stating that he was wanted in New York for bigamy and that he had swindled numerous women across America.

'We have numerous complaints against him on file and he is wanted badly here,' continued the letter, adding that since the treaty between Great Britain and America did not allow Hyne / Witzhoff to be extradited for bigamy, the American police were investigating the possibility of extraditing him on other charges.

22 JANUARY **1890** William John Brown and his wife Mary Ann appeared at the Police Court charged with causing their children to go out begging on the streets. Seven-year-old Gertrude had already appeared before the Bench the previous week, charged with begging in Park Row, Clifton. She told the policeman who arrested her that her mother had sent her out and, when the constable took her home to Temple Backs, he found the house in a filthy condition.

Before the magistrates, the Browns denied having sent their four children out begging, although they admitted that they had sent them into the streets with matches to sell. Magistrates fined them each 10s plus costs, or fourteen days' imprisonment and ordered the removal of the children to the Bristol City Workhouse.

23 JANUARY **1896** Harriet Emily Elizabeth Ware of Cotham woke at 7.30 a.m. Her husband lay beside her in bed and she gently stroked his face to wake him. The couple kissed and the next thing Harriet remembered was hearing a loud bang and feeling a sharp pain. As Harriet stumbled out of bed and ran to her mother's bedroom, she heard another bang and saw a flash of light. She remembered little more until she came round in hospital, discovering a bullet wound in the lower right-hand side of her abdomen.

Accountant William Henry Ware shot his wife and then shot himself through the heart. At an inquest on his death, the jury were told that he suffered from epilepsy and had been behaving strangely for the past year, making false accusations about Harriet's fidelity and then begging her forgiveness. Harriet was concerned when he purchased a revolver the week before the shooting, but her husband assured her that he intended the weapon as protection against burglars and promised that he would lock it in the safe at work.

The inquest on Ware returned a verdict of 'suicide while of unsound mind'. His wife survived for six days before submitting to peritonitis, a condition caused by the shooting.

1863 Coroner Mr J.B. Grindon held an inquest at The Bacchus, Temple Street, on the death of Sarah Wilmott and her illegitimate son.   24 JANUARY

Sarah had been in service in St Augustine's when she unexpectedly returned home to her parents in Temple, complaining of feeling ill. Her mother wanted to send for a surgeon but Sarah wouldn't allow it, claiming that she had already seen a doctor and been told that she just needed to rest.

After a couple of days, Sarah's mother suspected that her daughter might be pregnant and called in midwife Mrs Farr, who found Sarah bedridden and in a state of exhaustion. She denied having given birth, but a search of her room revealed the dead body of a baby boy under her pillow.

Sarah died within hours and Dr Fryer gave the cause of her death as exhaustion, stating that her baby was premature and was most probably stillborn. The inquest jury returned a verdict in accordance with the medical evidence.

1873 As William Gill delivered coal on Avon Street, a few lumps fell from his cart and were picked up by two little boys, Henry Crouch and Henry Jacobs.   25 JANUARY

This infuriated fifty-year-old Gill, who aimed a kick at Crouch. Next, Gill picked up Jacobs and tossed him into the air, catching him as he fell and shouting, 'Take that you little *******.' He then threw Jacobs up again, but this time failed to catch him, letting Jacobs crash to the ground, his head hitting the pavement with a sickening thud. 'There you may lie,' Gill told him, before mounting his cart and driving off.

Martha Curtis witnessed the incident and remonstrated with Gill, telling him that he should be ashamed to treat a poor little boy like that. Meanwhile, Henry Jacobs was taken home, where he remained unconscious for some time.

Eleven-year-old Henry seemed to recover, to the extent that he was able to return to work. However, he continued to complain of headaches and, after a couple of weeks, was taken to the Children's Hospital. Unbelievably, nobody thought to tell the doctors about his head injury and he was initially treated for rheumatism. When somebody finally thought to mention the bang on

A winter funeral. (Author's collection)

Henry's head doctors determined that he was suffering from concussion, from which he died a few days later.

Gill was charged with his manslaughter and appeared at the Bristol Assizes in April 1873. He denied the charge against him, claiming that it was a case of mistaken identity and that he knew nothing whatsoever about it. Henry Crouch and Martha Curtis both positively identified him as the man who had injured Jacobs, but their accounts of the incident didn't tally, either with one another's or with the deposition given by the victim before his death. The cart was variously pulled by one or two horses and Gill wore either a smock frock or a dark brown coat.

The differences in testimonies were so acute that the jury was forced to give Gill the benefit of the doubt, finding him not guilty.

26 JANUARY **1875** Five-year-old Charles Salmon, of St Paul's, was a sickly, rather delicate child. His parents consulted Dr Fendick, who prescribed medicine, but Charles was unable to keep it down and, since his condition appeared to be worsening, his mother took him to hospital, where he died the next day. A post-mortem examination attributed his death to jaundice and blood poisoning, but his devastated parents were convinced that it was due to the disgusting state of the communal lavatory at their home.

At the inquest on Charles's death, the coroner took a great interest in the water closet, which was in an appalling state according to Mrs Salmon. Mr Salmon told the inquest that he was always the first person to get up in the house and that the smell emanating from the toilet made him feel quite ill, particularly in warm weather. No amount of water would clear the obnoxious odour and a child from the house next door had recently died from unexplained symptoms, which the Salmons believed were connected with their toilet.

Mrs Salmon described a long battle with the Board of Health, whose response was to send a man to throw some lime down the pan, which had not helped. At the request of his jury, who were obliged to go and inspect the toilet and were almost overcome by the stench, the coroner agreed to write an official letter to the Medical Officer of Health.

27 JANUARY **1868** Twenty-four-year-old William Blackmore lived in lodgings on Thomas Street with his six-year-old son, Thomas. The whereabouts of Thomas's mother are not recorded, but William obviously resented having to care for the boy and had a long history of ill-treating him.

His abuse and frequent drunkenness prompted his landlady, Sarah Chibbens, to give him notice to quit her premises and, on 27 January, Blackmore announced his intention of taking his son to the Workhouse at Stapleton. Father and son were seen at four o'clock in the afternoon, walking alongside the River Froome towards the Workhouse, but they never arrived. Two hours later, Blackmore returned to his lodgings alone and said that he had met his sister in Bristol. While he was talking to her, Thomas wandered off and he had lost him. Thomas told his landlady that he had been to four different police stations to report the boy missing.

The following morning, Thomas's body was pulled from the River Froome about two miles from where he was last seen with his father. A post-mortem examination found the partially digested remains of bread and bacon in his stomach, a meal he was known to have eaten at three o'clock the previous afternoon, hence it was estimated that he died between five and six o'clock on 27 January.

Coroner Mr H.S. Wasbrough held an inquest at The Crown and Dove on Bridewell Street, during which Blackmore's long history of neglect and ill-treatment of his son was catalogued in great detail. When the jury learned that William had not reported the boy missing, neither had he spoken to his sister, who had fallen out with him as a result of his brutality to Thomas, they returned a verdict of 'wilful murder' against him. He was committed for trial at the next Bristol Assizes.

His trial opened on 27 March before Mr Justice Blackburn. William vehemently denied having murdered his son and, although the evidence against him was strong, it was purely circumstantial. Having deliberated the case for twenty minutes, the jury gave him the benefit of the doubt and pronounced him 'not guilty'.

1847 The barge, *Endeavour*, sank near the mouth of the Avon during a heavy gale. Captain William Livings and bargeman Mr Powell both drowned. Although Livings's body was quickly recovered, there was no trace of Powell until watermen John Gillet and William Tilly found him lying in the mud at Sand Point on 2 February.

The body was towed back to Rownham Ferry, where it was handed over to PC Joseph Burge. Knowing that an inquest would be needed, Burge tried to find somewhere for the body to rest, while awaiting the attention of the coroner. He approached several public houses, but all refused to allow him to place the corpse in their outhouses, believing that they would be held responsible for the burial costs. Burge approached the relieving officer, who could suggest nowhere to put the body and eventually, Burge was forced to leave Powell lying in full public view next to the wall of the Rownham Tavern, Hotwells. (The policeman did cover the corpse with straw, which he had to pay for out of his own pocket.)

Hearing that the same had happened to the body of William Livings, the coroner called it 'a scandalous outrage upon humanity'. The jury returned a verdict of 'accidentally drowned'.

29 JANUARY   **1863** An inquest was held by coroner Mr J.B. Grindon on the death of thirty-five-year-old John Bull, who died following an incident at work.

Bull was a warehouseman at Phipp & Co.'s wharf on Redcliffe Street and, on 22 January, he was standing talking to a colleague when he was suddenly hit by a 14lb weight, which had fallen through a pulley hole in the loft above where he stood. He was taken to the General Hospital with serious head injuries and died there on 27 January.

The only person in the loft at the time of the incident was a labourer named Selway, who was known to dislike Bull intensely. Selway admitted that he had been near the pulley hole and that his foot had accidentally touched something, which might have been the weight. Although Mr Stiles from Phipp & Co. questioned every one of the workers, all denied any knowledge of how the weight fell.

The inquest jury was left to determine whether Bull's death was a freak accident or a deliberate attack. With no evidence to support the latter theory, the jury returned a verdict of 'accidental death'.

30 JANUARY   **1890** Four teenage boys were buried in an ash heap in St Philip's. Ashes from the city of Bristol were heaped into huge mounds, which were regularly screened, as the waste was used for a variety of purposes, including soap making and masonry. The ash heaps provided a highly dangerous playground for the local children, many of whom were sent by their parents to collect cinders to use in place of prohibitively expensive coal.

Screeners had undermined a large ledge of ash and the boys decided to light a bonfire beneath the overhang, which collapsed on them. Richard Smith (15) was fortunate in that he was buried only up to his waist and, at length, was able to extricate himself and raise the alarm. Although rescuers scrabbled through the ashes with their bare hands, John James Smith (14) and George Shepherd (16) were suffocated. George Milsom (16) was pulled out alive, although badly burned, having fallen onto the fire.

The jury at the subsequent inquest recorded verdicts of 'accidental death' on both boys, adding that strenuous efforts should be made to prevent children from playing there.

31 JANUARY   **1892** Navvy Timothy 'Mad Harry' Franklin was a giant of a man, who gained his nickname by being wild in his ways. At 3 p.m. on 31 January, he was rampaging drunkenly around Shirehampton, shouting and using obscene language. PC Dorrington was summoned to deal with him.

Dorrington tried to persuade Franklin to go home, but Franklin responded with a stream of expletives. Soon the two men were struggling desperately and Dorrington hit Franklin on the head with his staff to subdue him. A large crowd gathered and eventually some men stepped in to help Dorrington and, with considerable difficulty, Franklin was taken to Shirehampton police station.

On his arrival, he was found to have an injury on the left-hand side of his head. PC Vaughan washed away the blood and called in chemist George Edward Glossop, who dressed the wound. Franklin was then charged with being drunk and disorderly and with assaulting a police officer. He was placed in a cell, still ranting and raving.

Regular checks were carried out on him and at nine o'clock, he was seen to be sleeping. At ten o'clock, he was lying unconscious on the cell floor, bleeding heavily from a wound on the right-hand side of his head.

Glossop was summoned again but suggested calling in a doctor. The police sent for Dr Wright, who found Franklin still unconscious, with his pupils dilated and his breathing heavy. Although Wright administered restoratives, Franklin died soon afterwards and a post-mortem examination showed that he had two head wounds, one on each side. Beneath the wound on the right-hand side was a fatal four-inch-long skull fracture.

Wright was unable to determine the cause of the second wound, stating that it could either have resulted from a fall or from a blow. He added that it was very similar to the first wound, which Dorrington admitted to inflicting with his staff.

At the inquest into Franklin's death, held by coroner Dr E.M. Grace at The George Inn, Shirehampton, PCs Dorrington and Vaughan insisted that Franklin only had one wound when he arrived at the police station, as did chemist Mr Glossop. It was theorised that Franklin had fallen in his cell, hitting his head on the floor, wall or bedstead. The inquest jury accepted this explanation and agreed that Franklin's fatal wound had not been inflicted by PC Dorrington.

FEBRUARY

The city centre, 1954. (Author's collection)

1910 Fifty-eight-year-old Joe Gainard died in a fire at Easton Colliery. At the inquest on his death held on 4 February, the jury were told that a candle was accidentally dropped as repairs were being carried out on an engine at the pit. The flame ignited the accumulated fluff and grease beneath the engine and twenty-nine men were cut off by the resulting fire. All were rescued, with the exception of Gainard, who was older and much heavier than his colleagues and who was later found to have been suffocated by smoke.

In returning a verdict of 'accidental death', the jury suggested that the area should be kept cleaner in future and that lamps should be used for illumination rather than candles.

1892 Mrs Perry of Keynsham left a key to her cottage with her neighbour, Emily Jane Lear. That afternoon, the Perrys' lodger called for the key but, while he was waiting for Mrs Lear to fetch it, Samuel Perry came home and began kicking his house door in.

Mrs Lear rushed out to tell him that she had the key, offering to let him in and light the lamp for him, as his wife had gone out.

'You stop where you are and tell her to come and mind her work,' Perry responded drunkenly. Mrs Lear told him that she didn't know where his wife was, then gave him the key and went back home.

Twenty minutes later, Perry walked into the Lears' house uninvited and began to search for his wife. Mr Lear persuaded him to leave, but shortly afterwards there was a loud bang and Mrs Lear realised that she and the baby on her lap had been shot through the window.

William Lear ran outside and told Perry that he had just shot Emily and the baby. Perry threatened to shoot him too, so Lear wisely fled indoors, bolting the door behind him. Perry broke the door open and, for the next fifteen minutes, Lear struggled to prevent him from entering his house, during which time Lear was punched, bitten and kicked. Eventually, Lear escaped and ran to the police station. Meanwhile, as gardener James Cantle was walking past

High Street, Keynsham. (Author's collection)

Lear's cottage, he was confronted by Perry waving his gun around. As Cantle ducked behind a pillar, Perry fired at him, fortunately missing.

William Lear had severe facial injuries, while Emily had shotgun pellets in her left arm and temple. The baby had pellets in the lip and left arm. Samuel Perry, who had previous convictions for violence, was committed for trial charged with shooting Emily Jane Lear and James Cantle and wounding William Lear, all with intent to murder.

Tried at the Somerset Assizes in March 1892, Perry's counsel offered a guilty plea to unlawfully wounding the Lears. Mr Justice Wills agreed that it would be difficult for the prosecution to prove intent to murder and, since James Cantle hadn't actually been injured, the plea was accepted. Perry was sentenced to nine months' imprisonment with hard labour.

3 FEBRUARY   **1858** Before her marriage to clergyman Samuel Smith, Sarah Mills was engaged to John Leech. Their engagement ended when Sarah met Samuel and Leech then married another woman.

In January 1858, Leech received a letter, in which Sarah wrote that she was recently widowed and hinted at resuming their former relationship. Since Leech's wife had also died, he responded enthusiastically. There was a flurry of letters between the former lovers, who agreed to meet in Bristol on 3 February.

When Leech arrived, almost the first person he saw was Samuel Smith. Yet, when he met Sarah minutes later, she argued that Samuel had died six weeks earlier and that Leech was mistaken.

At Sarah's request, she and Leech bought train tickets to Yate and, when they arrived, she proposed that they walk over Yate Common. In spite of a warning that it was too dark from the stationmaster, Mr Suffolk, Sarah insisted that she knew her way. Suffolk lighted them as far as the common, noticing on his return to the station that the couple were being followed by a man. Not long afterwards, Suffolk and his staff heard shouting and went to investigate.

They found Leech grappling with Samuel Smith, the man who had been following him. Smith told them that Leech had attacked him and this looked very feasible to the railway workers, since Leech was covered in blood on top of Smith. By the time Leech had convinced the railwaymen that he was the innocent party, the Smiths were long gone.

They were arrested at their home in Bristol, where several pieces of Leech's property were found in their possession. Mr and Mrs Smith appeared before magistrates and were committed for trial at the next Assizes, both charged with 'maliciously cutting and wounding with intent to murder or do grievous bodily harm'.

The jury learned that Smith had purchased a pistol the day before the attack, giving a false name. In a written statement, which he read out, Smith accused Leech of committing adultery with his wife and said that he had told Sarah that he was prepared to forgive her if she lured Leech to Bristol so that he might have his revenge. Smith swore that he had bought the pistol for protection, never intending to use it.

The jury found both defendants guilty as charged, but recommended mercy for Sarah on the grounds that she had acted under her husband's influence and had committed no violent act. Mr Baron Channell recognised this and sentenced Samuel to four years' imprisonment. Sarah was discharged to appear if called upon in the future.

1881 A private ferry, operated by Albert Gill, had crossed the New Cut at   4 FEBRUARY
St Phillip's Marsh for almost two years. The ferry was attached to a chain but, since the chain didn't span the entire width of the river, a piece of galvanised iron wire rope had been spliced to it.

As Gill ferried four men across, the chain parted and the boat filled with water. Gill and passenger Mr Hamilton were thrown into the river, while the other three passengers, Mr Bevan and his son and Mr Dyer, were swept away on the ferry by the strong current.

Several attempts were made to rescue them, but all were beaten by the force of the water. Eventually, Bevan junior was washed from the boat and swam for his life. He reached the shore by Bath Bridge and quickly raised the alarm.

The gaol ferry was launched and ferrymen Surry and Brownsey waited in the middle of the river for the arrival of the runaway boat. As it passed, they managed to grab Mr Bevan, but Dyer continued down river at a pace. Fortunately, the boat slowed as it neared the Vauxhall ferry and Dyer was rescued in a state of complete exhaustion.

Bevan and Dyer were rushed to the General Hospital and are believed to have survived their ordeal. Gill and Hamilton were both drowned.

1883 Eight-year-old Samuel Cross appeared at Bristol Police Court charged   5 FEBRUARY
with stealing 2s. The complainant was the boy's own mother, Amelia, who told the Bench that Samuel stole the money from a box on the mantelpiece and spent it on fireworks, matches and sweets.

The magistrates were appalled that a mother would bring so young a child before them, especially as Amelia's demeanour demonstrated an utter absence of any kindly feeling towards her son. They immediately discharged Samuel, much to Amelia's disgust. She protested that if the child wasn't 'put away', she would leave him, since she had a living to make.

She was still muttering about the injustice of the outcome when the magistrates ordered her to leave the court, which she eventually did, with Samuel trailing disconsolately behind her.

1900 Thirty-eight-year-old James Rossiter appeared at Bristol Police Court   6 FEBRUARY
charged under the Inebriates Act with being a habitual drunkard. The Bench heard that Rossiter – a married man with several children – had already appeared before magistrates fifty-one times and, since 1884, had spent more time in prison than out. In 1898 and 1899 alone, he had received ten convictions for drunkenness.

The magistrates ordered Rossiter to be detained in an inebriates' home for twelve months.

7 FEBRUARY   **1883** Arthur Henry John Yeo was found in near freezing conditions by a policeman, sleeping in a doorway near Colston Hall.

Eleven-year-old Arthur's mother had died two years earlier, leaving Arthur in the care of his father, who promptly absconded. The boy was taken in by a neighbour, Mrs Long, who kept him without payment for two years until his father returned and reclaimed the boy, only to subject him to abject cruelty.

Arthur was often banished to sleep on a bench in the back yard of his house, while his father entertained prostitutes inside. He was starved, inadequately clothed and often barefoot, his feet running with blood.

At Bristol Police Court, Yeo denied ill-treating his son, assuring magistrates that the boy had a good home and plenty of food. However the magistrates reasoned that, if this were the case, Arthur would never choose to sleep outdoors. He was sent to Clifton Wood Industrial School, where he was to stay until the age of sixteen. His father was ordered to contribute towards his support.

8 FEBRUARY   **1899** Carter Charles Slade tipped some granite chippings at the new Wills' factory, and then set off to fetch another load. As he reached the end of North Street, he realised that people were shouting and pointing, trying to attract his attention to the back of the cart.

Slade pulled up and walked from the driver's seat to the tail of the cart, which promptly tipped up, sending him sprawling onto the road. From his position on the ground, Slade could see something wedged under his cart and, when he checked, he found that it was a little boy.

The child was very shocked but had no obvious injuries. He was able to tell Slade that his name was Worthy Enice Bell and that he lived at King William Street, Bedminster. Slade drove the little boy home, where his mother took him straight to the General Hospital.

House surgeon Albert Paling could find no external injuries but, since Worthy was obviously suffering from severe shock, he guessed that the boy might be bleeding internally. Paling operated and discovered that the bleeding stemmed from a rupture in the child's liver. Although the hospital gave the seven-year-old a blood transfusion, he died from his injuries the following day and a post-mortem examination revealed that a large piece of his liver had been torn off.

Since nobody knew how or when Worthy came to be under the cart, the inquest jury returned a verdict of 'accidental death'.

9 FEBRUARY   **1837** George Brown, John Brooks Knight and John Belcher were detained in the Bristol Bridewell.

In the two weeks or so that the three men were imprisoned, they complained numerous times that their cell was freezing cold and so damp that they could sweep the water off the walls with their hands. Such was their discomfort that they asked to share a cell so that they could huddle together for warmth. The one cot was too small for all three, so they placed their bedding on the floor.

On the night of 8 February, turnkey John Kelly warmed the cell before the men retired for the night, placing a fire in a pot on the bedstead. The prisoners were locked up for the night at six o'clock and by half-past five, all three men were enjoying the relative comfort. The fire was removed when the cell doors were locked but before long, Brown complained of stomach cramps. Belcher told him to try and sleep, falling asleep himself minutes later.

When none of the three appeared for breakfast, Kelly was sent to see why, finding Brown and Knight apparently dead and Belcher groaning on the floor. Surgeon Mr Ruddock managed to save Belcher's life, although his cell mates were beyond assistance.

At the inquest on the deaths, Ruddock stated that the two men had died from suffocation by the 'carbonic acid gases' [*sic*] produced by the fire. With the window and door tightly closed and no ventilation in the cell, the gas, which was heavier than air, sank to floor level and when the men lay down to sleep, its concentration was sufficient to kill them. Had they remained standing upright they would have been fine.

The jury returned a verdict in accordance with the medical evidence, adding that they didn't believe that the Bridewell was a fit place for prisoners to sleep in.

10 FEBRUARY

1900 Catherine Cocking was brought before magistrates at the Police Court charged with assaulting her twelve-year-old son.

Mr E.J. Watson, who prosecuted on behalf of the National Society for the Prevention of Cruelty to Children, told the court that when Peter John Cocking arrived home from school on 5 February, his mother was drunk. Peter filled a kettle to make his father's tea, but his mother took objection to this, cursing him and punching him hard in the stomach. She then tried to kick him as he lay on the floor, but was unable to coordinate her movements, so picked up a chair and hit him with it, cutting his mouth.

The boy's father told magistrates that he had adopted Peter when he was a baby and that his wife persistently ill-treated him whenever she was drunk.

Since Catherine was already bound over to keep the peace, having previously been charged with biting Peter in November 1899, magistrates fined her £1, plus costs or fourteen days' imprisonment.

11 FEBRUARY

1889 Jane and John Withey, along with their four children, slept in the same room of their house in St Philips. At half-past ten at night John was aroused by one of the children screaming out that their mother was bleeding from her mouth and nose.

John called in the neighbours, who found that Jane was dead and set about laying out her body. Elizabeth Nutt positioned herself at her left-hand side and failed to mention to anybody that Jane had a deep stab wound on her left shoulder, which was only discovered when the police noticed blood on the linen sheet beneath her. Rather than dying from a burst blood vessel as her husband maintained, Jane had been murdered and, as the only other adult in the house, John was the prime suspect.

He gave conflicting versions of what had happened that night, suggesting that his wife had been cutting bread and the knife must have slipped underneath her. He told police that Jane had been out, whereas the children said that the whole family went to bed together and he neglected to mention quarrelling with Jane earlier that evening. When the police found the knife concealed in the feather bed, Mrs Nutt admitted that she hid it there 'for the sake of the children' and reluctantly produced Jane's clothing from a bundle of rags, with cuts corresponding to the knife wound. After the inquest on Jane's death, her husband was arrested and charged with her 'wilful murder' and Elizabeth Nutt with being an accessory after the fact.

Tried at the Bristol Assizes, Withey was found guilty and sentenced to death and Mrs Nutt was sentenced to five years' penal servitude. Shortly before Withey's execution, his oldest son, Frederick John, admitted to magistrates that he had pulled the knife from his mother's side. A telegram was sent to the Home Secretary, informing him of this new development and suggesting that the execution was delayed. However, since he had made a full confession to prison chaplain Revd J. Drew, Withey kept his appointment with executioner James Berry on 11 April 1889.

12 FEBRUARY 1895 Warden Mr Sharland of the Barton Regis Workhouse was called to one of the bedrooms at 7 a.m., where he found four inmates lying unconscious.

He immediately tried to bring them round, but it wasn't until four hours later that three of them showed any signs of recovery. The fourth – an eighty-two-year-old retired shoemaker – died later that day without ever regaining consciousness. Surgeon Mr E. Bernard found that William Pierce had suffered gas poisoning and died from apoplexy as a result.

At the inquest on his death, held by coroner Mr E.M. Grace, it emerged that the 18ft x 8ft room was heated by a gas fire, which was left on low overnight in frosty weather. The flame had gone out during the night of 11/12 February and, since the windows and door were closed, the room gradually filled with gas.

The inquest jury returned a verdict of 'accidental death'.

13 FEBRUARY 1879 Ten-year-old Henry Tomlin of St Philip's was poking around in a cupboard looking for a bradawl. He noticed a packet of flour and mentioned it to his mother, who happened to be making a pudding at the time.

The flour was thrown into the mixture and soon the whole family were suffering from sickness and diarrhoea, with the exception of Mr Tomlin, who was working nights and was asleep when the pudding was eaten.

At the Infirmary, house physician Dr James Scott realised that the family had ingested some kind of irritant poison. He treated their symptoms and they gradually recovered, apart from five-year-old Charlotte, who died shortly after her admission to hospital.

Samples of vomit, stomach contents and viscera, along with the remains of the pudding, were sent to city analyst William Walter Stoddart, who found that the pudding contained a massive amount of arsenic. There were also traces in the samples taken from Charlotte and her family. Stoddart was amazed that Mrs Tomlin and the other six children had survived, a miracle he put down to their purging of the poison through excessive vomiting.

At an inquest held on Charlotte's death by coroner Mr H.S. Wasbrough, Mr Tomlin was questioned about the arsenic, which had obviously been on top of the cupboard for some time, since its paper wrapping was black with dust. Tomlin and his family had lived in the house for three years and had not purchased the arsenic, or even been aware of its presence. Tomlin admitted to buying mouse powder, but had burned what was left after using it. Besides, there was far more arsenic in the packet than any chemist would ordinarily have sold.

Since the 'flour' discovered by Henry and mixed into the pudding was obviously arsenic, the inquest jury returned a verdict of 'death by misadventure' on Charlotte.

1894 Coroner Mr H.G. Doggett held an inquest at the General Hospital on the death of fifty-two-year-old night watchman, William Perry.   **14 FEBRUARY**

Although slightly crippled, Perry seemed in good health when he set out to watch a shed on the Welsh Back. His landlord, James Barry, took him some tea just before 11 p.m. and spoke to Robert Matthews, the watchman from the adjacent shed. Mathews told Barry that he had seen Perry just five minutes earlier. However, when Barry went to Perry's shed, there was no sign of him.

He walked from one end of the shed to the other, calling for Perry, but there was no response. Just as he was about to leave, he noticed the toe of a boot peeping out from beneath a huge pile of sacks. When Barry moved the sacks, he found Perry underneath them, standing bolt upright and apparently dead.

Barry shouted for Matthews, who ran for help. The noise attracted the attention of a passer-by Mr Pullen, who tried to resuscitate Perry, believing that he was merely stunned. When that didn't work, Perry was stretchered to hospital, where surgeon Mr J.L. Firth certified him dead.

At the inquest, Firth stated that he had found no external marks of violence on Perry and no broken bones. Yet, at the same time, Perry did not

Bristol General Hospital, 1910. (Author's collection)

look as though he had suffocated. He appeared to have suffered some kind of serious injury and died from shock, although Firth could find no such injury and could not therefore reliably determine the cause of Perry's death. The inquest jury returned a verdict of 'accidental death'.

15 FEBRUARY   **1865** James Pierce appeared at the Police Court charged with stealing furniture from Jesse Lawrence of Redcliff Hill.

The Bench heard that Pierce had lodged with Lawrence and his wife of sixteen years for about three months, during which time Harriet Lawrence, a fanatical chapel-goer, had taken an intense interest in Pierce's spiritual welfare, making it her goal to see him 'saved'.

Sailor Mr Lawrence went on a voyage on 31 January, returning three days later to find that his wife had obviously been interested in far more than the lodger's salvation, since the couple had run away, taking most of the furniture with them.

Lawrence tracked them to Trenchard Street, where they were living as man and wife. Not surprisingly, an argument broke out between the Lawrences and Harriet punched her husband in the face, giving the magistrates a charge of assault to ponder.

With Harriet swearing like a fishwife in the background, the magistrates dismissed the charge of theft against Pierce on the grounds that she had supervised the removal of the furniture from her marital home. Turning to Harriet's assault on her husband, the magistrates asked Lawrence if he would take her back with the furniture.

'Let the young man take her,' retorted Lawrence, although as the couple left the court, he was obviously considering the idea, especially as Harriet seemed willing to mend her ways. The census of 1871 shows them living together in Bedminster with a female lodger.

16 FEBRUARY   **1841** Coroner J.B. Grindon opened an inquest on the death of Caroline Frost.

Caroline was believed to have died from natural causes but, almost immediately after her death, rumours began to circulate that she had been fatally beaten by her husband. The rumours reached the coroner, who decided to hold an inquest, forcing the funeral to be abandoned as Caroline's body was being conveyed to the churchyard.

Twenty-eight year-old Caroline died from a brain tumour the size of a walnut. However, there were also marks of violence on her face and, although doctors were certain that the tumour had caused her death, they were not sure if the tumour had resulted from violence.

The inquest heard that Caroline's husband threw a key at her about four months before her death, which hit her eye and disrupted her vision. Additionally, it was revealed that Caroline was a hard drinker and had been involved in two drunken brawls with other women, injuring her nose and forehead.

The coroner eventually recorded that Caroline died from a brain tumour. As there was nothing to suggest that her husband had beaten her, he was released without charge and the gossips were hopefully silenced.

1900 Charles and Beatrice Compton let rooms in their house in Bedminster to
Cornelius Henry Flowers and his wife Elizabeth. However, due to Cornelius's
fondness for alcohol and his tendency to attack his landlord and landlady
while drunk, he was given notice to quit.

On 17 February Cornelius attacked Beatrice, biting her fingers and, when
Charles tried to protect his wife, Cornelius bit off the end of his nose.

Brought before magistrates at the Police Court, Cornelius denied biting
anyone. He maintained that, four days earlier, Beatrice had got drunk and
attacked him with a brush and that since then he had been terrified of her.
If her fingers got bitten, it was because she put them in his mouth and the
injury to Charles's nose occurred when he fell through a window.

Although Elizabeth Flowers backed her husband's statement, the
magistrates weren't convinced. They sentenced Cornelius to two months'
imprisonment with hard labour, adding that they hoped it would teach him
not to behave like a wild beast in future.

1895 Coroner Mr H.G. Doggett held an inquest at the Beaumont Hotel, St
Philip's, on the death of four-month-old Ernest Percival George.

Ernest was born with a small birthmark on his ear and his mother, Kate,
consulted with Dr Lee, who proposed doing nothing about it. Dissatisfied,
Kate took her baby to the Children's Hospital, who referred her back to Dr
Lee, with the suggestion that the ear might be 'vaccinated'. Lee still refused
to treat the naevus so Kate went back to the hospital, where Frederick's ear
was operated on.

Although Kate bathed the wound diligently, Frederick's ear turned black
and so she took him to another doctor, Michael McDonnell, who prescribed
ointment. Frederick's face became terribly swollen and McDonnell diagnosed
erysipelas – a bacterial skin infection – and although he treated the baby,
Frederick died from septic poisoning.

The inquest jury returned a verdict that Frederick 'died from blood
poisoning, probably due to the operation on the ear.'

1900 Inspector Taylor of the Society for the Prevention of Cruelty to
Children visited the home of Walter Trapnell in Easton and found all seven
of his children barefoot and half-naked. Trapnell was in bed and told Taylor
that he had recently been dismissed from his job for drunkenness.

Having found out that Trapnell's family were entirely dependent on
handouts from the neighbours, Taylor ordered him to get a job, but every
time the Inspector visited the house, Trapnell lay in bed while his wife and
children starved.

Trapnell was brought before magistrates on 28 April charged with
'neglecting his children in a manner likely to cause suffering and injury to
health.' Along with Inspector Taylor, the chief witness against him was his
long-suffering wife, Isabella, who related that her husband was quite happy
to share in any food she managed to obtain, but flatly refused to find paid
employment to support his family. The magistrates succeeded where Taylor
had failed – in sentencing Trapnell to two months' imprisonment with hard

labour, they at least ensured that he would actually get out of bed and do some work.

20 FEBRUARY   1895 Two labourers from the Bristol Gas Company were thawing a frozen gas pipe on Stratton Street, St Paul's, using a torch of tarred rope and a bottle of naphtha for pouring down frozen pipes.

There were about thirty small boys in the area, who ignored the labourers' repeated orders to go away and, while the men were climbing a ladder to inspect a gas light, the boys picked up the torch and began playing with it. One poured the naphtha over the torch and there was a sudden explosion.

Passer-by Henry Thomas Smith saw one boy with his clothes on fire and beat out the flames with his bare hands. He and three boys – Thomas Bentley, Fred Potter and William Scadding – were taken to the Infirmary, where Scadding died from his burns the next morning.

At an inquest held by Mr H.G. Doggett, the main consideration for the jury was whether fourteen-year-old Charles Pring poured the naphtha over the torch out of pure mischief or with the intention of reviving the flame, which had almost burned out. Doggett told the jury that, if the former were the case, Pring would be indicted for manslaughter.

The jury determined that Scadding 'died from shock due to extensive burns caused by his clothes having been set on fire by some ignited naphtha.' The coroner told Pring that the jury had dealt with him very leniently and censured the labourers for their carelessness in leaving the naphtha unattended in the street.

21 FEBRUARY   1888 As labourer Thomas Mogg was walking to work at about 7 a.m., he found an unconscious man on the lane leading to Jenkins's Lime Works in Montpelier.

The man was taken to the Infirmary, where he died three days later without regaining consciousness. He was identified as James Henry Joseph Small (62) and a post-mortem examination revealed that he had a fractured skull.

At an inquest held by coroner Mr H.S. Wasbrough, the jury were told that there were signs that somebody had slept on the top of a lime kiln at the Works. It was theorised that Small was that person. He had seemingly toppled off the kiln and fractured his skull, having been overcome by fumes from the lime. The inquest jury returned a verdict of 'accidental death'.

22 FEBRUARY   1908 Twenty-five-year-old Francis Arthur Brown, the son of the proprietors of The Drawbridge Hotel in St Augustine's, was very depressed following a bout of influenza. Over the past four weeks, his friends had taken several revolvers and pistols from him, which he acquired for the purpose of committing suicide.

Some time previously, Brown was courting a young woman named Cissie, but they eventually parted and Cissie married somebody else and went to live in Cardiff. Now, Brown contacted Cissie Parsons and asked her to meet him in Bristol on a matter of great urgency.

The Drawbridge
Hotel, St Augustine's.
(Author's collection)

On 22 February Brown and Mrs Parsons met at the home of a mutual friend on Stoney Lane. Cissie was later to say that Brown's behaviour seemed 'strange'. He sang a song called 'There's a Home for Little Children', then asked if they could go into a different room, where they could talk privately. When Cissie agreed, Brown shot her before turning the gun on himself.

Although seriously injured, Cissie Parsons recovered from the unprovoked attempt on her life. Her assailant died instantly.

1875 At the Infirmary, coroner Mr H.S. Wasbrough concluded a four-day-long inquest on the death of forty-year-old Ellen Hurley.

23 FEBRUARY

On 26 December 1874, Ellen was drinking in The Goat in Armour on The Quay when a fight broke out between Patrick McCarthy and James Mahoney. Courageously, Ellen stepped between them to try and break it up. A third man, James Keeler, asked 'What do you interfere for?' and told her, 'Keep back.' With that, he punched Ellen in the chest and kicked her heavily on the shin.

Ellen collapsed and was picked up by Mary Taylor, who took her to hospital, where doctors treated a severe cut on her knee. Although they wanted to admit her, Ellen refused, saying that she had young children to look after and insisting on returning home. In February 1875, she developed erysipelas and eventually died.

The inquest heard from a number of witnesses, all of whom gave conflicting evidence. Some stated that they had seen Keeler kick Ellen, but others were equally sure that he hadn't. While most stated that Ellen was sober at the time, a few argued that she was very drunk. However, the deciding evidence for the jury came from surgeon Mr H.M. Chute.

Chute was positive that Ellen's injury was caused by a kick, but could not be absolutely certain that the erysipelas, which ultimately killed her, resulted from the wound. While the jury were satisfied that Keeler had injured Ellen in a 'gross, unprovoked and cruel attack', they could not be sure that Keeler's actions had caused her death and returned a verdict of 'death from natural causes'.

The coroner told Keeler that he had been extremely fortunate to avoid committal for manslaughter and trusted that his narrow escape would serve as a warning to keep a check on his violent temper in future.

24 FEBRUARY   1854 A Spanish vessel, *Rosario*, crewed entirely by Spaniards and *Highlander*, which had a mixed crew of English, Scottish and American sailors, were docked at Bristol Port.

One of the *Highlander's* crew saw a Spaniard abusing a young woman and intervened to protect her. A fight broke out between the two men, which was ended by passing police officers, who separated the combatants and sent them back to their ships. There was another fight between the two crews later that evening, after the Spanish sailors allegedly attacked the men from *Highlander.*

Unfortunately, the following day, both crews chose to drink in the same pub, The Hole in the Wall on Prince's Street. Recognising that there might be trouble, the landlord wisely separated them, sending the *Highlander* crew to an upstairs room. Shortly afterwards, a lone sailor from *Highlander* arrived at the pub and was attacked by the Spaniards. His shipmates heard the disturbance and went to his rescue but, being unarmed, quickly scattered when they realised that the Spaniards all had knives. Three men were stabbed in the affray. One of them, Cornelius Murphy, was an innocent bystander, who just happened to get in the way of a knife-wielding Spanish sailor. Murphy, Robert Hoskins and John Beale were taken to the Infirmary, where Murphy died soon after admittance.

His assailant was identified as Juan Antonio Castro and, when the subsequent inquest on the death of Murphy recorded a verdict of 'wilful murder' against him, he was committed for trial at the Gloucestershire Assizes. On 1 April, Castro was found guilty of the lesser offence of 'manslaughter' and sentenced to one year's imprisonment.

25 FEBRUARY   1907 Mr Gore was boiling tar in a saucepan on the fire at his home in Knowle, ready to be used for a household job. As Mrs Gore got her six children ready for bed, she happened to glance at the saucepan and realised that it was about to boil over.

She lifted it off the grate but, as she did, the contents splashed onto the fire and exploded in a ball of flames, setting light to the children's clothes. As everybody tried to escape the conflagration, their exit was barred by one of the children who had collapsed in front of the door. With difficulty, Mr Gore managed to wrench the door open and push the child out.

Mr and Mrs Gore and their three-year-old daughter, Gladys, managed to escape, although all were badly burned. George Edgar (10), Alice Maud (9), William Henry (6), Winifred Mary (3) and baby Arthur Herbert all perished in the flames.

Note: Contemporary newspapers reported that Winifred was the only child saved. However, official records seem to indicate that the one surviving child was Gladys.

1881 Albert Edward Clarke of St James's died at the Infirmary, aged one month.

Albert's mother was disturbed by his constant crying and her landlady recommended laudanum, saying that she had always used it on her own children. She fetched the laudanum for Mrs Clarke and suggested that five or six drops would be a safe dose.

Mrs Clarke was not familiar with the properties of laudanum. Without measuring it, she put some of the liquid into a spoon and topped it up with water before feeding it to Albert.

The infant's crying ceased almost immediately and he fell into a deep and peaceful sleep. However, when Mrs Clarke checked him an hour later, his mouth was open and his tongue protruding. Unable to rouse Albert, Mrs Clarke rushed him to the hospital, where surgeon Mr A.A. Lendon diagnosed opium poisoning. In spite of the efforts of Lendon and his staff, who kept Albert alive by artificial respiration for almost twenty-four hours, the baby died the following morning. Lendon told the inquest that a safe dose of laudanum for an adult would be no more than four drops and that, for a baby of Albert's age, a quarter of a drop was a dangerous dose.

The inquest jury returned a verdict of 'death by misadventure' and the coroner instructed the police officer in charge of the case to make enquiries into how the landlady had managed to procure such a large quantity of the deadly drug.

1899 Richard Frost and Harriet Fitzwaller were arrested for keeping a disorderly house at Clarence Road, New Cut. Harriet blamed Frost, saying that he refused to work and had forced her into prostitution.

When the couple appeared at Bristol Police Court, the police stated that they had been keeping the house under surveillance for some time and had observed a constant stream of men and women visiting. When arrested, Harriet was carrying nearly £6 in her purse and had a bank book in her possession, showing a balance of £10.

Solicitor Mr H.S. Wansbrough, who appeared for Harriet, told the magistrates that she was in poor health and had acted under the influence of Frost, who was described as 'a good for nothing fellow'. The magistrates sent him to prison for six weeks and fined Harriet £5 plus costs.

1876 Coroner Mr H.S. Wasbrough held an inquest on the death of fourteen-year-old Frank William Sandall.

On 22 September 1875, Sandall decided to visit his former workplace, Greenslade's Manufactory on Thomas Street, rather than going to his own work. Workmen heard a tremendous crash and turned to see Sandall being whirled around the shaft of a machine, which then spat him onto the floor. One of Sandall's arms was completely ripped off and the stump fractured, and both of his legs were broken. Rushed to the General Hospital, he lingered until 26 February 1876.

The machinery was usually guarded but the fencing had been temporarily removed while repairs were carried out. Carpenter Thomas Pironet told the inquest that he was actually rebuilding the guard when the accident happened, having cut the necessary boards but not finished replacing them.

Since Sandall had no right to be on the premises, the coroner told the jury that the only conclusion they could come to was that his death was accidental and a verdict to that effect was returned.

29 FEBRUARY 1892 Thomas B. Leach appeared at Bristol Police Court charged with 'failing to make himself efficient'.

The case was brought by Captain Vines of the 1st Gloucestershire Volunteers, who stated that Leach had failed to attend the requisite drills in order to make himself efficient. When Vines spoke to Leach about his non-attendance, Leach told him that he had been bitten by a dog and was undergoing hospital treatment.

Vines asked Leach to provide a doctor's certificate to that effect, writing to him three times with the same request, but Leach simply ignored the letters, forcing Vines to bring him before magistrates.

Leach gave the same excuse for missing drills to the magistrates, but could not provide a doctor's note, nor offer any explanation for ignoring the letters. He was fined 35s – the amount of grant lost to the Volunteers through his not being efficient – and ordered to pay the court costs.

MARCH

Colston Hall, 1905 (*see* 15 March). (Author's collection)

1 MARCH

1852 Magistrates spent much of the day dealing with incidents arising from a strike at the Great Western Cotton Works. The predominantly female workforce had three main grievances. They believed that improper fines and deductions were being taken from their wages and that their agreed working hours were not being adhered to. They also objected to the recent installation of a wicket gate at the Works. The gate was just fifteen inches wide and all personnel had to pass through it when leaving the factory. Needless to say, this delayed the women considerably and, on the previous Thursday, they rebelled, refusing to leave unless the main gate was opened.

Manager John Ashworth was called to deal with the chaos and appeared in the factory yard with some dogs. The workers alleged that he set the dogs on them and also that he hit one of their number, Emma Williams, with a stick and kicked her when she was down. As a final outrage, he ordered the engineers to set up hoses, with which he drenched the protesting women. The response was a volley of stones, thrown from both inside and outside the Works, which damaged machinery and buildings and injured several people.

The women admitted before magistrates that they often stopped their looms while the engine that drove them was still working – a practice that the management insisted caused damage to the machines. However, the women claimed that the engines were not stopped until several minutes after the agreed time for work to end.

Ashworth protested to the magistrates that he had acted perfectly reasonably to quell the riot. He denied having struck any of the women or setting the dogs on them and stated that the extent of his usage of the hoses had been exaggerated. After hearing evidence throughout the day – much of it conflicting – the magistrates found Ashworth guilty of an unjustifiable assault and fined him 5*s*.

2 MARCH

1879 Emily Tripp, a barmaid at a music hall, went to church without her boyfriend, clerk Frank Sedgebear. When she left, she stopped to speak briefly to a male acquaintance, unaware that Frank was watching.

Emily and Frank went for a walk together that evening and, as they walked along Dove Street, Frank began interrogating Emily about why she was talking to another man. She refused to tell him, so Frank pulled out a revolver and shot her.

Emily ran away and Frank fired again. Fortunately for Emily, the first shot hit the steels of her corset and shattered, while the second hit her below her ribs on her right-hand side, passing through her body and exiting on the left, missing all of her vital organs. Before anyone could apprehend Sedgebear, he put the revolver into his mouth and pulled the trigger, dying instantly.

At an inquest held on his death the next day, the jury learned that Frank had stolen the gun and six bullets from a relative who had recently visited him. Before setting off for his walk with Emily, he remarked to her landlady that he didn't think that she would be coming back.

The jury returned a verdict of *felo de se* – an archaic term meaning 'murder of oneself' – and ordered twenty-two-year-old Frank's body to be buried at midnight.

1892 Seventy-year-old Philip Tovey appeared before Mr Justice Hawkins at the Gloucestershire Assizes charged with unlawfully wounding his wife and with attempting to commit suicide on 27 January.

Mr Justice Hawkins. (Author's collection)

The court heard that Tovey and his wife Ann had been married for forty-three years and that Tovey had always been a good husband and father. However, his behaviour had become somewhat strange. After drinking heavily the night before, he went into his wife's bedroom at their house in Redfield and hit her several times on the head with a hammer. Mrs Tovey screamed and her daughter, Alice Brown, rushed upstairs to see what the matter was. While Alice tended to her mother, her father slipped quietly downstairs and cut his throat.

Although Mrs Tovey developed erysipelas, both she and her husband recovered from their injuries. The Assize jury found Tovey guilty of both charges but recommended mercy. At this point the judge called Ann Tovey back into the witness box.

Having established that she was prepared to ensure that her husband did not drink, Hawkins discharged Tovey on his own recognisance to appear if called for judgement in the future. The couple, who wept throughout the proceedings, embraced tenderly and left the court hand-in-hand.

1881 Deputy-coroner Mr E.M. Harwood held an inquest at the Infirmary on the death of sixty-eight-year-old Mary Mahoney, who died there on the previous day.

Widow Mrs Mahoney had visited a shop on Bridge Street, owned by Mr Richards. According to shop assistant Henry Ralph Humphries, she was very drunk and refused to leave the shop when asked to do so and, as Humphries tried to eject her, Mrs Mahoney fell.

Mr Richards sent her by cart to the home of a relative, Charles Pfeiffer, who took her to the Infirmary. There, Mrs Mahoney gave a deposition to the magistrates' clerk Mr Holmes Gore, in which she stated that Humphries had deliberately pushed her, knocking her over.

A number of witnesses testified at the inquest, including Pfeiffer, who insisted that Mrs Mahoney was not drunk. However, the majority stated that Mrs Mahoney had pulled down some nuts from the shop shelves and then slipped on them and fallen over.

The inquest jury recorded a verdict of 'death by misadventure', exonerating Humphries of all blame for Mrs Mahoney's death.

1896 Servant Alice Harrison, aged fourteen, was employed by Mr Langley (or Longley) of St George's Road. As she sat in the front room looking after the family's baby, a friend of her employer's son walked in, picked up an airgun that was lying in the room and, without speaking, shot at Alice.

Fortunately, the pellet passed harmlessly through her skirts. She managed to escape from the room uninjured, despite being fired at again.

Later that evening, Alice remonstrated with fifteen-year-old Ernest West, who promised not to touch the gun again. Minutes later, as Alice was bending down to pick up a flat iron, a pellet was fired under the kitchen door, hitting her eye.

West was brought before magistrates at Bristol Police Court charged with unlawfully wounding and causing bodily harm to Alice. The case was adjourned and Ernest was remanded several times. However, by the end of May, it was suggested that the shooting was a terrible accident and that while there was culpable negligence on West's part, there was no intention of causing any injury to Alice.

Alice agreed that she might be prepared to drop the charges if she was financially compensated for the loss of the sight in one eye. Despite being poor, West's parents managed to scrape together £5, but Alice held out for £100.

Cleverly, West's solicitor reminded her that the gun belonged to her former employer, Mr Langley. He offered to unconditionally hand over £5 if his client was discharged, intimating that Langley might bear some of the responsibility for her injury. Alice accepted and West was cautioned and freed. There are no reports to suggest that a claim against Langley was ever pursued.

6 MARCH   **1901** *The Times* reported a four-day trial at the Bristol Assizes of David Allport and Louisa Eleanor Chappell (aka Louisa Allport), for the attempted murder of Allport's son, Arthur, known as 'Bertie'. There were further charges against both prisoners of neglecting Bertie and his younger brother Walter.

The court heard that Allport married in May 1890 and his wife gave birth to three children, one of whom died in infancy. The couple separated in 1898 and the children remained with their mother. One year later, the Allports reconciled but were only together for a month before separating again.

In September 1899, Allport moved to City Road, Bristol, bringing both boys with him. He advertised for someone to look after them and a Mrs Williams took Bertie to live in her own home, where he stayed until his father reclaimed him on 25 June 1900. At that time, he was a perfectly healthy little boy.

By then, Allport had met Louisa Chappell, who gave birth to his child in August 1900. Soon afterwards, Bertie was reported to be suffering from diabetes and consumption. Rather than calling a doctor, Allport locked Bertie in his bedroom, which had no fire and very few bedclothes. When a doctor finally saw the boy some weeks later, he found that Bertie did not have a disease, but was suffering from starvation. Bertie weighed only half the weight of a normal seven-year-old and was so emaciated that his stomach rested on his spine. Bertie was taken to hospital and given proper food, making a full recovery in time.

It was suggested in court that the Allports had deliberately starved Bertie, who was heavily insured by his father, an agent for the Wesleyan and General Assurance Society. The sum of £25, payable on Bertie's death, was a fortune to a couple who were heavily in debt and Louisa had been heard to say that

The Azzize Courts,
Bristol, 1897.
(Authors collection)

she would dance at the boy's funeral, while Allport had already ordered a mourning suit and made arrangements for the laying out of his son's body.

Although Allport and Louisa denied all the charges against them the jury found them guilty and Allport was sentenced to fifteen years' imprisonment, Louisa to five. Custody of Bertie and Walter was given to Reverend Benjamin Waugh, who agreed to care for them until they reached the age of sixteen.

1899 Butcher James Smith of Bedminster decided he would skin and joint a cow – horrifically, he neglected to kill it first.   7 MARCH

Smith's neighbours and traumatised butcher boy tried to prevent him hacking at the live cow with an axe and a knife, but he could not be persuaded to kill the animal until the following day, by which time he had cut out several chunks of the animal's flesh and slashed it numerous times in an attempt to skin it.

When Smith appeared before magistrates at the Police Court, they insisted that he was examined by a doctor, saying that it was impossible that a man in his right mind would do such a thing. Smith was found to be insane and sent to an asylum.

1886 George Sage and his son Philip shared a bedroom in a rented apartment on Barrow Lane, St Philip's. For some time, George had complained of feeling the cold, so Philip bought a small portable stove to heat their bedroom at nights.   8 MARCH

There was no chimney in the room and landlord Henry Ayre warned Philip that the accumulation of fumes could be dangerous. Philip reassured him, saying that he only used cinders from the living room fire and always left a window or door slightly open for ventilation.

Nevertheless, both Philip and his father were found dead in bed on the morning of 8 March. An inquest jury later ruled that both had 'accidentally suffocated by fumes from an open stove placed in the bedroom for the purpose of warming it.'

9 MARCH

1847 Steeplejack John Shipway was working 50ft above ground on the construction of a new sugar refinery at Counterslip. As he and one of his workmen carried a heavy iron girder across a scaffold plank, the plank suddenly snapped, plunging both men to the ground.

They were picked up, unconscious and bleeding from multiple injuries, and taken to the Infirmary, where Shipway was found to have a broken leg. More seriously, he had also ruptured his small intestine and it was from this injury that he died that night.

At an inquest held the following day by coroner Mr J.B. Grindon, the jury were shown the broken plank, which was 2.5in thick and appeared perfectly sound, even though it was old. It had been used with other planks to make a bridge, spanning 8ft between a wall and a scaffold pole. Shipway and his workman were walking entirely on the plank that broke, rather than spreading their combined weight over the adjacent boards.

The jury returned a verdict of 'accidental death' on Shipway, a very experienced steeplejack, who left a wife and four children. At the time of the inquest, Shipway's unnamed workman was still alive, although his condition was said to be serious.

10 MARCH

1859 Mary Ann King and Ann Hyman were next-door neighbours who just couldn't get along. They spent much of their time arguing and it was almost inevitable that their constant quarrelling would eventually come to blows.

Even as the women appeared at the Lawford's Gate Petty Sessions, where Ann Hyman charged her neighbour with assault, they were still bickering. Mary Ann called Ann, 'a gossiping old woman who deserved to have her nose cut off', and told the magistrates that, whenever she had visitors, Ann would listen at the door and then spread their conversation throughout the parish. Ann indignantly swore 'before God and man' that she did no such thing, accusing Mary Ann of hitting her.

Unable to settle the matter, magistrates dismissed the case, telling the women to sort it out between themselves and, if they could not, to live farther apart in future.

11 MARCH

1891 Thirty-year-old Elizabeth Mifflin died at her father's home in Lower Montague Street after a brief illness, her death shrouded in mystery.

Elizabeth, who was unmarried, worked as an accountant for a firm on Castle Street and left for work as normal on 28 February. She was not seen again for four days.

When she returned, Elizabeth refused to say where she had been. She also seemed unwell, although she assured people that it was only a cold. However, as she grew sicker, her father insisted on a doctor being called. Sadly, Dr Imlay's visit was too late, as Elizabeth died soon after his arrival. A post-mortem examination showed the cause of death to be peritonitis, which had resulted from the forceful insertion of an instrument, for the purpose of inducing an abortion.

Elizabeth was a particularly secretive woman, who, judging by the letters she received, seemed to have a number of admirers. In her office desk, police found correspondence from Folkestone, Bath and Cardiff and two letters from Bristol, in which the handwriting appeared to have been disguised. The police traced the writers of all the letters with the exception of those from Bristol.

Elizabeth's one confidante was a cook at work and, even then, she revealed very little about her private life. The cook was able to tell police that Elizabeth visited Bath almost every month to attend concerts at the Sydney Gardens and that she had a female friend there. She had holidayed in Folkestone and had recently received several gifts, including a silver-mounted umbrella. The cook also said that Elizabeth consulted a herbalist shortly before her death.

Coroner Mr H.S. Wasbrough opened an inquest, which was to extend over four sittings. It was obvious that the cause of death was a botched abortion and Dr Greig Smith told the inquest that, given Elizabeth's temperament, it was just possible that her injuries may have been self-inflicted, although he believed it highly unlikely. The inquest jury agreed, returning a verdict of 'wilful murder against some person or persons unknown'.

1866 James Fox appeared before magistrates at the Council House charged with 'breach of the peace'.

The complaint was brought by George Oliver, who told the Bench that, on the previous Sunday, he had observed Fox and another person running a race on the New Cut. Between 400 and 500 people had congregated to

12 MARCH

The Council House, 1904. (Author's collection)

watch them and were using the most disgusting language imaginable. Not only that, but Fox and his opponent were in a state of semi-nudity.

Magistrates thanked Oliver for bringing this 'intolerable nuisance' to their attention, binding Fox over in his own recognisance and ordering him to provide a surety of £5 or be sent to prison.

13 MARCH **1859** George Britton of Bitton had little success with the opposite sex. The young collier was the butt of constant name-calling and teasing from the village girls, who compounded their taunting by sending him caustic Valentine's cards. On 13 March, George finally snapped, waylaying the ringleader of his tormentors on her way home from chapel and kicking and beating her.

Bitton, 1916. (Author's collection)

Although Mary Ann Sparks sustained no more serious injury than a few bruises, her Sunday best bonnet was damaged irreparably.

At the Lawford's Gate Petty Sessions, George pleaded guilty to the charge of assault and was rebuked by the magistrates for his cowardice in striking a woman. He was fined 10s plus costs or a month's hard labour.

George's mother stepped forward to pay his fine but he brushed her aside, saying that he would rather go to prison than pay Mary Ann's costs.

14 MARCH **1888** Jane Roberts appeared at the Bristol Assizes charged with wounding her fifteen-month-old son, James, with 'felonious intent'.

On 8 February, another of Jane's sons, William, was having a sleep prior to working the night shift at a local factory. He was rudely awakened by screaming and, when he ran downstairs, his mother told him, 'I have killed my child.' William snatched James out of her arms and Jane ran out of the house.

She arrived at St Philip's police station and told Inspector Hardy, 'For God's sake send to my house; I've killed my child. I took hold of his legs and dashed his face on the floor.' A constable was despatched to the house but found that neighbours had taken James to the Infirmary, where Dr Swain found him so facially bruised and battered that he was almost unrecognisable.

Jane had been married for twenty-eight years and had always been a good wife and mother. She had never ill-treated her children, had not been drinking and showed no signs of insanity. Yet, in spite of her confessions to both William and the police and the overwhelming evidence against her, she was acquitted. Fortunately, baby James made a full recovery.

1872 An exhibition closed at the Colston Hall, at which the star attraction was Millie Chrissie, 'the two-headed nightingale'. 15 MARCH

Fused together at the spine, Millie and Chrissie McKoy were African-American conjoined twins from North Carolina, who had been enslaved since birth. By the time they were six years old, they had been sold three times and, although the Enslavement Act of 1863 abolished slavery, the girls chose to stay with their then owner, Joseph Pearson Smith.

The contemporary newspapers enthused about the girls' talents, although the reporters often struggled to know how to refer to them, calling them 'she', 'they' and even 'it'. 'There are two distinct, well formed busts, two very pleasing and cheerful faces, two sets of arms and two sets of legs', wrote the reporter from *The Bristol Mercury*. He added, 'although the faces are of negro type and of a rich mulatto colour, they are more intelligent than such faces are in general.'

The twins could read and write and spoke five different languages. They played the piano and the guitar and, as their billing suggests, had beautiful singing voices and danced 'with lightness and grace'.

Although the twins were undoubtedly exploited, they achieved a financial independence practically unheard of for women in the 1800s. However, a fire in 1909 reduced them to poverty and they died from tuberculosis in 1912.

Colston Hall, 1908. (Author's collection)

16 MARCH

1879 Frederick Walters was tried at the Bristol Assizes for the attempted murder of his estranged wife, Elizabeth.

The couple had mutually agreed to separate. Soon afterwards, Frederick called on Elizabeth at her work in a laundry to say goodbye and, putting his arm round her as if about to kiss her, cut her throat with a razor. He was apprehended by her colleagues and locked in an outhouse to await the arrival of the police, who found him driving a chisel into his own throat.

Fortunately, Elizabeth survived and Frederick's self-inflicted wound was not serious. Found guilty of 'attempted murder', he was sentenced to fifteen years' penal servitude.

17 MARCH

1853 Isaac Tucker, a skilled shoemaker, had worked for Mr Kempster at Clifton for twenty years. As Kempster approached retirement age, he suggested that Tucker took over his business and, on 12 March, Tucker moved his family into the house and shop at Prince's Place, Clifton.

On 17 March, Isaac sent his wife out on an errand, leaving their two little girls in the charge of servant Mary Ann Howell. Soon afterwards, Tucker took five-year-old Caroline and three-year-old Mary Jane upstairs to his workshop, where he cut their throats with a shoemaker's knife, before ending his own life in the same way.

At the subsequent inquest, it emerged that Tucker was a steady, sober and industrious man and a loving husband, who idolised his two daughters. However, since agreeing to take on Kempster's business, he had been wracked by a fear of failure and was terrified of being unable to provide for his family. His anxiety had apparently induced him to murder his daughters, rather than see them in poverty. The inquest jury determined that Tucker killed Caroline, Mary Jane and himself while in a fit of insanity.

18 MARCH

1881 Fifty-year-old clay miner George Lacey died in the General Hospital from injuries received two days earlier in a work accident.

Lacey, who was employed by the Crown Clay Company at Trooper's Hill, Crew's Hole, was riding with another miner in a 'tram' – a truck used for transporting clay underground. The tram was pushed by a third miner, George Crew.

Joseph Reed, who was kneeling in front of Lacey in the tram, banged his head on a beam supporting the mine ceiling. The impact pushed him into Lacey, whose body was bent backwards over the edge of the vehicle, fracturing his spine and damaging his spinal cord.

At the inquest into his death, Inspector of Mines Mr R. Donald Bain stated that, although it was not common practice, there was no rule against men riding in the trams and therefore there had been no breach of the Coal Mines Regulation Act. Bain had inspected the mine after the accident and found it safe in every respect. The inquest jury returned a verdict of 'accidental death'.

19 MARCH

1888 Nun Catherine Felice Anne Mason sued Dr H. Marshall and Dr Shaw of Clifton and Mother Superior Adelaide Gauchard at the Bristol Assizes, for having her committed to the Brislington Lunatic Asylum. Madame

Gauchard was further charged with malice and fraud for her part in Miss Mason's committal.

In the *Nisi Prius* Court, Mr Justice Field and a specially commissioned jury agreed with the doctors that Miss Mason was of unsound mind. Furthermore, they found that at the time of her committal, Miss Mason was 'in such a state that she was likely to do mischief.' Field therefore found for the defendants, ordering Miss Mason to pay their costs.

1855 Hill's Bridge (aka Bath Bridge), which spanned the canal between Bath Parade and Totterdown, was a large, cast-iron single arch, built by the Colebrookedale Iron Works in 1805. In 1808, a defect in the stonework on which it rested caused its collapse, resulting in several deaths and injuries and, on 20 March 1855, there was another equally serious accident, when a coke barge, *John*, hit the ironwork.

20 MARCH

The bridge quivered violently for a few moments before collapsing, throwing carts, gigs and pedestrians into the canal. Although several people swam to safety, it was thought that many more had drowned, imprisoned in the mass of tangled ironwork.

There was great difficulty in determining the exact number of casualties and fatalities, since nobody knew precisely how many people were on the bridge at the time of the disaster. As an added complication, it was believed that bodies were washed out to sea by the changing tides.

Missing and presumed dead were carter William Bevan and William Cooksley, who was last seen talking to Gwynne Thomas at one end of the bridge. When the barge struck, Cooksley was plunged into the water, while Thomas miraculously remained safe on the side of the bridge.

By 11 April, Cooksley's body was the only one to have been recovered. At the inquest on his death, held by coroner Mr J.B. Grindon, fourteen of the fifteen jury men were satisfied with a verdict of 'accidental death'. The fifteenth held out for a charge of 'culpable negligence' against barge captain John Domican, who was arrested immediately after the incident. (Domican had always insisted that a strong tide had accidentally pulled the barge into the bridge support.) The coroner accepted the majority verdict and there is no evidence that Domican was ever charged.

1859 Margaret Hayes went to Temple Meads Station to see off a group of her friends, who were travelling to London. As she waited for the train to pull out, Margaret realised that there were several soldiers on board, en route to Chatham.

21 MARCH

She recognised that they belonged to the same regiment as two of her brothers and struck up a conversation through the train window with one of them, who agreed to pass on a message for her.

Just then, the train pulled off and Margaret walked briskly along the platform in order to finish giving her message. Unfortunately, she neglected to look where she was going and collided with one of the pillars supporting the station roof. As she rebounded, she stumbled onto the railway line and two of the train's carriages ran over her head and arms, killing her instantly.

Coroner Mr Grindon held an inquest later that day, at which the jury returned a verdict of 'accidental death'.

22 MARCH   **1744** Two Irishmen, Andrew Burnett and Henry Payne, were hanged at Durdham Downs, Clifton, for the 'wilful murder' of Richard Ruddle, on 26 October 1743. It was believed that robbery was the motive. The two men had mistaken Ruddle for a farmer, Mr Winter, who they were expecting to cross the Down carrying a large sum of money.

After their executions, the men were hung in chains as a warning to other would-be thieves and murderers, before finally being laid to rest in Clifton. A hundred years later, almost to the day of the murder, their bodies were unearthed by builders digging the foundations for a new house on Gallows-Acre Lane.

23 MARCH   **1881** An inquest was held at The Lamb and Anchor Tavern, Clarence Street, on the death of forty-eight-year-old tailor Thomas Cook.

Cook, his wife and some of their friends had eaten mussels for supper on the night of 21 March. Soon afterwards, Mrs Cook began to vomit and developed a rash all over her body.

The next morning, just as Mrs Cook was beginning to feel better, her husband complained of feeling unwell and took to his bed. He had no particular symptoms until the following day, when he complained of feeling nauseous. Minutes later, he lay back on his bed and died.

The inquest learned that Cook had previously been in excellent health, apart from suffering from flatulence. None of the friends who ate the mussels suffered any ill effects and besides, the doctors pointed out that any symptoms resulting from eating bad food would generally arise immediately afterwards, as they had in Mrs Cook.

With no apparent reason for Cook's sudden demise, the jury returned a verdict of 'death from natural causes'.

24 MARCH   **1899** Henry and Priscilla Barnes of Hotwells Road went out drinking, leaving their three children, aged eight, seven and two years, alone at home. Neighbours heard the youngest child screaming and found that Emily Alice had been burned when the fire grate fell on top of her.

With no sign of her parents, the police were summoned and PC Charles Tripp carried Emily to the Infirmary. House surgeon Harold Frederick Mole found that her burns were not as severe as they first appeared but, since she was unusually thin and very dirty, he decided to admit her. Meanwhile, Emily's parents returned home at eleven o'clock that night. PC Tripp tried to explain what had happened in their absence, but Henry was too drunk to understand and Priscilla was also sufficiently drunk to be 'muddled'.

Sadly, although she initially appeared to be making a good recovery, Emily died on 26 March. At an inquest held by deputy coroner Mr A.E. Barker at The Crown and Dove Hotel on Bridewell Street, the jury found that she had died from a convulsion caused by her burns, adding that they believed that her death was a direct result of negligence by her parents.

Henry and Priscilla Barnes appeared at Bristol Police Court charged with ill-treating all three children. Neighbour Thomas Dyer, who originally found Emily, likened the Barnes' rooms to a dung heap, adding that he was forced to hold his nose when passing to avoid the stench. Inspector Ottley of the National Society for the Prevention of Cruelty to Children confirmed Dyer's assessment of the children's living conditions, saying that when he visited the house on 4 April, it was filthy, swarming with fleas and with very little furniture.

Priscilla Barnes insisted that she had not been out of the house for longer than half an hour and denied being 'muddled with drink'. Her husband stated that he had been out of work for several months but now had a good job and was trying his best to furnish his home, although, according to his neighbours, most of his wages went on alcohol.

It was not the first time that Henry and Priscilla had been summoned for neglecting their children and magistrates sent both to prison with hard labour, Henry for two months and Priscilla for one.

1865 Abraham and Eliza Long ran a butcher's shop in Hotwells. Having previously been widowed, Eliza had one son, Tom Anstey, by her first husband.

As Eliza sat doing the shop's books at half-past ten at night, Abraham told her to fetch in the meat that was hanging outside the shop. Eliza called after him that she didn't feel well, but Abraham had already left the room and didn't hear her.

The Longs' servant, Emma Bevan, offered to do it but, being only twelve years old, she didn't do a very good job. At that point, Tom came in, having spent all day out delivering. He was tired, hungry and wet through but, seeing the meat, thought he'd better put it right before his stepfather saw it.

Abraham walked into the shop as Tom was moving the meat and immediately raged at the boy for not doing it properly. Eliza intervened on her son's behalf, trying to tell her husband that the servant was responsible but Abraham rounded on her and hit her.

'You shall not strike my mamma,' Tom told him, at which Abraham raised his hand, intending to punish the boy for daring to correct him. Eliza grabbed Abraham around the waist and yelled at Tom to run. However the diminutive woman was no match for her stronger husband and Abraham dragged her through the shop and into the street in pursuit of his stepson.

Eliza could hold him back no longer. She saw Abraham rush at Tom then reel back, clutching his chest. As Abraham staggered on the pavement, Tom walked calmly back into the shop and replaced a knife on the butcher's block.

Abraham Long died from a single stab wound early the following morning and his twelve-year-old stepson was tried at the Bristol Assizes in April for 'felonious slaying'. Tom's counsel, Mr Edlin, did a sterling job for his client, tugging the jury's heartstrings by describing a forlorn, fatherless little boy, who watched his mother suffer endless abuse at her husband's hands.

Judge Baron Channell was less emotive, calling on the jury to determine whether someone as young as the defendant could fully appreciate the nature of his act. The jury determined that he couldn't and found him not guilty.

26 MARCH

1899 Deputy coroner Mr A.E. Barker held an inquest on the death of Frederick John Martin, who died in an accident at John Cox & Co. Tannery, in Bedminster.

Martin, whose job was colouring leather, was sent by his foreman to collect hides from the floor of the drying room. When he didn't return, Thomas Cook went to look for him, finding that the boy had been practically decapitated by the huge fan that dried the skins.

The fan was an experiment and had only been in use for fifteen days, hence it was not guarded. Nevertheless, each of the workers in the department had been individually warned not to go anywhere near it. The fan was thought to be reasonably safe. It was sited so that anyone wanting to walk past it would have had to contort himself into a most unnatural position to do so. It seemed as though Martin had tried to save time by throwing the hides under the fan, rather than carrying them along the passage, as he was expected to do.

The inquest jury returned a verdict of 'accidental death', suggesting that the fan should be properly guarded. The company were later fined £5 plus costs for neglecting to guard the fan and a further 10s for failing to keep a register of young persons employed in their factory.

27 MARCH

1906 In the early hours of the morning, a fire broke out at Derham's Boot Factory on St James Street. There was a high wind at the time and it quickly became obvious that many of the cottages surrounding the factory were in jeopardy.

The aftermath of the fire at Derham's Ltd Boot Factory, 1906. (Author's collection)

The police evacuated all homes in the neighbourhood, with many people being temporarily accommodated at the Central Police Station. There was an epidemic of measles among local children at the time, which increased problems for the police, who had to keep them isolated.

The factory was demolished to the ground by the blaze, during which one fireman lost his life and another was seriously injured by falling masonry. The dead man, Mr Wale, left a widow and eight children.

Funeral of Fireman Wale, 30 March 1906. (Author's collection)

1840 As they were undressing for bed, Temperance Williams and her husband Thomas of Whitson Street, St James, got into a petty argument about some vinegar. Thomas, who was drunk at the time, pulled off one of his boots and threw it at his wife, cutting her temple.

Thomas was devastated when he realised that he had injured her. He fetched a neighbour, Elizabeth Johns, who managed to stop the blood pouring from Temperance's head, then he escorted his wife to the Infirmary, where he was described by doctors as 'much distressed'.

Temperance was treated at the hospital for three weeks before she was discharged and said to be cured. However on 16 April, she was stricken with erysipelas, from which she died six days later. On her death, Thomas was charged with her manslaughter and committed for trial at the next Assizes.

On his first appearance at Gloucestershire Assizes, a principal witness was ill and the case was deferred until 31 March 1841, when Thomas appeared before Mr Justice Coleridge.

The court was told that surgeon William James, who conducted the post-mortem examination, found inflammation of the brain and had recorded the cause of Temperance's death as erysipelas arising from the wound in her temple. However, under cross-examination by defence counsel Mr Self, James admitted that the erysipelas could have been caused by any number of things, including drinking cold water while overheated.

Thomas's sister, Ann Williams, testified that she had visited the couple on 15 April, when Temperance had fallen over and knocked herself unconscious. Another witness recalled drawing a pint of cold water from the pump for Temperance, who had complained of feeling hot and gulped the water straight down.

Thomas and Temperance – who had three children – had been married for nine years and were said to be very happy together. Mr Self reminded the jury that Thomas had an excellent character and that nobody could be certain quite how his wife contracted the erysipelas that ultimately killed her. He asked the jury not to let his client live with the stigma that his was the hand that killed his wife and the jury obliged him, finding Williams not guilty.

1851 Soldiers Andrew Daley and John MacFarlane appeared at the Gloucestershire Assizes charged with the 'wilful murder' of policeman John Pym (or Pim). His death occurred in May 1849, but both defendants were posted to India immediately afterwards and were brought back to face trial by order of the Home Secretary.

When Pym told the two men to go home because they and two prostitutes were causing a disturbance on Thomas Street, he was dreadfully beaten and eventually died from erysipelas. The two defendants claimed mistaken identity and, although some of the eyewitnesses were sure that this was not the case, the two prostitutes were confused. Mary Ann Crumac was not convinced that the defendants were the men she was with on the night of the attack, whereas Jane Hellier recognised MacFarlane but was unsure about Daley. Some witnesses claimed to have seen a third soldier running away, who was never apprehended.

The defendants' company sergeant, Sergeant Whitworth, witnessed the fight. As well as giving both men excellent character references he added that he had clearly seen another man striking Pym and had also heard Daley say to someone, 'Don't kill the man.' Another soldier stated that he had seen Daley picking Pym up after the attack and others said that they had seen a bloody stick at the scene of the murder, which did not belong to either of the accused.

In the face of the contradictory evidence, the jury eventually returned guilty verdicts of manslaughter on both defendants. Both were sentenced to be transported for fifteen years.

30 MARCH   **1850** Alfred Dancey (or Dauncey) appeared before Baron Platt at the Gloucestershire Assizes charged with 'wilful murder'.

On 23 December 1849, Henry Coggan, William Braund and Edward Horgan spotted Dancey and another boy named Collins playing leap-frog over the posts on Bedminster Bridge. When Horgan jokingly encouraged them by shouting 'over', the boys rounded on him and called him rude names. Horgan made as if to chase them, before rejoining his companions, but Collins and Dancey continued to harass them. Horgan, tired of the insults, cuffed both boys. To his surprise, Dancey pulled out a pistol and threatened to shoot him.

Coggan, Braund and Horgan walked away, but Collins and Dancey followed. Horgan tried throwing a stone at them, but it missed and eventually Collins picked up a life-belt from the riverside and threatened William Braund with it. Braund told him to put it away and a scuffle developed between them. Restrained by Coggan and Horgan, Dancey shouted to Braund, 'I'll shoot you if you don't let Collins go.'

'You don't mean that,' Horgan said, but Dancey insisted that he did. Before anyone could stop him he ran towards William Braund, who was just getting to his feet. When he got within three yards of Braund, Dancey fired. The pistol ball entered Braund's left side under his armpit, passing between his ribs and severing his windpipe. He was killed instantly. Dancey ran away, but there were several witnesses to the affray and he was quickly apprehended.

At his trial, his defence counsel insisted that the pistol had fired at half-cock and thus Braund's death was a tragic accident. At worst, it was an act perpetrated in the heat of the moment, after Dancey was provoked by Braund and his companions, so could amount to nothing more than manslaughter.

Platt seemed to agree with the latter scenario and encouraged the jury to consider the lesser offence. They found Alfred Dancey guilty of manslaughter and Platt sentenced him to be transported for a period of ten years.

At the time of the shooting, Alfred Dancey was just fourteen years old. He sailed for Van Dieman's Land on the *Equestrian* on 27 August 1852.

31 MARCH   **1876** Large boulders from Birchwood Quarry were usually stacked next to the line at Brislington, ready for loading onto trains. Somehow, one of these enormous stones was dislodged from the pile, possibly by the vibrations of a

The Flying Dutchman. (Author's collection)

passing train and it rolled onto the tracks, over which *The Flying Dutchman* was expected to pass at any minute.

Quarry foreman John 'Jack' Chiddy averted certain disaster by moving the stone off the line. However, he was unable to get clear of the passing train and was hit, dying almost instantly. He left a widow and seven children.

There was no compensation for such work-related accidents and a collection taken among the passengers of the train amounted to only £3 17s. Chiddy's case was subsequently raised in the House of Commons by Lord Elcho and although there were no official funds available, the resultant publicity touched the hearts of the British public and enough money was donated to allow Elizabeth Chiddy to build a cottage for herself and her children. A memorial stone to Chiddy's heroic deed was also erected close to the scene of the accident.

APRIL

The Tramways Centre. (Author's collection)

1873 John Roche appeared at the Bristol Assizes charged with unlawfully wounding PC Edward McCarthy, with intent to do grievous bodily harm. Roche lived with Martha Smith, although theirs was a tempestuous relationship, punctuated by violent quarrels. Having thrown John out, on 20 March, Martha returned home after a night out and found him lounging on her sofa. She asked him to leave and, when he refused, she fetched a constable to evict him.

PC Edward McCarthy tried to persuade John to leave but he flatly refused to go anywhere and began hitting Martha. McCarthy threw Roche out of the house after a struggle, but moments later Roche returned and when the policeman tried to take him into custody, Roche pulled out a knife and stabbed him in his side. McCarthy managed to hit Roche on the hand with his staff, breaking his knife and so disarming him.

Luckily, his wound wasn't too serious and McCarthy survived to see Roche sentenced to twelve months' imprisonment with hard labour.

1878 Servant Mary Jane Chapple (or Chappell) always seemed to be unwell and was sacked from her station at Clifton Hill because she was unable to do her work. True to form, she spent her last day in bed complaining of stomach ache, before leaving on the morning of 2 April.

After her departure, her employer Mrs Sarah Brown noticed that one of the lavatories was partially blocked. When the problem didn't resolve itself, she called in a plumber, who found the blockage to be a dead baby.

Mary Jane was arrested and charged with 'concealing the birth of an infant'. Her employers and fellow servants had not suspected that she was pregnant and Mary Jane denied all knowledge of the tiny corpse in the water closet. Nevertheless, she was found guilty of concealment at the Bristol Assizes and sentenced to three months' imprisonment with hard labour.

1938 Fifty-year-old George Frederick Button Sayers was found dead in his home in St Paul's. Sayers lived with his wife and three children, Rose (18), Nellie (14) and a ten-year-old son. His father-in-law lived with the family and another son, Frederick Albert Button Sayers, was an able seaman, serving aboard HMS *Forester*.

George was a drunken tyrant, who terrorised his family and took an unhealthy and active interest in very young girls. His wife despaired of his behaviour and sent several letters to Frederick, saying that she was desperate to start her life afresh and begging him to stand by her.

When Frederick came home on shore leave he went to stay with his fiancée at Wyke Regis, where his mother sent him a telegram on 2 April asking him to come home. Frederick did as he was asked and, on 3 April, when his father went upstairs for a lie-down, Frederick attacked him with a hatchet and a razor and killed him.

Frederick was charged with his father's 'wilful murder' and, while he was awaiting his trial, an un-posted letter to his mother was found on his ship. In it, Frederick wrote:

You have got to tell me the truth. There can be no arguments at all. Either he has or he hasn't. Myself, I think he has. Looking back over his record, I cannot find one redeeming feature. No wonder that I loathe and detest him. This is the last straw. I have made up my mind that he has no right to live. I shall do it and take the consequences. If you try to warn him or tell him, I shall never forgive you. I shall kill him as sure as I am sat here.

At his trial at the Bristol Assizes in July 1938, Frederick evoked the sympathy of the court and there was a round of spontaneous applause when he was found guilty of the lesser offence of manslaughter and sentenced to just nine months' imprisonment. 'Nothing can justify the crime you committed but I have been able to feel that what you did, although not justified, may be explained on grounds which do afford real mitigation,' said the judge. He added that he sincerely hoped the naval authorities would allow Sayers to continue with his promising career after his release from prison.

4 APRIL

1872 Fourteen-year-old Ellen Kent appeared at Bristol Police Court charged with wandering about Bedminster without being under proper control.

Ellen, from Cheltenham, had absconded from the Industrial School at Stanhope House in Cotham, by stripping herself naked and wriggling through a ventilator grill, which measured no more than six inches square. She had first thrown her clothes through the hole.

The magistrates took one look at Ellen – described in the contemporary newspapers as 'a plump girl' – and stated that they didn't believe that the dimensions of the ventilator grill were accurate. Having been assured that they were, the Bench asked Ellen for her to promise to behave better in future. Ellen duly gave her word and was handed back to the school managers.

5 APRIL

1847 Thirty-six-year-old Thomas Welsh appeared at the Gloucestershire Assizes charged with killing and slaying his wife, Catherine.

On 9 January, Thomas and Catherine were quarrelling at their home in St Augustine's. Neighbours heard Catherine cry, 'For God's sake, Thomas,

Shire Hall, Gloucester (site of the Assizes). (Author's collection)

don't beat me any more', and saw Thomas raise his hand to his wife. The next minute, Catherine tumbled down the twelve steps leading to her rooms, landing unconscious at the bottom. Thomas ran downstairs and grabbed her arm, dragging her up the stairs and into their room, slamming the door behind him.

The neighbours notified the police and PC Henry Charles and surgeon Mr W. James went to investigate, finding Catherine lying on the floor, still unconscious. Thomas, who was drunk, tried his best to prevent them from examining his wife, asking PC Charles, 'What shall I be done to if she dies?'

Catherine did die and on conducting a post-mortem examination, Mr James found that she had a fractured skull with swelling of the brain, which he believed was caused by a fall.

At Welsh's trial, his defence counsel Mr Symonds conceded that Welsh might have been 'correcting' his wife when, by some misadventure, she accidentally fell down the steps. Symonds called a character witness, who swore that Welsh always treated Catherine kindly and humanely.

The jury found him guilty, tempering their verdict with a recommendation for mercy and Welsh was sentenced to twelve months' imprisonment.

1840 Martha Brain, who worked as a domestic servant for Captain Farr and his family, was unwell. For some months, the family and Martha's fellow servants had suspected that she might be pregnant, something which Martha vehemently denied. Yet, as she sat in the kitchen at Bathurst Basin, Bedminster, complaining of feeling poorly, it was evident that her abdomen was much smaller than it had been of late and Mrs Farr directed charwoman Mrs Hale to search the house for a baby.

The body of a newborn baby girl was found in the boiler and Mrs Farr sent for surgeon Thomas Prowse, who examined the body and found extensive wounds on the baby's face and neck. Her carotid artery was severed, her tongue almost cut out and her lower jaw was broken. Prowse had no doubt that the child had been born alive within the previous twenty-four hours and, on examining Martha, he determined that she had recently given birth.

Martha was too ill to attend the inquest, so the coroner went to interview her at the Farr's home, where she was confined to bed. 'I never heard it or saw it move,' insisted Martha and, in spite of the fact that no knife or similar weapon had been found, the inquest jury returned a verdict of 'wilful murder' against her.

Martha was sent for trial but was judged unfit to plead. She was detained in prison until 31 March 1841, when she was finally called to the Gloucestershire Assizes. The judge instructed the jury to acquit her on the charge of 'wilful murder', at which she pleaded guilty to concealing the birth of her daughter. Since she had already served nearly a year in prison, she was sentenced to four months' penal servitude with hard labour at Gloucester County Jail.

6 APRIL

1893 Sixty-one-year-old Catherine Doolan died in the Infirmary following an accident with a horse-drawn tram.

7 APRIL

On 6 April, William Joliffe of the Bristol Tramways Company was about to drive his tram across the new bridge at St Augustine's when he noticed several people standing by a hoarding. William knew from experience that there were only inches between the side of the vehicle and the hoarding, so he called to them to get out of the way. Everyone moved except Miss Doolan and when Joliffe repeated his request, she suddenly ran towards the tram. Although Joliffe applied his brakes, he was unable to avoid hitting her and she was jammed between the side of the tram and the hoarding.

People ran to assist her, removing part of the hoarding to free her, before sending her to the Infirmary, where she died the next morning. A post-mortem examination conducted by surgeon Henry Lawrence Ormered revealed that she had suffered no injuries whatsoever in the accident, not even the smallest bruise. Ormered believed that Miss Doolan had died from fright and the jury at her inquest concurred.

8 APRIL

1887 When smoke was seen billowing from a house on William Street, Totterdown, neighbours broke in and found the body of seventy-two-year-old Elizabeth Spurrl lying on the kitchen floor, an empty paraffin bottle at her side.

Mrs Spurrl was drying washing at the time and it was thought that she threw paraffin onto the fire to make it burn better and speed up the drying process, resulting in a burst of flames setting light to her clothes. Her husband was out at the time of the fire, visiting the grave of their daughter, who had died earlier that year.

9 APRIL

1877 William Ord and Frank Leslie Poulton went to Leigh Valley to collect ferns. Frank climbed some rocks and was reaching for a particular specimen when his foot slipped.

'Hello, I'm off,' he said jokingly to William as he rolled gently downwards. However, his speed increased so much that he was unable to stop himself

A painful fall.
(Author's
collection)

rolling off the top of the arch of the railway tunnel and falling 25ft onto the line below.

William scrambled down, finding him lying on his back across a large stone, obviously severely hurt. William ran for assistance and Frank was carried home to Cotham, where surgeons found that he had fractured his thigh.

The bone was set but, when it showed no signs of healing, it was decided that Frank's leg must be amputated. Although eighteen-year-old Frank survived the operation, he died within forty-eight hours.

At an inquest held by coroner Mr H.S. Wasbrough, the jury were asked to decide whether the amputation had caused or hastened Frank's demise. When surgeon Mr John Ewens testified that the operation was Frank's only chance of survival, the jury returned a verdict of 'accidental death'.

1898 Eighteen-year-old George Reader died in Taunton Hospital from the effects of an accident on 24 March.

10 APRIL

George was working as a builder's labourer on some alterations to Messrs Wills' tobacco factory at Bristol, when he trod on a nail. The wound was poulticed and George went straight back to work, making no complaint about his foot until more than a week later.

By 2 April George was limping badly and on 4 April he could no longer work and was forced to consult a surgeon, who unaccountably treated him for pleurisy. He decided to go home to his parents in Taunton to recuperate and, when his condition showed signs of worsening, a second doctor was summoned. Dr MacDonald quickly realised that Reader had lockjaw and admitted him to Taunton Hospital. However, it was too late to save Reader's life and he died two days later.

An inquest was held by West Somerset coroner Mr T. Foster Barham, where the jury returned a verdict of 'accidental death', making no comment about the fact that a young man who sought medical advice for a badly injured foot was treated for lung disease.

11 APRIL   **1890** *The Bristol Mercury* printed an account of the death of Edward Lyons, which occurred on the evening of 8 April.

Seventeen-year-old Lyons was returning home with his family after a night out when they unwittingly became involved in a disturbance. Seeing the police approaching, Edward's brother, William, feared he might be arrested and so ran away.

In a panic, William raced to the Tontine Quay and jumped into the harbour. Edward was a strong swimmer, whereas William was not and, believing that William might need rescuing, Edward promptly dived in after him. While William climbed out of the water, Edward sank.

A large crowd of people collected but nobody made an attempt to rescue Edward until John Ryan found a boat hook and snagged him. By that time, Edward had been struggling in the water for fifteen minutes and all attempts to revive him failed.

The inquest jury returned a verdict of 'accidental death by drowning' and Coroner Mr Wasbrough publicly censured those who stood by and watched him die, without attempting to save him.

12 APRIL   **1802** Maria Davis and Charlotte Bobbett were hanged at Bristol – Davis for the murder of her fifteen-month-old son, Richard, and Bobbett for aiding and abetting her. The child had become a burden to Maria, whose husband was killed in Ireland just after his son's birth and she and her friend Charlotte hatched a plan to abandon him, hoping that someone would find him and look after him. After considering and discounting various sites, they finally settled on Brandon Hill as the perfect place. Unfortunately, they chose to leave the baby on a bitterly cold night in January and the child froze to death.

13 APRIL   **1821** John Horwood became the first person to hang at Bristol New Gaol. He was executed a few days after his eighteenth birthday for the murder of Eliza Balsum at Hanham.

After his execution, his corpse was presented to surgeon Richard Smith of the Royal Infirmary, for use in his dissection classes. Smith had the boy's skin preserved and used it to bind a book, detailing the murder, trial and execution. The black book, with its embossed skulls and crossbones at each corner, bears the Latin legend *Cutis Vera Johannis Horwood* – the skin of John Horwood – and is held at the Bristol Records Office.

14 APRIL   **1896** Seventeen-year-old labourer Thomas John Hall appeared at the Bristol Quarter Sessions charged with an indecent assault on his mother, Ada. The full details of the offence, described as 'the most abominable offence of

indecency conceivable', were considered too shocking for publication, but Hall maintained that he was simply trying to get a penny out of his mother's pocket. In his son's defence, Hall's father stated that his wife was not strong and was sometimes known to behave strangely.

Nevertheless the jury found Thomas guilty as charged and he was sentenced to six months' imprisonment.

1861 William Willey rented three adjoining properties on Hotwells Road, the middle one of which was The Hope and Anchor pub, over which Willey lived with his wife and six children.

15 APRIL

On 15 April, police officers Gelding, Brain and Pepperell noticed that the pub was on fire. They rushed to warn Willey, who was most aggrieved by their attempts to put out the blaze. He shouted at the policemen for sounding their rattles to summon assistance and tried to prevent them entering his premises. 'Can't a man do what he likes in his own home?' he asked.

Once the blaze was extinguished, the police found that the house had been deliberately fired at fourteen different points. Floorboards had been removed, to allow a through draught and there were 2,700 pieces of wood piled up beneath the floor, as well as wood shavings and straw mixed with tar.

Although Willey told the police that he was not insured, it later emerged that he had taken out a policy with Sun Fire Insurance a few months earlier. At that time, he applied for other policies but the Sun was the only company willing to accept his business.

Willey was charged with unlawfully setting fire to his home while his wife and children were inside, with setting fire to his home with intent to defraud the Sun Fire Insurance Company and with setting fire to the house of his landlord, Richard Yorke, with intent to defraud said landlord. The death penalty still applied for the first charge, although at Willey's trial at the Gloucester Assizes, Mr Justice Keating stated that he did not believe that there was sufficient evidence to prove that indictment, leaving the jury to focus on the other two offences. Found guilty, Willey was sentenced to twenty years' penal servitude.

1894 Daniel Harrington and Mary Jane Solari had been courting for almost a year, although Harrington was not above using his fists on Mary Jane whenever she displeased him. On 15 April, he hit her several times, splitting her lip.

16 APRIL

Nevertheless, Mary Jane spent the night with him at his lodgings on Gloucester Lane and the next morning, the couple went to The Forester's Arms on Merchant Street. Her lip was painful and still oozing blood, so Mary Jane went to the hospital that afternoon, where it was stitched.

Witnesses saw her with Daniel on Nelson Street later that evening, when both seemed to be drunk. They began arguing and Daniel hit Mary Jane again, so hard that her head whipped back, banging against the wall of the house outside which she was standing. As she slumped to the floor, Daniel said, 'Now you have got it,' and walked away.

Mary Jane died within minutes from a haemorrhage on the surface of her brain, caused by either a blow or a fall. Harrington was charged with manslaughter but, at his trial, his defence counsel Mr Lloyd maintained that Mary Jane had started the quarrel and was so drunk that the slightest touch would have caused her to fall over. When Harrington hit Mary Jane, she was attempting to scratch his eyes out and Harrington, who was trying to prevent her from doing so, could not possibly have anticipated that his blow would have such severe consequences.

When the jury found Harrington guilty of manslaughter, he begged the judge for mercy, saying that it wasn't his fault, since Mary Jane followed him around everywhere and he was unable to free himself from her unwanted attentions. The judge took into consideration the fact that he had already spent eleven weeks in prison awaiting his trial and sentenced him to a further four months' imprisonment.

17 APRIL

1879 Rosa Ball was cleaning, her five-week-old baby propped in an armchair, supported by a pillow. Wanting to borrow a piece of firestone, she popped next door to her neighbour, Martha Palmey and, when she returned five minutes later, she found her baby head down in the bucket of cleaning water, which she had left close to the armchair.

She snatched up the infant and ran back to Martha, who began to massage the baby and sent for midwife Mrs Sleeman, who lived just a few doors away. However, the infant gasped just once and then stopped breathing and neither Martha nor Mrs Sleeman was able to revive it.

At an inquest held by coroner Mr H.S. Wasbrough, the jury heard that the baby was illegitimate, although Rosa was expecting to marry the father shortly. It was a much-loved, well cared for child and the coroner determined that there was no reason to suspect any improper conduct other than carelessness on Rosa's part. The inquest jury returned a verdict of 'accidental death'.

18 APRIL

1892 As twenty-five-year-old Henry John Hemmings stood watching some men working in a yard in St Philip's, he suddenly dropped to the floor. The workmen sent for surgeon Dr Hannan, who quickly ascertained that Hemmings was dead, having been shot in the back. Nobody had heard a gunshot and the position of the wound ruled out any possibility that Hemmings had committed suicide.

Shortly after midnight, the police arrested two of the workmen – eighteen-year-old George Hedges and thirty-four-year-old Thomas Hill – charging both with 'wilful murder'. It emerged that Hedges was in the habit of practising shooting in the yard and his gun had gone off accidentally, killing Hemmings.

Hill was eventually released without charge and Hedges was committed for trial at the Bristol Assizes, the charge against him reduced to manslaughter. The jury accepted that the shooting was a tragic accident and he was acquitted.

19 APRIL

1891 An inquest was held at the Infirmary on the death of ten-month-old Ellen Shaddick, who was run over by a cart on 15 April.

Ellen's mother stated that her six-year-old daughter, Elizabeth, was sitting on the doorstep of her home on Captain Cary's Lane, nursing the baby when a boy ran past and snatched her hat, running off with it. Elizabeth gave chase and the boy threw the hat into the road.

Elizabeth ran to pick it up without looking to see if the road was clear and a passing cart ran over her foot. Elizabeth immediately dropped Ellen and the cart wheel ran over the baby's head, fracturing her skull.

The inquest jury returned a verdict of 'accidental death', laying no blame on Elizabeth or the cart driver, William Kelly. However, they told the coroner that they believed that the little boy who had precipitated the tragic chain of events should be flogged.

1900 Early in 1900, Queen Victoria made a personal gift of chocolates to every British soldier serving in South Africa in the Anglo-Boer War. Towards the end of March, Bristol people were offered the opportunity to win a box of these chocolates in a raffle to be held on 20 April at The Angel Hotel, Redcliff Street. The tickets cost 1s each and the proceeds were to be donated to the local war fund. Unfortunately, as the ticket holders were to discover, the raffle was a hoax.

20 APRIL

The police found that 1,000 tickets had been printed by Chappell's of Redcliff Street and thus identified the seller, twenty-three-year-old Charles Vincent Matthews. Matthews swore that he had been promised a box of chocolates by a friend in the Gloucestershire Yeomanry and had the tickets printed in anticipation of its arrival. He sold only a dozen tickets and, when the promised prize didn't arrive, his conscience had pricked him and he destroyed the remainder. However, printer Harold Victor Chappell told police that the last time he saw him, Matthews had said that he had sold 660 tickets.

Matthews was brought before magistrates at Bristol Police Court in June 1900 charged with obtaining 2s by false pretences from Mary Cook and a further 2s from Rosa Ward, both of whom stated that Matthews had sold them tickets by canvassing house-to-house. Since Matthews was unemployed and couldn't afford to repay the money, he was sent to prison for six weeks. He married only a few days before his appearance in court.

1900 Fifty-four-year-old John Croot of St Philip's had been drinking steadily for four days and had run out of alcohol. He asked his wife to fetch him some and, when she told him that it was too late and that everywhere would be closed, he viciously assaulted her, kicking her leg and cutting it so badly that she needed six stitches.

21 APRIL

Croot was brought before magistrates charged with assault. Esther Croot stated that this was the third time her husband had assaulted her since Christmas and she didn't want to live with him any more. Although Croot asked the magistrates to deal with him leniently and promised never to drink alcohol again, they sentenced him to six months' imprisonment with hard labour.

Croot had only recently been released from prison, serving a three-month sentence for assaulting Esther but, when sober, was said to be one of the kindest, quietest men in Bristol. Esther obviously relented as the couple were still living together in 1901.

22 APRIL **1881** Isaac Britton (or Brittan) of St George's had allegedly assaulted his wife, injuring her very badly. In consequence, a number of local boys hissed and booed at him and he saw red. Seizing a stick from one of them, he waved it around and threatened to kill them. The boys scattered, with Britton in pursuit.

Britton threw the stick at one, John Holly, hitting him and knocking him over. Holly scrambled to his feet and tried to escape by running down a narrow lane but collided with a donkey cart. As he lay on the ground, Britton caught up with him and kicked him hard in the stomach.

Holly died two days later and was found to have a ruptured intestine, leading to a charge of manslaughter against Britton by the coroner and one of 'feloniously killing and slaying' by the magistrates. Britton was therefore tried for both offences at the Gloucestershire Assizes. However, as Holly was helped home, he told two people that he had hurt himself on the shaft of the donkey cart, even though he later told his mother that Britton had kicked him. The jury therefore gave Britton the benefit of the doubt and acquitted him.

23 APRIL **1866** During 1832, it was estimated that cholera killed at least 626 people in Bristol, with 1,979 succumbing to an epidemic seventeen years later. General improvements in sanitation led to a decrease in fatalities during the next epidemic, with only 430 victims recorded in 1854.

On 23 April 1866 a single case of cholera was reported, the sufferer dying within eighteen hours. At that time, Bristol had an extremely forward-thinking medical officer, David Davies, who immediately took action to prevent another epidemic. The characteristic symptom of cholera is 'rice water' diarrhoea – watery faeces with flecks of mucus, which have the appearance of water in which rice has been washed. Davies realised that the diarrhoea carried germs and made a determined effort to stop their spread.

He set up a widespread programme of disinfection, with corpses wrapped in their bed sheets, liberally doused with sulphate of iron or carbolic powder and buried immediately. He recruited a team of twenty-eight women – each of whom had her own allotted district of Bristol – who visited houses, persuading people to disinfect their lavatories night and morning.

Depots for free disinfectant were set up throughout the city and people were instructed to disinfect anything that might have come into contact with infected stools. Whenever a new case was reported, the privies, drains and sewers of the affected household and their neighbours' were immediately disinfected. Communal pump handles were chained up or removed.

When a death occurred, the victims' beds and bedclothes burned. Other inhabitants were removed from the house, which was then cleaned, fumigated and whitewashed throughout. Those who recovered from the disease were monitored and subjected to stringent disinfection regimes.

The fact that the 1866 outbreak of cholera claimed only twenty-nine victims in Bristol is entirely credited to Davies, who was unremitting in his battle against the disease. In comparison, Swansea in Wales and its surrounding area experienced 521 deaths in the 1866 outbreak.

1862 Frederick Sims of Newfoundland Gardens made a second appearance at the Council House charged with assaulting his ten-year-old son, Joseph, and also his wife, Elizabeth.

Two days earlier, Joseph appeared before magistrates still bearing a chain around his waist, with which he alleged that his father had chained him to a bed post on 12 April. (Although Joseph managed to break the chain that tethered him, his father refused to relinquish the key to the padlock that locked it in place.)

Frederick freely admitted to chaining up his son, saying that he could do nothing else with him. He reminded magistrates that Joseph had appeared before them before and been sent to the Bridewell, having stolen money from him. On his release, Frederick alleged that Joseph had stolen his shirt studs and sold them to buy a pistol, with which he then threatened to shoot his sister. He also told the magistrates that Joseph persistently ran away from home, sometimes absenting himself for three or four nights.

When Joseph's mother remonstrated with her husband about his treatment of their son, she was beaten for interfering. Frederick said that every time he came home from work, his wife complained about Joseph's mischief and pilfering yet, when he tried to punish the boy, Elizabeth took her son's side and refused to allow it.

Joseph was released from his chain and the magistrates discharged his father on the condition that he found two sureties of £25 to guarantee his good behaviour for the next six months.

1861 Emily Smith of St George's accused Eliza Cribb of being a prostitute. In response, Eliza dragged Emily to a ditch by her hair and was beating her head against the bank when Ann Melsom heard the child's terrified screams and tried to intervene. Ann was rewarded with a mouthful of bad language and a punch in the face and, to make matters worse, Eliza's mother was now inciting her daughter to even greater violence, urging her, 'Go into her, 'Liza, give it to her.'

Eliza, described in the contemporary newspapers as 'an Amazon' and 'a virago', appeared at Lawford's Gate on 2 May charged with two counts of assault. Eliza admitted both charges, believing that she was within her rights to chastise Emily Smith, but the magistrates disagreed, fining her 5s with costs or fourteen days' imprisonment for assaulting Emily and the same for her assault on Mrs Melsom.

1888 Eight-year-old Charlotte Drew died, after returning home from school two days earlier complaining of a headache and nausea. Questioned by her parents, Charlotte told them that one of the teachers had hit her on the head.

Coroner Mr Wasbrough requested a post-mortem examination and surgeon Mr A.S. Goff found that death had resulted from 'congestion of the brain', although he could find nothing to suggest the cause. Goff found no external marks of violence and suggested that, while a blow on Charlotte's head could have caused the congestion, it would have to have been a very severe one. Since Charlotte had been suffering from a heavy cold in the days before her death, Goff felt it far more likely that this had led to her brain becoming congested.

The inquest jury returned a verdict that 'death was the result of congestion of the brain, with no primary cause established.'

27 APRIL 1888 William Charles Huggins worked at a steam saw mill on Easton Road. At the side of the building was a tall chimney, which leaned outwards at a dangerous angle. Huggins was terrified that the chimney would fall on him and avoided walking past it whenever he could. If he absolutely had to pass it, he would eye it nervously before sprinting by as fast as possible.

On 27 April, a fire broke out at the mill and employees rushed to rescue what tools and paperwork they could from the burning building. Although the workshop was razed to the ground, there was just one fatality – William Huggins died when the chimney collapsed and buried him in the ruins.

Ironically, arrangements had just been finalised for the demolition of the chimney in three weeks time.

28 APRIL 1896 When the parents of Robert and Elizabeth 'Betsy' Smith died, they left their cottage in Winterbourne to their children, on condition that they remained unmarried. Thus, when Robert married, he forfeited his right to live in the cottage, leaving Betsy as the sole occupier, although Robert owned the adjacent land.

Robert suffered from heart and lung disease, which prevented him from working. He suggested to Betsy that he and his family should be allowed to move into their parents' cottage, but Betsy refused.

On 28 April Robert felt well enough to work on his land. Betsy was sitting sewing when her brother walked into the cottage and, without speaking, began to rummage through the kitchen cupboards. When he found what he was searching for – a hammer – he suddenly attacked Betsy, hitting her several times on the head.

Betsy managed to stagger to a neighbour's cottage. A doctor was called and she was taken to the General Hospital, where her condition was described as 'critical'. Robert was later found dead, hanging from a beam in an outhouse at the cottage. (Coincidentally, his brother hanged himself from the same beam ten years earlier.)

Gloucestershire coroner Mr E.M. Grace held an inquest on Robert's death, at which it was surmised that, sixty-one-year-old Robert hung himself 'whilst of unsound mind', believing he had already killed his sister.

Sixty-five-year-old Betsy is believed to have survived her brother's murderous attack.

29 APRIL 1900 PC Greenslade watched as Isaac Roach drove his trap along Henleaze Road. The trap careened from one side of the thoroughfare to the other and back, much to the obvious amusement of Roach and his female passenger.

Henleaze Road, 1906. (Author's collection)

Suspecting that Roach may be drunk, Greenslade managed to stop the horse, finding its driver so intoxicated that he was incapable of standing up.

Roach was summoned to appear before magistrates at Lawford's Gate charged with being drunk in charge of a horse and trap. Found guilty, he was fined 10s and costs, with the option of spending fourteen days in prison.

1894 Forty-two-year-old Sarah Simmons was admitted to the General Hospital, where she died at five o'clock the next morning.

Sarah was a servant at The Hen and Chickens pub in Bedminster. She had worked there since 3 April and was a respectable and temperate woman, who was proving a reliable and conscientious employee. Shortly before Sarah's admission to hospital, barmaid Emily Meere went upstairs to their shared bedroom and found her lying unconscious on the floor. The room reeked of spirits – as did Sarah's breath – and she quickly fell into a coma, from which she never awoke.

When Sarah was undressed, nurses found a length of rubber tubing in her pocket, which also smelled strongly of alcohol. Sarah's bedroom at the pub was used for storing cases of spirits in six-gallon jars and, after her death, one of the jars was found to be half empty.

When surgeon Mr J.L. Firth conducted a post-mortem examination, he found that all of Sarah's organs were healthy with the exception of her lungs, which were congested. Although Firth couldn't be absolutely sure what had killed Sarah, the only explanation he could offer was that she had died from alcohol poisoning, having removed the bung from one of the jars of spirits and sucked out a large quantity through the piece of tubing. Yet, although it was not impossible for Sarah to have gained access to the liquor, there were two heavy boxes on top of the case, which did not appear to have been moved.

For want of a better explanation, the jury eventually returned a verdict of 'death as a result of coma, in all probability induced by alcoholic poisoning.'

30 APRIL

MAY

Clifton Suspension Bridge. (Author's collection)

1876 Seventy-year-old James McGuire of Tankard's Close often drank himself into a stupor and it was left to his grandson James Griffiths to put him safely to bed. On 1 May, lodger Mary Bond returned home in the evening to find grandfather and grandson sitting around the table with two women, Emily Hooper and Ann Ley. McGuire was almost naked and some of the furniture was broken.

As Mary was going upstairs, she saw Griffiths hit his grandfather on his side with a champagne bottle and from her room she heard several loud bumps. Mary called down to Griffiths, telling him not to hit his grandfather and the young man replied, 'I'll knock him on the head if he doesn't go to bed.'

McGuire eventually went to bed and was found dead there a little while later. The police found scratched paint and drops of blood in the room and a smashed champagne bottle downstairs, on which analyst Mr Stoddart found specks of blood.

When a post-mortem examination revealed that McGuire was covered with bruises and abrasions and appeared to have died from a blow, Griffiths and the two women were charged with his manslaughter. Although the women were later discharged, Griffiths appeared at the Bristol Assizes.

The court heard that McGuire was incapable of standing and that his grandson and Emily Hooper had carried him upstairs, Griffiths holding him beneath his armpits and Hooper holding his feet. Ann Ley testified that McGuire habitually got so drunk that he fell about and that earlier on the day of his death, he fell into the grate and hit his head. The champagne bottle was accidentally broken when he fell over.

At this, the jury informed the judge that there was insufficient evidence for them to convict Griffiths of manslaughter and he was discharged with a caution.

1880 Six-year-old Herbert Dudley Laudale and his brother were left in the care of their aunt and a nursery nurse while their father was in Calcutta. Herbert had a bad cold and Rachel Laudale ordered her maid to run a hot bath for him, but as soon he was lowered into the water Herbert began to scream.

He was a rather excitable child and his screams and struggles to get out of the bath were nothing unusual, but after six or seven minutes his eyes suddenly rolled back in his head. The nurse drew Miss Laudale's attention to Herbert's strange expression and the two women decided to lift him out of the bath. As the nurse bent over to pick him up, she realised that the bathwater was extremely hot.

Herbert died the next morning, his death attributed to shock to his nervous system caused by extensive scalding of his legs and lower torso. An inquest held by coroner Mr H.S. Wasbrough heard that Miss Laudale tested the temperature of the water with her hand before putting Herbert in, but Dr Shingleton Smith pointed out that this was a very unreliable method, adding that it was better to use an elbow if a thermometer was not available. The inquest jury returned a verdict of 'death by misadventure'.

3 MAY

1899 Maurice Organ and Hugh Heyward were transporting five tons of timber from Leigh Woods to Bedminster, in a cart drawn by four horses. As they descended the steep Rownham Hill, the cart began to accelerate. It collided with the horse between the shafts, which in turn pushed the horse in front of it until all four animals were trotting as fast as they could. Maurice, who had been applying the brake, was left behind and watched in horror as the cart careened down the hill with Hugh in pursuit, hitting a bank at the bottom and overturning. Twenty-two-year-old Hugh was trapped beneath the load and it took almost thirty minutes to extricate him, by which time he was dead.

At an inquest held by coroner Mr S. Craddock, Maurice stated that he had transported similar, often heavier, loads along the same route for three years without problems. He believed that on this occasion the cart wheels skidded in the gutter and were unable to gain any purchase on the road surface. The inquest jury returned a verdict of 'accidental death'.

4 MAY

1888 As miner Walter Gould was working below ground at the South Liberty Colliery his lamp suddenly went out, plunging him into darkness. Disoriented, he walked the wrong way along a tunnel and fell almost 200 yards down an open shaft. His mangled body was recovered by his father, a fellow miner.

At the inquest on his death, held at the Plough Inn, Bedminster Down by coroner Mr Craddock, the jury returned a verdict of 'accidental death', adding a recommendation that the shaft should be fenced off immediately.

5 MAY

1888 John Keast of Martin Street, St Paul's, heard a child screaming. He leaped out of bed and rushed to the door, where he was met by a thick cloud of smoke.

Although Keast knew that Mrs Emily Hunt and her baby were upstairs, his immediate concern was for his own child, but as soon as his son was safe, Keast ran back into the house, finding a baby lying on the staircase. He carried the child outside, before going back to look for Mrs Hunt.

When he reached her room, he found her on the floor, her feet in the open doorway. As he bent to lift her, her clothes crumbled beneath his hands and he quickly realised that she was dead.

An overturned paraffin lamp lay on the floor, the brass flattened as if it had been stamped on and it was evident that somebody had tried to douse the fire with water. At the inquest, coroner Mr Wasbrough theorised that the lamp had fallen over close to Mrs Hunt's baby and she set her skirts alight trying to stamp out the fire.

She apparently threw water at the flames, but when that proved futile ran downstairs to put the baby in a safe place before returning to her room to remove her burning clothes, some of which were found on the landing. Since Keast had not heard Emily shouting for help, the coroner surmised that she had probably been suffocated by the smoke.

In returning a verdict of 'accidental death', the jury agreed with the coroner who believed that Emily might have saved herself if she had not tried to rescue her child.

1859 As John Noble walked home late at night, he met Richard Stadden (or Staddon) and Mary Ann Colston on the corner of St Thomas's Lane and strolled a short distance with them. When Noble excused himself to go into a dark alley for 'a necessary purpose', Mary Ann followed him and there was some activity between them, which culminated in Noble paying Mary Ann 6d.

6 MAY

As Noble and Mary Ann made their way back to the road, Stadden suddenly grabbed Noble by the throat and strangled him until he became unconscious. When he came round, all his money had been stolen. Noble sought out a policeman, who quickly located Stadden and Colston in a nearby house.

The couple appeared at the Gloucestershire Assizes on 9 August charged with robbery and violence. Both were found guilty and, since it was not their first offence, Mr Justice Byles sentenced Stadden to four years' imprisonment and Mary Ann Colston to eighteen months with hard labour.

1888 Thirty-year-old Arthur William Masters was found dead in his cell at Horfield Prison. He had served just three days of the twenty-one day sentence awarded by magistrates for assaulting his wife, Mary Anne.

7 MAY

A post-mortem examination by gaol surgeon George Gardiner showed that Masters had committed suicide by forcing a piece of rag down his throat with a wooden spoon, the handle of which protruded from his mouth when his body was discovered.

At an inquest held at the prison by coroner Dr E.M. Grace, the jury returned a verdict of 'suicide whilst of unsound mind'.

1862 James Roberts, a war hero who lost a foot in the Crimean War, went to visit his sister-in-law Charlotte Walker with his wife, Betsy. Roberts seemed in good spirits, but when he arrived home to Great George Street he went upstairs to where his two daughters lay sleeping and attacked them with a poker.

8 MAY

Betsy snatched up her badly injured children and ran across the road to Charlotte's house. With neighbour Elizabeth Hayden, she and Charlotte carried the girls to the police station, from where they were escorted to the Infirmary. Fourteen-month-old Clara died from a fractured skull and five-year-old Alice Elizabeth had severe head injuries, although she survived.

Roberts was arrested on 9 May and charged with Clara's 'wilful murder'. According to Roberts, he had lived on bad terms with his wife for some time and wanted to separate, but Betsy was afraid that her children would 'come to want'. Her husband assured her that he would kill them before that happened and, in the face of more 'aggravation' from Betsy on their return from her sister's house, he did just that.

When the case came to trial at the Gloucestershire Assizes on 12 August 1862, Charlotte Walker testified that James and Betsy were laughing and joking together when they visited her on the night of the murder and were 'good tempered and sociable' when they left.

Charlotte and other witnesses stated that after his discharge from the Army, Roberts purchased a horse and cart and started up a haulage business, which, with his pension, gave the family a good living. Yet he became addicted to drink and sold everything, including the horse and cart, to finance his habit. Consequently, the family were deeply in debt and had only dry bread to eat.

Roberts himself finally acknowledged that the murder was 'all owing to drink and bad temper', and since he had a family history of insanity, the jury acquitted him on those grounds. He was ordered to be detained during Her Majesty's Pleasure and was sent to Broadmoor Criminal Lunatic Asylum.

9 MAY **1866** At about ten o'clock in the morning, George Green of Portishead became the first person to commit suicide by jumping off the Clifton Suspension Bridge.

Green purchased a ticket from toll collector Mrs Lavis, who noted that he looked sad and that he kept passing his hand across his forehead, as if he were in pain. As he neared the middle of the bridge, a phaeton driven by Mr Fussell passed and, recognising Green, Fussell gave him a nod. Green raised his hand in acknowledgement then suddenly vaulted over the 4ft-high high railings. He turned and twisted several times in the air, before landing heavily in the mud 250ft below the bridge.

A view from Clifton Suspension Bridge. (Author's collection)

A group of workmen laying water pipes rushed to him but found him dead. At the inquest on Green's death, held by Mr H.S. Wasbrough, it was said that Green had been showing signs of mental derangement for some time. The jury determined that, 'in a temporary fit of insanity, the deceased threw himself from the Clifton Suspension Bridge into the river Avon, by means of which he was immediately killed.'

10 MAY **1881** Isaac Howard was committed for trial by magistrates charged with raping domestic servant Sarah Ann Hall.

The couple were both members of the Salvation Army and, after meeting for three months at the twice-weekly services, were engaged to be married. After the service on 9 May, Isaac volunteered to see Sarah safely home, an offer she gladly accepted. However, according to Sarah, she was far from safe, as Isaac bundled her into a field and 'ravished' her. When the deed was done, Sarah fled to a nearby house and Isaac was quickly arrested.

At his trial, Isaac insisted that Sarah had consented to having intercourse with him and then had second thoughts after the act. He was acquitted.

1885 Newspapers countrywide printed the miraculous story of Sarah Ann Henley. Broken hearted after a lover's tiff, on 8 May Sarah decided to end it all by jumping from the Clifton Suspension Bridge. She was wearing a billowing dress with crinoline petticoats, which acted as a parachute, slowing her fall and cushioning her landing in the mud at the side of the Avon.

She was rescued fully conscious and taken to hospital, where it was discovered that, in spite of having fallen nearly 250ft, she didn't have a single broken bone. Sarah went on to live well into her eighties.

1874 Edward Price and Mary Ann Shannon lived as man and wife on St Augustine Street, although Price worked at Mangotsfield and usually stayed there during the week.

On 12 May, Price and Mary Ann went to Mangotsfield together. They spent a few hours drinking in The Crown before heading back to Bristol, but when they arrived at Mangotsfield Station they found they had missed the train. They went back to the pub, remaining there until closing time, then set off to walk the six or seven miles home.

Mary Ann was a few yards in front of Edward when she was suddenly set upon by a gang of ruffians, who began to kick and beat her. Price managed to pull her away from the men and the couple retreated to the porch of the pub. However, the gang followed and, restraining Price, dragged Mary Ann to Mangotsfield Common, where for the next two hours they sexually assaulted her, covering her mouth with their hands to prevent her from screaming.

Mary Ann's ordeal finally ended when a nearby resident heard a commotion and went to investigate. The men fled as the witness approached, leaving Mary Ann exhausted, battered and bruised, her clothes torn from her back.

Another local resident, Mr Powell, heard the men running past his house and recognised three of them – George Britton, Joseph Haskins and Charles Bullock. It was quickly established that they too had been drinking in The Crown and had left in the company of Aaron Summerhill, William Sheppard and Sydney Bracey.

All six were arrested and appeared before magistrates charged with attempting to commit an indecent assault on Mary Ann Shannon and with stealing 4s, a thimble and a handkerchief from her. (All laughed, joked and made ribald comments throughout the proceedings.) There was little evidence against Summerhill, Sheppard and Bracey, who were discharged, but the others were committed for trial at the next Gloucestershire Assizes.

There, all three were found guilty of 'assault with intent to ravish'. Haskins and Bullock were sentenced to six months' imprisonment, while Britton, who was considered the ringleader, received a sentence of twelve months' imprisonment.

13 MAY

1895 Alice Starr had been in service but returned to her parents in Lewin's Mead in disgrace, having fallen pregnant. On 12 May, in severe pain, she was taken to St Peter's Hospital by a neighbour, but couldn't be persuaded to stay and fled home.

The next morning, the body of a baby girl was found in an outhouse behind the Starrs' house. Their landlady, Clara Thomas, was woken at four o'clock that morning by the sound of somebody moving around and, looking through her bedroom window, saw Alice's mother going to the back of the premises. When the police were informed, Alice and Mary Ann Starr were arrested.

St Peter's Hospital.
(Author's collection)

Alice was charged with manslaughter and with concealing the birth of her child, Mary Ann with concealment only. Both were tried at the Bristol Assizes. Alice gave conflicting statements, saying that she fainted after giving birth and remembered nothing but also that she recalled going downstairs and out into the yard.

Surgeon George Thomas Miles told the court that there were no signs that the baby had suffered any injuries and it appeared to have died for want of proper attention shortly after birth. Miles also stated that, although it was physically possible for Alice to have gone downstairs, he personally doubted that she would have had the strength, so soon after giving birth.

The jury accepted Miles's opinion, finding Alice not guilty of both charges. Mary Ann, however, was found guilty and sentenced to two months' imprisonment with hard labour.

14 MAY

1900 Robert Winter (17), William Thomas (16) and Henry Wilmot (12) appeared at the Police Court charged with gambling in the public streets in St Paul's on a Sunday morning. John Haberfield (15) was charged with committing a similar offence in Redcross Park, while Arthur Jefferies was charged with playing football in the streets.

Magistrates heard that Sunday gambling and football playing had now reached such a pitch that the police were obliged to send out plain-clothed officers to apprehend those perpetrating this 'intolerable nuisance'. As an example to others, the magistrates dealt with the four boys harshly, fining Jefferies 2s 6d, Winter, Thomas and Haberfield 5s each, and committing Wilmot to the Workhouse for three days on account of his youth.

1944 During the Second World War, Bristol was one of the most frequently bombed cities in the British Isles, the principle enemy targets being the docks and aircraft factories. The last air raid in Bristol on 15 May 1944 was a comparatively minor one, with the loss of just one life.

In all, there were more than seventy air raids on Bristol during the hostilities, resulting in the deaths of more than 1,300 civilians. Many more people were injured and several of Bristol's historic properties were destroyed, including the Bishop's Palace, the Dutch House and the Children's Hospital. Bristol's civilian war dead are remembered on a memorial at the ruins of St Peter's Church in Castle Park, itself a target of enemy bombs.

The Dutch House (destroyed during the Second World War). (Author's collection)

1898 Fifteen-year-old Mildred Nethercott visited Charles Greenway, a monumental sculptor at Arno's Vale, on the pretext of asking him to call on her father. While there, she elicited a contribution of one shilling for her church mission charity. Unfortunately, the donations collected by Miss Nethercott from Greenway and several other Bristol businessmen went no further than her own pocket.

Charged at Bristol Police Court with obtaining charitable contributions by false pretences, Mildred was sent to the Liverpool Reformatory School, where she was ordered to remain for four years.

Her father, Henry, told magistrates that his daughter had always been a good girl and had only offended since she had taken to bicycle riding.

1888 Coroner Mr H.S. Wasbrough held an inquest on the death of five-month-old Frank Jenkins, who died from the effects of his clothing catching fire nearly a month earlier.

Frank's mother, Ellen Elizabeth Jenkins, of Hotwells, told the inquest that she had gone out to do some shopping, leaving Frank and his four-year-old brother in the charge of their sister, Annie. Given a copper by a neighbour, Annie went to the shop and purchased a toy lantern, which she lit and gave to her brothers to play with, before going out to play with her friends.

The lamp set Frank's clothing alight and his brother scooped him up and rushed him downstairs. Neighbour Mrs Spillett heard screaming and went to see what the matter was. Seeing Frank in his brother's arms, enveloped in

flames, she beat the fire out with her hands and rushed the baby to a doctor,
who sent him straight to the Children's Hospital. Frank was badly burned on
his right leg, foot and elbow and died on 17 May from 'exhaustion'.

Mr Wasbrough told the jury that there was little doubt that Frank's death
was a tragic accident, adding that eleven-year-old Annie had committed a
fearful neglect of duty. She should have been well aware of the dangers of
playing with fire and she had also gone out instead of doing what she was
told and minding her little brothers. Wasbrough sincerely hoped that this
would be a 'life lesson' for the child, telling her that if she had been just a
little older, she would have been answerable in law for her brother's death.
The jury returned a verdict of 'accidental death' and joined the coroner in
censuring Annie for her part in the tragedy.

18 MAY   **1877** Samuel Biggs of Barton Regis ran away with another woman, leaving
his wife and their five children dependent on parish relief for their survival.
They were taken to the Workhouse and efforts were made to trace Samuel.
However, after a year they were discharged and provided with 'outdoor
relief'.

By chance, a police officer found Samuel living with his lover in Devizes,
Wiltshire, using the alias Samuel Jones. Since maintaining Samuel's wife
and children had cost the Union a total of £120, he was summoned to
appear before magistrates at Bristol Police Court charged with deserting his
wife and family. He was additionally charged with deserting from the South
Gloucester Militia.

Found guilty, he was sentenced to three months' imprisonment with hard
labour for the first offence and fined £2 for the second, with the option of
another month's imprisonment in default

19 MAY   **1880** John Webster appeared at Bristol Police Court charged with being a
'wandering lunatic', after a policeman arrested him for causing a disturbance

and an obstruction by preaching to a large crowd on the streets. The subject of Webster's sermon was Sodom, Gomorrah and the Gates of Heaven and, after the arresting officer told the Bench that Webster was clearly insane, the accused treated the magistrates to a lengthy harangue on the Books of the Prophets.

When they were finally able to get a word in, the magistrates hurriedly discharged Webster to the care of his daughter, on receiving her assurances that he wouldn't be allowed outside in future.

1856 Fourteen-year-old Henry Jones appeared at Bristol Police Court charged with stealing a plum loaf. Magistrates heard that he had a long record of petty thefts and had only just been released from prison.

Henry told magistrates that his father was a drunkard, who neglected and ill-treated his family. The constable who arrested him confirmed this, saying that the boy lived in a shocking state of poverty and that his mother was on the verge of death. His father squandered all of his earnings on drink and Henry's thefts had been items of food, which he shared with his family to keep them from starvation.

Henry pleaded to be sent to Reformatory School and the magistrates remanded him for two days while they made enquiries. When he was brought back before them, they called his father to the Bench and lectured him on his duties towards his son. Mr Jones agreed to teach the boy his own trade and Henry was discharged with a caution.

20 MAY

1859 William Wright appeared at the Council House charged with assaulting his mother-in-law, Mary Loscombe, and with breaking a window at her shop on Hotwells Road.

Wright dragged his wife around the room by her hair and, when Mrs Loscombe objected to his treatment of her daughter, he picked up a chair and beat her with it. Mrs Loscombe lived over her shop, but was so afraid of Wright's violence that she no longer slept at home.

It was not Wright's first appearance before magistrates for assaulting his wife and her mother and, in March 1859, he was bound over in the sum of £20 to keep the peace towards his mother-in-law for a period of three months. Magistrates ordered that he should forfeit his bail and asked his solicitors to appear before them the following week. Meanwhile they sentenced Wright to four months' imprisonment with hard labour.

21 MAY

1858 A group of children went to bathe in Malago Brook, Bedminster. They had dried and dressed themselves, when fifteen-year-old William Garland arrived and asked them to go back in to show him the depth of the water. When they refused, Garland grabbed Henry Giles and tossed him into the stream.

Weighed down by his clothes, Giles struggled to stay afloat, eventually grabbing some grass on the bank and hanging on for dear life. The shouts of his companions attracted the attention of a milkman, who pulled him out, foaming at the mouth and almost drowned.

22 MAY

Garland was named by one of the boys as the culprit and was later identified at the police station by Henry, the milkman and by another boy, Henry Bessell. However, Garland insisted that they were all mistaken, since he had been nowhere near the brook that day. Magistrates didn't believe him and fined him 40s plus costs or six weeks' imprisonment, warning him that, if it hadn't been for the timely intervention of the milkman, the case could have ended tragically and he would probably have been transported.

23 MAY   **1852** Coroner Mr J.B. Grindon held an inquest at The Giant's Castle on Philip Street on the death of thirty-four-year-old Henry Luff, a married man with five children.

Luff worked at Finzel's sugar refinery and, earlier that day, John Griffiths heard a strange noise coming from one of the engine rooms, which he described as sounding 'like the flapping of a broken engine strap.' Griffiths found the shaft of the engine turning and Luff spinning round with it, caught fast by his leather apron.

A glance was enough to confirm that Luff was dead – both his legs were torn off, his right arm hung limply and all the fingers were missing from his left hand. Luff was apparently fitting a new strap on the shaft when his apron became entangled in the moving parts. It was common practice to fit new belts while the machinery was in motion, as it was believed to be easier.

The jury returned a verdict of 'accidental death', laying no blame on Finzel's for permitting this dangerous practice.

24 MAY   **1903** Sidney John Anthony Gower (14) and Frank Marks (4) died in the Infirmary from injuries received the previous day at The Bristol Post Office Sports, held at the County Ground.

The boys were among 8,000 spectators watching a five-mile motorcycle race involving four competitors – T.H. Tessier and G. Barnes of London and E. Kickham and P. Bailey of Bristol. Kickham broke a chain and retired at the end of the first lap, while the three remaining competitors completed three

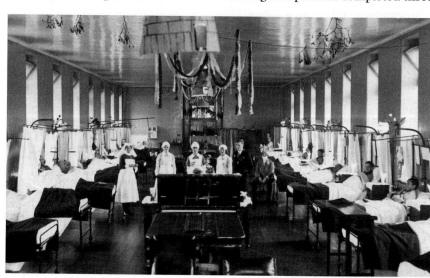

Bristol Royal Infirmary, 1927. (Author's collection)

miles of the race before disaster struck. Barnes was about to overtake Bailey, who was a lap ahead. As he did so, Bailey looked round and his motorcycle veered off course.

Barnes managed to pass him on the outside of the track, but he and Bailey collided and both riders and their bikes were thrown into the crowd. Panic stricken spectators rushed onto the track, narrowly avoiding Tessier, who had not seen the accident and so continued racing. While Bailey escaped relatively unscathed, Barnes and ten spectators were rushed to the Infirmary. Barnes and two spectators were able to leave after treatment and another two were discharged the following morning.

It is believed that there was one more fatality as a result of the incident, the victim being a thirteen-year-old boy.

1910 An inquest was held on the deaths of thirty-five-year-old Clara Rose and her ten-year-old son, Harold. 25 MAY

Clara lived as man and wife with Frederick Harvey, an inspector on the Clifton Suspension Bridge and Harold was their son. The couple had been arguing recently and, on 23 April, Frederick moved out of their home.

Clara sent Frederick their savings of £65 with a note saying that if she couldn't have him then she didn't want his money. When Frederick sent some men to remove some of his belongings from the couple's home, they found Clara dying in a bedroom and Harold already dead.

The inquest jury found that Harold was poisoned by his mother, who then committed suicide while insane.

1861 An inquest was held at St Peter's Hospital on the death of three-year-old Matilda Oliver of St Philip's. 26 MAY

On the previous day, Matilda's mother, Catherine, walked calmly into the Central Police Station and told PC William Windmill, 'I am your prisoner.'

'What for?' asked Windmill.

'For hanging one of my children,' Catherine replied, handing over the key to her rooms on John Street. When Windmill checked the premises, he found Matilda hanging from the bed rail and, although he cut the child down, life was extinct.

Catherine, an epileptic, was widely known as 'Flighty Mrs Oliver' and had borne twelve children, six of whom survived. Although she was an extremely zealous chapel-goer, there were rumours that she overindulged in alcohol. Her behaviour in the past had been decidedly strange – a devoted mother, she once abandoned her family and walked to London, saying that she wanted to get into hospital there. According to her husband, Henry, she sent the children outside naked and once pawned every stick of furniture and item of clothing from their home.

Catherine explained that she had murdered her daughter after years of abuse and ill-treatment at the hands of her husband. Committed for trial, the main consideration for her jury was whether or not Catherine was insane.

Surgeon Mr Crosby Leonard, PC Windmill and the surgeon of Bristol Gaol, Mr Alfred Bleeck, testified that they believed that Catherine was of sound mind at the time of the murder, if a little 'eccentric'. However the jury chose to believe Catherine's neighbours, who detailed her ill-treatment at the hands of her husband and her strange ways, finding her not guilty on the grounds of insanity.

27 MAY   **1888** Nobody had seen or heard Henry and Eliza Clements of Church Street, Temple, for four days. Their landlord, Charles Cole, believed that they were in their room but was unable to rouse them and, when he peered through the keyhole, he could see Eliza lying on the floor and hear her snoring.

When she hadn't moved some hours later, Cole forced open the door to be met with a scene reminiscent of a slaughterhouse. The room was covered in blood from floor to ceiling and Eliza Clements was dreadfully injured – three of her fingers were almost severed, she had a deep stab wound in her chest and the whole of her forehead and most of the front of her brain had been hacked off with a bill hook. Her dead husband sat in a chair nearby, wearing just his shirt. He had six self-inflicted stab wounds in his left breast made by a table knife, which lay on the floor by his chair.

Amazingly, Eliza was still alive and conscious. Cole sent for the police and PS Brimble procured a cab to take her to the General Hospital. There she was able to tell surgeons 'my husband beat me', and explain that after a quarrel on 24 May, he tried to cut her throat. She grappled with him, cutting her fingers on his knife and he then stabbed her. The last thing she recalled was seeing him coming towards her with the bill hook. She remembered feeling a blow to her head, then nothing more.

Eliza soon lapsed into unconsciousness and was expected to die within hours. Incredibly, she survived until 8 July, by which time an inquest had long since reached a verdict of *felo de se* on her husband. Eliza was pregnant and her baby died with her, a post-mortem examination revealing that what remained of her brain was riddled with abscesses and filled with pus.

Henry Clements apparently loved his wife to distraction but was terribly jealous. The couple married on 8 December 1886 but, prior to her marriage, twenty-six-year-old Eliza had given birth to two illegitimate children, something that her husband could neither forgive nor forget.

At the inquest into Eliza's death held by coroner Mr H.S. Wasbrough, the jury returned the only possible verdict – that of 'wilful murder' against Henry Clements. By coincidence, Clements's brother had been a victim of murder ten years earlier (*see* 31 July).

28 MAY   **1894** Thomas Marshall of St Jude's appeared at Bristol Police Court charged with assaulting his eleven-year-old son, John. The Bench heard that, after spending the evening drinking, Marshall sent his son for some fried fish. John came home with the wrong sort and, when he refused to take it back to the shop and change it, his father beat him with a belt, cutting his head and leaving bruises all over his body.

Marshall insisted that he had only given John a few licks and that the cut on his head occurred when he accidentally bumped it on a table. 'He laughed and jeered at me,' pleaded Marshall and added, 'That is a thing a father could hardly stand.'

Magistrates sent him to prison for one month with hard labour.

1898 The afternoon and evening of 29 May were unprecedented in the annals of the Bristol Fire Brigade, who received a total of six call-outs, stretching resources to their limits.

29 MAY

The afternoon began with a fire at Charles Hare and Company White Lead Works on Little Avon Street, St Philip's. Two hours later, a workshop fire on Cloud's Hill Road endangered the Baptist Chapel there.

A storeroom at Reynolds & Sons on the Tontine Quay, St Augustine's then caught fire and, while the brigade were dealing with that, they learned that another fire had broken out, after a paraffin lamp exploded in a house on College Street. Fortunately, by then, the fire at the Tontine Quay was almost under control, freeing some of the firemen to attend with the manual engine.

The final call to a house on Hotwells Road came in the early hours of the morning of 30 May. Thanks to the barking of their collie dog, Mr Hussey and his family were able to escape with their lives. The dog was not so fortunate, becoming the only fatality of the day.

1857 Ambrose Marshall appeared at the Council House charged with violently assaulting his wife, Ann, by striking her on the face with a coconut.

30 MAY

In the course of an argument between them, Bedminster greengrocer Marshall began pelting his wife with cabbages. Fortunately, his aim was poor but Marshall then flung a weight at Ann and, when that also missed, he turned to the display of coconuts. The second one found its target, hitting her on her cheek and giving her a terrible black eye.

In his defence, Marshall told the magistrates that his wife had struck the first blow and he was only retaliating. He was sentenced to one month's imprisonment with hard labour.

1856 Irish labourer Patrick Haggarty of St Philip's died at the Infirmary.

31 MAY

One week earlier, Haggarty was romping with a young widow. He gave her a playful hug and immediately felt a sharp pricking sensation in his chest. The woman was a seamstress and was in the habit of sticking needles in the bodice of her dress, one of which had pricked Haggarty as he pulled her close. Initially, Haggarty believed that the needle had merely scratched him but, when the pain increased, he went to the Infirmary, where Dr Green determined that it was lodged in his chest.

An operation was performed at midday on 26 May, when the surgeon was able to grasp the needle with forceps and extract it. The needle had pierced Haggarty's lung and heart and, when it was removed, Green realised that the eye end had broken off.

At first, twenty-three-year-old Haggarty seemed to be recovering from his surgery, but then developed pneumonia. At an inquest held by Mr J.B. Grindon, the jury returned a verdict of 'accidental death'.

JUNE

Police funeral in Bristol (*see* 19 June and 22 June). (Author's collection)

1885 Before his death in 1882, Isaac Rogers made a considerable amount of money keeping The Chequers Inn and running the ferry at Hanham. His personal fortune included outright ownership of a house, Nightingale's Rest.

After Isaac's death, his widow married a man named Pillinger, a local man who had spent many years in Australia. The new Mrs Pillinger also had two sons living there and the couple decided to emigrate, much to the chagrin of Mrs Pillinger's youngest son, Lewis. When the Pillingers tried to sell Nightingale's Rest to finance their journey, Lewis made such a commotion at the auction that he was arrested and bound over for three months to keep the peace.

Lewis, who was living with his mother and stepfather, moved out and took lodgings with a neighbour. As the time for the Pillingers' departure approached, Lewis went to his mother and asked her either to take him with them or to leave him some of the proceeds from the sale of the house. The Pillingers refused to do either.

Lewis purchased a revolver and, on 1 June, went back to his mother's house to ask her again. When she said no, he shot his stepfather in the face.

Pillinger struggled with his stepson for possession of the gun and it eventually dropped to the ground. As soon as he lost the gun, Lewis Rogers ran off, his stepfather in hot pursuit. A strong swimmer, Lewis ran to the nearby River Avon and plunged in. His stepfather believed that he intended to swim across the river and escape on the opposite bank, but instead the boy swam to the dam, where he sat for a while before jumping back into the river, throwing up his arms and sinking in the deep water. He made no attempt to swim and his body was recovered the next morning.

Pillinger was attended by a surgeon, who found that the bullet had passed through his lower jaw, taking out four of his teeth. He survived the attempted murder by his stepson, who then committed suicide while the balance of his mind was disturbed.

1900 Painter Charles Denning was working at rope makers Terrell & Co., Brislington, where he was painting a skylight. A plank was balanced on the ceiling beams to allow Denning to reach the skylight and, according to witnesses, he frequently changed his position on the plank, standing up, sitting down and even walking along the 4in-wide beams.

At just after midday, he was seen balancing with one foot on the plank and one on the beam, a cigarette in his mouth. Seconds later, he crashed to the floor.

He was taken to the General Hospital with a compound fracture of his right arm, injured ribs and head and facial injuries. It wasn't until forty-three-year-old Denning died from pneumonia on 8 June that the extent of his head injuries was realised – a post-mortem examination discovered two skull fractures, with lacerations to the brain.

At an inquest held by coroner Mr H.G. Doggett, the jury recorded a verdict of 'accidental death', apportioning no blame to either Terrell's or to Denning's employers, Wilkins & Sons, for not providing safety ropes.

3 JUNE

1843 Mary Hunt, an elderly woman living alone in Brislington, was awakened in the middle of the night by three ruffians who told her, 'Give us your money or death shall be your portion.'

Holding a knife to her throat, one of the men placed her underneath her mattress and knelt on it. When Mary fainted, the men assumed she was dead and left, taking her silver watch and numerous other articles and leaving the mattress weighted down with a heavy box. Luckily Mary survived and was able to identify her attackers as Isaac, Thomas and Robert Watkins.

The three men appeared at the Somerset Assizes charged with burglariously breaking and entering the dwelling house of Mary Hunt and stealing 'divers' [sic] articles and with assault with intent to murder.

Although no defence was offered for Robert, Isaac's two daughters testified that they had been with him all night on 3 June, while a woman stated that she sat up with a sick child at Thomas's house and that he was asleep in bed at the time of the burglary.

The jury didn't believe the alibis and found all three guilty of burglary and of wounding Mary Hunt, but determined that there had been no intent to murder.

All three were sentenced to death, although their sentences were later commuted to transportation for life. The father of two of the defendants suddenly dropped dead shortly after their arrests. His death was attributed to the situation of his two sons, which 'preyed much on his mind'.

4 JUNE

1898 Christopher and Bessie Muller of Bedminster appeared at the Police Court charged with having neglected and ill-treated Arthur Hickman.

Bessie advertised for a child to adopt and was offered nineteen-month-old Arthur. She was paid 3s a week to care for him but the reality of a baby didn't match her dreams of having 'a companion'.

In the six months that the Mullers had charge of the little boy, he became almost skeletal. He was beaten, bathed in cold water and shut in the coal cupboard when his crying became too irritating. He had such severe nappy rash that his body was ulcerated.

Arthur was eventually rescued by a neighbour on 16 May and taken to Bedminster police station, where Superintendent Crocker was so appalled at his condition that he immediately telephoned the Society for the Prevention of Cruelty to Children.

In court, both defendants denied neglecting Arthur, ship's mate Mr Muller pleading that he was away at sea a lot of the time and left the child's care to his wife. Nevertheless, magistrates found both guilty as charged. Mr Muller was fined 40s plus costs, while his wife was sent to prison for six weeks. It was her second attempt at fostering a baby, the first having died from an abscess on the brain.

5 JUNE

1848 Coroner Mr J.B. Grindon supervised an exhumation at St Paul's following allegations about Thomas Wellington Hill, the husband and father of the three deceased.

Maria Hill and her sons Edward and John died in October 1847 and Thomas wasted no time in claiming the £3,000 due on Maria's death from the National Loan Fund Assurance Society. The insurance company found Mrs Hill's death suspicious and delayed payment while they investigated further. Although Hill threatened them with legal action, the company requested that his wife's body was exhumed and a post-mortem examination carried out.

As the graves were opened, thirty-three-year-old Hill committed suicide by taking essential oil of almonds, leaving a note reading, 'my mind is bowed down by heavy imputations cast on me – advantage taken of me by powerful persons to crush me, which they have just done.'

Although the Hills' deaths were originally attributed to 'gastro-enteric fever', analyst Mr W. Herapath showed that all three had ingested a fatal dose of arsenic.

At the inquest on Maria Hill, the jury were told that her husband had insured her life only four months before her sudden death, at an annual cost of £117, even though his yearly income was only £100. Witnesses including Maria's mother, Mary Gould, and Eliza Floyd, who had nursed Maria in her final illness, testified that Maria and Thomas seemed happily married and that Thomas always treated her kindly. Eliza had personally fed Maria all her meals and medicines and stated that the food was prepared downstairs by Thomas Hill and his sister Harriet. Both Mary Gould and Hill's mother, Ann Hill, told the inquest that Thomas had also insured their lives and paid the premiums on their policies.

Although nobody could offer any concrete evidence that Thomas Hill had either obtained arsenic or administered it to his family, the inquest jury returned a verdict of 'wilful murder' against him. With regard to the two boys, verdicts of 'poisoned by arsenic' were returned, although the jury found no evidence to say by whom it was administered. At Hill's own inquest, the verdict was 'suicide while temporarily insane'.

1830 Brothers Joseph and Henry Grant, aged seventeen and twenty-years-old, drowned while bathing near the Glass House. They were out walking with a friend, who tried to persuade them not to bathe as the water was too cold. However, the Grants ignored his advice.

6 JUNE

As they bathed, Henry's foot slipped and he fell into deep water. Joseph swam to assist him and managed to get him part of the way towards the bank but lost his hold and, before long, both men were out of their depth. Their friend, who couldn't swim, was unable to help and, after raising the alarm, ran to the men's home on Culver Street to alert their father of their predicament.

Their father raced to the scene, arriving just in time to see his drowned sons pulled from the water. Meanwhile, back at his home, a man knocked on the door and told Mrs Grant that her husband had sent him to collect a sheet and 3s, which was to be given to the boatmen as a reward for their efforts in searching for the bodies. Mrs Grant handed over the requested items and the man dropped the sheet and fled with the money.

1851 Robert and Louisa Carpenter appeared for the second time at the Council House, accused of starving their daughter, Christiana.

7 JUNE

At their first hearing, fifteen-year-old Christiana was carried into court on a chair, refusing to look at her father and stepmother as she detailed their cruelty towards her. According to Christiana, she had been locked in her room for more than three months before managing to escape. During her incarceration, her bed was never changed and she was allowed clean clothes only twice a week. She had a chamber pot for bodily functions, which was emptied daily by her brother. Christiana maintained that she was starved and beaten for months, eating little more than dry bread, with the occasional piece of meat or cheese.

Her parents were remanded to the Bridewell, to the disgust of spectators in court, who had to be restrained from lynching them.

At the Carpenters' second appearance before the Bench, they were allowed to cross-examine Christiana and her replies to their questions didn't tally with her earlier statements. In the face of her contradictory testimony, the magistrates suggested that she might be confused and asked her to leave the court while they examined other witnesses.

The first of these was Sarah Petherham, who lodged with the Carpenters and stated that Christiana was never locked in her room and her door was usually wide open. Miss Petherham passed the open door numerous times and spoke to Christiana and the girl had never once complained or asked for help. According to Miss Petherham, Christiana was often downstairs and was treated exactly the same as the family's other children.

When Christian's elder brother, John, corroborated Miss Petherham's testimony, prosecuting solicitor Mr Ayre didn't feel able to proceed with the case. The magistrates spoke to Robert Carpenter, who told them that he had no income whatsoever and, because of Christiana's allegations, was about to be evicted from his home. All of Carpenters' children were sent to the Workhouse during the investigation and magistrates decided that they should remain there for the time being, to give Robert a chance to get back on his feet. The case against Robert and Louisa was then formally dismissed and they left the court in tears.

8 JUNE

1881 George Davis returned to work at Brison's Brush Factory after a holiday with some trepidation. The eighteen-year-old was the butt of constant taunting and bullying by his workmates. According to Davis, his cap was repeatedly knocked from his head and, on occasions, a paste brush was forced into his mouth.

On 8 June, as Davis was carrying a bag of shavings, he fell over, injuring his nose and forehead on a large stone. Davis told his mother and the doctor who treated him that he was deliberately pushed, naming three boys as the culprits.

When Davis died from blood poisoning, it was left to deputy coroner Mr E.M. Harwood to determine whether his death was an accident or a direct result of the actions of another person or persons, which could justify a charge of manslaughter.

At the inquest at The Clarence Hotel, George's mother and a neighbour, Margaretta Cooksley, revealed that he had made specific allegations about three youths, Joseph Greenland, F. Hutchins and another boy named Hunt.

Greenland stated that Davis had simply overbalanced while carrying the bag of shavings. He denied being anywhere near Davis and insisted that he had not pushed him. His testimony was corroborated by clerk Robert Williams, who witnessed the fall and confirmed that Davis just slipped as he walked across some staging. Furthermore, Hutchins was elsewhere in the factory at the time and there was nobody named Hunt employed by the company. Once Dr Carter confirmed that Davis was 'weak-minded', the inquest jury returned a verdict of 'accidental death'.

1892 Mary Jane Wilcox spent the evening serving in her husband's pub, The Albion, on Newfoundland Road. The next morning, the Wilcox's servant, Ada Harding, called a cab and when it arrived, Charles Edward Wilcox asked Mr Brace the cab man to come to his wife's bedroom and assist him in carrying her downstairs. Brace found Mrs Wilcox in bed, covered with blood and, when he asked what had happened, Ada told him that she had fallen over and hit her head on a gas meter.

9 JUNE

Mrs Wilcox was taken to hospital, where she arrived smelling very strongly of alcohol, although quite rational. Asked how she had injured her head, Mrs Wilcox told surgeons that she had tripped over a mat in her bedroom.

Mrs Wilcox died on 13 June and at her inquest Ada Harding, Charles Wilcox and his brother-in-law, Henry Rosewarn, insisted that she had fallen and hit her head on the gas meter. However, several neighbours had heard sounds of fighting coming from the pub throughout the night, leading the inquest jury to return a verdict of manslaughter against Charles Wilcox.

Wilcox was later sentenced to sixteen months' imprisonment for the manslaughter of his wife. Ada Harding, who was on very friendly terms with Wilcox, was charged with being an accessory and, although she was acquitted, she was then charged with perjury, for which she received a sentence of four months' imprisonment. It is believed that Rosewarn was also charged with the same offence but unfortunately it has not been possible to ascertain the outcome of any criminal proceedings against him.

1893 Leslie Herbert Pearce (20) and Elizabeth Jane Smith (16) went by steamship to Conham to visit friends. They had arranged for Samuel Higgett (16) to collect them by boat that evening but, when they got to the appointed meeting place, there was no sign of him. Leslie and Elizabeth decided to travel back to Bristol by tram and had just started walking to catch one when Higgett arrived.

10 JUNE

He had hired a small rowing boat, capable of seating just two persons. Amy and Thomas Thomas, who were at the riverside to see their friends off, pleaded with Leslie and Elizabeth not to get into the boat, but they reassured them that it would be fine. The overloaded boat got just fifty yards before it capsized, throwing its occupants into the River Avon.

Unfortunately, although life saving equipment was kept at the nearby Bull Inn, Thomas Thomas wasn't aware of this and ran a quarter of a mile to find a boathook. By the time he returned, his three friends had drowned.

At the inquest, it was revealed that Samuel only expected to collect Leslie and had consequently hired a two-man boat. The jury returned verdicts of 'accidentally drowned' on all three victims, suggesting that the life saving apparatus should be more prominently displayed.

11 JUNE   **1898** *The Bristol Mercury* reported on the appearance at Bristol Police Court of Mary Ann Carroll, who was charged with being drunk and disorderly and with assaulting two policemen.

When PC 74A was called to St Jude's to deal with a disturbance, he found forty-eight-year-old Mary Ann fighting with a man and, when the constable asked her to go home, she attacked him. Eventually, the policeman pinned her to the ground awaiting the arrival of another constable, PC 21D. Both officers were punched and kicked several times as they took Mary Ann into custody.

Mary Ann had averaged six appearances in court every year for the past eight years, all for offences relating to drunkenness and, after one such appearance in 1896, had promised to sign the pledge. The magistrates sent her to prison for one month, with hard labour.

12 JUNE   **1888** On 8 June, two elderly sisters, Miss Rebecca Gough, who was deaf, and Mrs Ellen Handcock, who was blind, moved into an apartment on Victoria Street, Clifton. Their new home was on the second floor of a house, the first floor occupied by the Harris family and the ground floor used as a workshop by carpenter, cabinet maker and undertaker Alfred Hood.

Every morning at six o'clock, Hood's nephew Arthur Joynt unlocked the workshop to allow his uncle's staff to begin work. At about half-past six on 12 June, Mr Harris was awakened by the smell of smoke and realised that the building was on fire. Without pausing to dress, he ushered his wife and two children outside then ran back to try and rouse Miss Gough and Mrs Handcock but was forced to run for his life when the staircase burst into flames.

Victoria Street, 1906. (Author's collection)

While awaiting the arrival of the police and fire service, neighbours placed a ladder at the window of the old ladies' rooms and Mr West climbed up. He managed to grasp the wrist of one of the women but her sister clung to her so tightly that he was unable to rescue her. As he struggled, the women were gradually overcome by smoke before the floor burned through, plunging them to their deaths. Their bodies were recovered when the fire died down, as was that of fourteen-year-old Arthur Joynt.

It was impossible to discover the cause of the fire, although it was theorised that Joynt lit a gas ring to make himself a cup of coffee, dropping a lighted match onto an accumulation of sawdust on the floor. At the subsequent inquest, the jury returned verdicts of 'accidental death' on all three victims.

1899 Coroner Mr A.E. Barker held an inquest on the death of ten-week-old Laura Bateman of St Jude's, who died in Horfield Prison.

13 JUNE

Laura's mother, Eliza, was imprisoned for two months on 9 June for neglecting Mary, another of her daughters. Warder Emily Helms (or Elms) was disturbed by Laura's condition. She weighed only half the normal weight of an infant of her age and had absolutely no fat on her body. Prison surgeon James Edward Prichard ordered extra milk for Laura, who sadly died of starvation before it could have any beneficial effect.

At the inquest, the chief witness was Laura's father, William Daniel Bateman. Bateman related that his wife spent every penny of his income on drink and rarely purchased food for him or their three children. His testimony was supported by his landlady and by Inspector John Ottley of the Society for the Prevention of Cruelty to Children.

The conviction for neglecting Mary was not Eliza's first and the inquest jury had no hesitation in recording a verdict of manslaughter against her in respect of Laura's death. She was committed for trial at the Bristol Assizes on the coroner's warrant.

Eliza's trial opened in July 1899 and she was found guilty of Laura's manslaughter and also with 'neglecting her child in a manner likely to cause unnecessary suffering.' She was sentenced to twelve months' imprisonment with hard labour, to run concurrently with the month still to be served for Mary's neglect.

1860 Nine-year-old Ellen Whiting of Trenchard Street helped Mrs Griffiths of St Augustine's to look after her four children and occasionally did a little light housework. On 14 June, she went to work as usual but found plumber and glazier George Griffiths at home. As Ellen was dusting in the kitchen, Griffiths pulled her onto a sofa and raped her. Although she struggled and cried out, she was unable to escape and, when he had finished with her, Griffiths warned her not to tell anyone, promising to buy her a gold watch at Christmas for being a good girl.

14 JUNE

Ellen complained of a 'pain in her bowels' and her mother gave her some senna and sent her to bed. The following morning, Ellen cried and told her mother that she didn't want to go to work because Mr Griffiths had hurt her. Her mother took her straight to Mrs Griffiths but, under questioning from

Trenchard Street
(now the site of a
multi-storey car
park). (© N. Sly)

both women, Ellen refused to say any more about what had happened. Her
mother then took her to see Dr Bryant, who confirmed that she had been
violently assaulted and the rape was reported to the police.

Griffiths was tried at the Gloucester Assizes in August charged with
'feloniously assaulting and carnally knowing and abusing a child under ten
years old.' His defence counsel first tried to convince the jury that Ellen was
actually more than ten years old and then that she had made up the whole
story to avoid having to go to work. However, Ellen's confident testimony
convinced the jury that she was telling the truth and they found Griffiths
guilty. He was sentenced to five years' penal servitude.

15 JUNE   **1932** Death from heart failure at Southmead Hospital ended the thirty-year
addiction to morphia of John Stanley Robarts.

Fifty-year-old Robarts was admitted to the hospital in 1929 to undergo
a programme of detoxification. On his admission, he was taking eighteen
grains of morphia every day, half a grain being the normal fatal dose.

Robarts left the hospital just once in three years, when he went to visit his
sister in Bournemouth. On leaving, he was given a bottle of opium, which
should have lasted ten days but drank the entire bottle on his first day of
freedom.

16 JUNE   **1842** Street violinist Peter Castle appeared at the Council House charged
with being disorderly in Lewin's Mead.

A constable, described in the *Bristol Mercury* as being 'dull-souled', arrested
him at ten minutes past midnight, when he was playing his fiddle, accompanied
by a boy on a tambourine and surrounded by a crowd of dancing people.
Asked to stop playing because of the lateness of the hour, Peter took one look
at his appreciative audience and vowed to keep going for as long as he had the
strength to draw bow across string. He was promptly arrested.

At the magistrates' court, a stalemate developed between Peter, who insisted that the crowd were enjoying the music and the policeman, who was equally adamant that it was attracting complaints. Magistrates agreed to discharge him without penalty providing he gave his word that he would never play his fiddle on the streets again.

1900 Ann Mable of Hillgrove Hill put her one-year-old son to bed in his cradle, with the teat of his feeding bottle in his mouth. When she went to wake Wilfred the next morning, she found him dead.

A Siphonia Bottle. (The Web Childhood Museum)

The type of bottle that Ann used was known as a 'Siphonia Bottle', which had a long rubber tube attached to the teat. The tube had twisted around baby Wilfred's neck and Dr Norton, who examined the deceased infant and pronounced the cause of his death as strangulation, theorised that the tragedy had occurred when the baby rolled over during the night.

Siphonia bottles were commonly known as 'murder bottles', since the long rubber tube was almost impossible to clean and led to the deaths of many infants through gastroenteritis. However, for coroner Mr H.G. Doggett, this was the first incidence of strangulation by the tube.

1900 Alfred Cartledge, a twenty-eight-year-old labourer, appeared at Bristol Police Court charged with assaulting and unlawfully wounding his mother-in-law, Elizabeth Reece.

The Bench heard that on 8 June, Alfred's wife Alice and her mother were enjoying a glass of beer in the Ale and Porter Stores on Pritchard Street. Licensee John Thompson stepped out of the bar for a few moments and, when he returned, Alice was on the floor, being violently beaten by her husband. Mrs Reece tried to intervene to protect her daughter and was hit in the face.

In court, Mrs Reece alleged that Alfred had a penknife in his hand when he struck her, cutting her cheek. Alfred denied this, saying that Mrs Preece had tried to strike him with a glass and that, in defending himself, the glass had accidentally been pushed into her face.

Since John Thompson had seen Mrs Reece throwing a glass at Alfred, albeit after he allegedly struck her, the magistrates felt that they could not reliably determine whether or not Alfred had stabbed his mother-in-law. Nevertheless, they believed that a violent assault had been committed and fined Cartledge 10s plus costs or fourteen days' imprisonment.

1842 In the early hours of the morning, as PC Joseph Roberts patrolled his beat in St James's, he heard the sounds of a disturbance, which emanated from a fight outside a coffee shop.

The protagonists were two warring groups of Irish labourers. Roberts ordered them to break it up and go home, at which one of them picked up a stone and threatened to 'break his ******* head'. Roberts drew his staff and told the man to drop the stone, or he would strike him. The man complied but, as Roberts tried to arrest him, his compatriots began to pelt the constable with bricks, eventually seizing his staff and belabouring him with it. By then, PC Daniel Skinner had arrived, shortly followed by PC Thomas Colleypriest.

Roberts was taken to the Infirmary, where he made a deposition before magistrate James Ward. The three policemen knew the identities of those concerned and six men were quickly arrested and taken to the hospital, where Roberts identified them as his assailants.

On 22 June Roberts died and Charles, William and Jeremiah Dwyer, James Regan, Patrick Donovan and Dennis Callaghan were charged with his 'wilful murder'. They were tried at the Gloucestershire Assizes in August.

The jury returned verdicts of manslaughter against Charles and William Dwyer and Dennis Callaghan, finding that there was insufficient evidence against the other three defendants, who were consequently discharged. Since Charles Dwyer had been seen kneeling on Roberts and hammering him on the head with a brick, he was sentenced to transportation for life. His two partners in crime were each sentenced to ten years' transportation.

20 JUNE

1900 Ellen Elizabeth Taylor and her husband, Thomas, appeared at Bristol Police Court, Ellen charged with professing to tell fortunes and Thomas with aiding and abetting her.

From their premises in Upper Arcade, Ellen – otherwise known as Madame Zippia or The Gipsy Queen – professed to be able to read palms, while Thomas passed himself off as a phrenologist and 'physiogonomist', reading the bumps on people's skulls to tell their characters.

Most of those who visited the Taylors were young women, who were almost invariably told that they would marry a tall, dark, handsome stranger and that there was great wealth coming to them.

At their appearance before magistrates, Thomas Taylor defended phrenology as a scientific principle, insisting that the charge of 1s for the couple's services was entirely for phrenology and that the palm reading was thrown in as a free incentive. It was Taylor's contention that, if no charge were made for palmistry then no offence had been committed. Magistrates disagreed, fining each defendant £3 with £2 costs or one month's imprisonment.

21 JUNE

1851 Mining was going on as normal at the North Side colliery in Bedminster until just before eleven o'clock on the morning of 20 June, when a cart laden with coal collided with a wooden pit prop. In the blink of an eye, between fifty and sixty tons of earth, rock and timber fell into the shaft, trapping almost fifty men below ground.

Friends and relatives rushed to the pit head, desperate for news of their loved ones. One young woman slumped to the ground, cradling her baby and moaning that her father, son, husband, brother and uncle had all been buried alive.

Only two men in the upper shaft were known to be still alive as men began the slow, dangerous task of clearing the debris, working through the night. On the afternoon of 21 June, Edward Reynolds of the Malago Vale Colliery came up with a plan, which involved lowering a man in a covered bucket to the two known survivors, William Braine and Morgan Phillips. It was a risky idea and managers asked for a volunteer to be lowered. James North, described as 'rather an effeminate looking youth', stepped forward and at long last the two men were hauled up, exhausted but otherwise unharmed.

In view of the foul air below ground, neither Braine nor Phillips believed that anyone on the lower level could have survived. North volunteered to be lowered again and shouted and hammered on a piece of rock for ten minutes but got no response.

A canvas hose was borrowed from the Fire Brigade and lowered into the shaft in an attempt to get fresh air to the lower vein, while the men redoubled their efforts to clear the shaft and eventually they were rewarded with signs of life from below. At seven o'clock in the evening, the first three miners were brought to the surface and soon all the men were rescued alive. After spending more than thirty hours underground, there was not so much as a broken bone between them.

Tragically, William Bolt and Edwin William Javins – two of the miners who worked so heroically to save their trapped colleagues – were accidentally killed three weeks later, while trying to repair the collapsed shaft. Between them, they left twelve children. A third man was seriously injured at the same time but is believed to have survived.

1872 Coroner Mr H.S. Wasbrough held an inquest on the body of PC 224, William Counsell, who drowned in the Cumberland Basin in the early hours of that morning. 22 JUNE

Counsell was last seen alive by his sergeant at midnight. Shortly afterwards dock labourer William Lewis heard muffled cries for help and, suspecting that someone had fallen into the Basin, he and a colleague found a small boat and set out to look. Finding a policeman's helmet floating on the water, they immediately raised the alarm and the Basin was dragged for several hours before Counsell's body was recovered.

There were no suspicions of foul play and it was theorised that Counsell might have dozed off while sitting on the quay wall and fallen into the water. Although working night shifts, he hadn't slept that day as he was busy moving house and had complained of feeling very tired when he started his duty.

Counsell left a widow and three young children and, although his life was insured, he was slightly in arrears with the payments and it was suspected that this would invalidate his policy.

The inquest jury returned a verdict of 'accidental death'.

1859 As William Cox was driving cows up Barton Hill in St George's, one broke into Alfred Johnson's garden. 23 JUNE

Johnson protested and Cox became extremely belligerent, challenging him to a fight. When Johnson refused, Cox swung at him with the end of his stick, knocking out four of his teeth.

Cox was summoned to appear at Lawford's Gate Petty Sessions, where he gave a contradictory account of the incident. According to Cox, Johnson had rushed up to him wielding a hoe and had threatened to chop the cow's legs off. He then tried to take Cox's stick, at which Cox struck him in self-defence.

Cox's version of the incident was corroborated by his employer, who was with him at the time. Yet there was no doubt that Johnson was missing four teeth.

The magistrates asked the two men to settle out of court, but neither was willing to do so. Eventually, although they agreed that Johnson's display of bad temper had undoubtedly aggravated the situation, the magistrates found Cox guilty of assault, fining him £1 plus costs or one month's imprisonment.

24 JUNE **1898** Thomas William Chard fought with his wife, Annie, throwing several things at her and badly injuring her arm. Annie went to hospital and, on her return, her husband asked where she had been.

'I'll give you hospital', he threatened, picking up a broom and beating Annie with it until it broke over her head, leaving her unconscious.

Chard was arrested and appeared at the Bristol Assizes charged with feloniously wounding Annie with intent to do her grievous bodily harm. His defence counsel Mr Hawke related a tale of a couple who couldn't live together and yet couldn't seem to live apart. During their marriage, they had separated several times, mainly because Annie spent all of her husband's wages on drink. Hawke insisted that his client had been provoked into beating his wife by her conduct over the previous years.

Mr Justice Wright was unmoved by Hawke's impassioned speech and sentenced Chard to six months' imprisonment with hard labour.

25 JUNE **1859** Nine-year-old Emma King was collecting sticks in Mangotsfield with her mother when she was punched in the back by Sarah Bennett, who then threw several stones at the child.

Summoned to appear at Lawford's Gate Petty Sessions, Sarah vehemently denied assaulting Emma. She explained that Emma was pulling a hedge to pieces in her search for sticks and that she had merely remonstrated with the child, who had then 'sauced' her and called her names.

Emma and her mother insisted that an assault had taken place, while Sarah and her sister were equally insistent that it hadn't. Eventually the magistrates dismissed them from court to try and settle the matter agreeably between them.

When they were informed that this had proved impossible, the magistrates decided in favour of the complainant, fining Sarah Bennett 2s 6d plus costs or fourteen days' imprisonment.

26 JUNE **1928** Arthur Darbyshire was sentenced to seven years' penal servitude at the Bristol Assizes for a criminal assault on Dorothy Elizabeth Savery, a nurse in his employment. Darbyshire, who pleaded guilty to the charge against him, was a certified dipsomaniac, who was described by the counsel for the prosecution as 'a fiend incarnate when in drink.'

1877 George Richards appeared at the Police Court charged with neglecting to provide adequate food, clothing and lodging for his eleven-year-old son, Benjamin.

Mr Parr, who brought the prosecution on behalf of the Bristol Board of Guardians, told the court that he had visited the child's home after concerns expressed by his grandmother. Benjamin was very small for his age and emaciated – he was also filthy, barefoot, dressed in rags and crawling with vermin. Neighbours told Parr that Benjamin and his five-year-old sister were left alone at home all day and often stole food out of garbage pails. The children were regularly beaten and, at the time of Parr's visit, Benjamin had a wound over his eye, which his father inflicted with a red-hot poker.

The children's mother died a week before Christmas 1876, soon after the death of her ten-month old baby. Richards claimed that he had injured his kneecap and was unable to work, but the prosecution countered that he worked at his blacksmith's shop in St Philips for enough time to accumulate some cash, which he spent on drink.

After his wife's death, Richards cohabited with a young woman, who shared his passion for alcohol. When Parr visited the house, he found her lying naked in bed, possessing no other clothes except a shawl. Parr told the court that he removed the woman and Benjamin to the Workhouse and, before he could do so, he had to organise clothes for both of them. Although the rooms at Richards's house were relatively clean, the only furniture was a bed and a pewter quart pot, stolen from a public house, which was used for all domestic purposes.

Maria Rumney, the children's maternal grandmother, and several neighbours told the court that any attempt at intervention on behalf of the children brought forth threats of violence from their father. Mrs Rumney, who already had Richards' oldest son in her care, took in the little girl, while Benjamin recovered in the Workhouse.

Magistrates sentenced George Richards to six weeks' imprisonment with hard labour, telling him that were it not for the interference of his neighbours and Benjamin's grandmother, the consequences of his neglect could have been far more serious.

1932 Twenty-nine-year-old John Ryan was tried at the Bristol Assizes for robbery with violence. Ryan snatched a handbag from a young waitress, punching her in the face when she tried to wrestle it away from him. The woman told the court that her face was swollen for two or three days after the attack.

Found guilty by the jury, Ryan was sentenced to six months' imprisonment but also ordered by the judge to receive eight strokes of the 'cat o'nine tails'.

1844 Fourteen-year-old Thomas Farley worked at the Cotton Works, Barton Hill, where his duties included cleaning the wheel houses. As he picked up a piece of cotton waste, one of the wheels ran over his middle finger.

Farley was taken to the Infirmary, where the wound was dressed. As an orphan, he lodged with Samuel and Ann Morgan in Phoenix Street and on the following day – a Sunday – stayed in bed all day, claiming to be in great pain. He went to work as usual on Monday morning but was still in agony and, after returning to his lodgings for breakfast, took the rest of the day off.

Samuel Morgan took him to the Cotton Works that evening to see company surgeon, Emilius Scipio Mayor, who removed the dressings on Farley's finger and found a large contused wound, which was swollen and inflamed. The surgeon ordered a poultice for the finger and sent Farley home with his landlord.

By Tuesday, the Morgans were very concerned and went back to the Cotton Works to ask Mayor to call and see Thomas. Mayor was not there, but his assistant Mr Thwaites found the boy feverish, although not complaining of pain in his hand. Thwaites did not examine his wound but told the Morgans to keep the boy cool and to collect some medicine from the Works at six o'clock. The Morgans did as they were instructed, sitting up with Thomas all night, but he died at seven o'clock on the morning of 3 July.

A post-mortem examination carried out by Dr Riley determined that Thomas had died from 'constitutional irritation', caused by his injury. At the subsequent inquest, Riley stated that everything possible had been done for Farley, whose life had never seemed in danger after suffering what was a relatively minor wound. Although Riley suggested that the Morgans might have changed the poultice, he believed that Mayor and Thwaites had given appropriate treatment.

Ann Morgan told the inquest that she was not instructed to renew the poultice and, since Thomas had not complained of pain in his hand, she thought it best to leave it. The inquest jury pronounced themselves satisfied that Thomas Farley had received every possible medical care and returned a verdict of 'accidental death'.

A funeral procession. (Author's collection)

1851 An inquest was held by coroner Mr J.B. Grindon at The Lord Nelson, Ashley Road on the body of a newborn baby boy.

Labourer Arthur Roberts stumbled over the tiny corpse in a field of mangold wurzels and potatoes. There were no marks of violence on the baby, which was wrapped in the remnants of an old black gown and, with nothing to suggest either his identity or that of his mother, the inquest jury returned a verdict of 'found dead'.

The next day, a second inquest was held at the same place, after Roberts found another dead baby about 200 yards from the spot where he found the first. This time it was a girl and again there were no clues to her identity and no marks of violence. Once again, a verdict of 'found dead' was recorded.

JULY

A well-known Bedminster character. (Author's collection)

1867 The Millwrights' Arms on the Welsh Back was packed with sailors of every nationality, enjoying the music and dancing – not to mention the alcohol. Among them was a Greek named Andrew Martineo, a Swiss named Otto Alexander Krikner, and a man named Licuode, about whom very little was known.

An argument broke out between Krikner and Licuode and, when it looked like it was developing into a physical fight, the landlord threw them out. Nobody was quite sure what happened next, but there was a pitched battle between rival groups of drunken sailors, which culminated in Krikner being fatally stabbed. Several people who witnessed the stabbing identified Krikner's killer as Martineo.

Welsh Back.
(© N. Sly)

Martineo was arrested and tried for 'wilful murder' at the Bristol Assizes. According to his defence counsel, Mr Alexander, the identification of Martineo as the killer was a case of mistaken identity. Alexander pointed out that the stabbing occurred on a dark night and almost all the witnesses were either drunks or prostitutes, whose evidence could not be trusted. There were many sailors involved in the fight, several of whom carried knives. Martineo had no quarrel with the victim and the coat he was supposed to have worn at the time bore no traces of blood.

Nevertheless, the jury returned a verdict of guilty of the lesser offence of manslaughter, adding a recommendation for mercy. After consulting with another judge, Mr Justice Willes sentenced Martineo to ten years' penal servitude.

1898 Thirteen-year-old Elizabeth Cox appeared before magistrates charged with stealing money from little boys on the streets of Bedminster.

Elizabeth had developed a clever confidence trick. She approached children and told them that a gang of thieves were operating on certain roads, offering to keep their money safe for them. When the children gratefully agreed, she carefully wrapped their coins in paper and put the packets in her pocket. She later handed back empty paper packets, urging the recipients to keep the money wrapped up so that they didn't lose it.

Found guilty, Elizabeth was sent to Red Lodge Reformatory.

3 JULY   **1869** Fifty-seven-year-old Elizabeth Sherborne of Horfield fretted for weeks after her daughter married a publican and moved to St Philip's. Missing her daughter terribly, Elizabeth constantly complained of feeling sick and, on 2 July, she began vomiting and took to her bed.

Her daughter, Mrs Halmarack, was summoned, as were two doctors, who quickly realised that Elizabeth was dying. Mrs Halmarack sent neighbour Mrs Chapman to fetch some brandy for her mother, handing her a bottle from Mrs Sherborne's dressing table.

There appeared to be a little brandy left in the bottle, so Mrs Chapman didn't bother to rinse it out before getting it refilled. However, by the time she got back to Mrs Sherborne's house, the brandy had turned completely black.

Elizabeth died on 3 July and Mrs Chapman suspected that her daughter had poisoned her, particularly when Mrs Halmarack showed her a large sum of money that she had taken from her mother's room 'for safekeeping'. She also revealed that she had taken a gold watch and chain that had been promised to her.

However, when the bottle of brandy was found to contain nothing more harmful than a little iron and a post-mortem examination revealed no traces of any poison, the jury at the subsequent inquest returned a verdict that Mrs Sherborne died from apoplexy.

4 JULY   **1895** Coroner Mr H.G. Doggett held an inquest on the death of nine-year-old Frederick Lloyd Smith.

On 10 June, Frederick went to Soundwell for a Sunday school outing. Numerous stalls and fairground attractions were set up in a field and, as Frederick walked behind a shooting gallery, he was seen to suddenly clutch his head.

Henry Bull went to see if he was all right and found that the child's head was bleeding. Although Frederick insisted that he wasn't badly hurt, Bull decided to take him home, where his parents took him straight to the Infirmary. He was operated on the next day and a small bullet removed from his head.

Although Frederick initially seemed to be recovering, infection set in and he developed an abscess on his brain. He died on 2 July.

The police interviewed William Henry Bracey, who was in charge of the shooting gallery. Bracey stated that the gun was very low-powered, taking a pea-sized shot and about five grains of gunpowder. The fatal shot had been accidentally fired by Bracey's sister who, having taken two shots at the iron target, attempted to hit a glass ball, which played on a jet of water. The gun jammed and, as she handed it to her brother to fix, it accidentally went off, the bullet passing through the canvas screens and hitting Frederick.

Ward 6 at Bristol Royal Infirmary. (Author's collection)

In returning a verdict of 'accidental death', the inquest jury recommended that the public were protected by something rather more substantial than canvas.

1861 Mary Jefferies took supper to her husband, who was working the night shift at Roberts & Daines's Saw Mill on Marsh Lane. While there, her dress caught in the wheels of the machinery and she was dragged onto the circular saw. Her husband immediately threw the saw into reverse but his forty-one-year-old wife was quite literally cut to pieces, in full view of their eight-year-old son.

5 JULY

Although the machine was guarded, in returning a verdict of 'accidental death' the inquest jury recommended the installation of a substantial iron sheet barrier to prevent future accidents.

1861 At The Black Horse Inn, Kingswood Hill, coroner Mr W. Gaisford held an inquest on the death of Charles Haydon, aged eighteen months.

6 JULY

Charles fell down a well while playing in the garden. Although the water was only six inches deep, he died from hitting against the walls as he fell. When the police inspected the garden, they found not one, but two unguarded wells, with nothing to prevent anyone from walking into either.

The inquest jury returned a verdict of 'accidental death' and it emerged that Charles was the third Haydon child to die as the result of a tragic accident. One child was 'overlain' – accidentally suffocated while in bed – and a second was suffocated by bedclothes. The coroner censured the parents for their carelessness, ordering them to guard both wells immediately and threatening that in the event of a similar occurrence in future, they would be charged with manslaughter.

1859 James Guest appeared at Lawford's Gate Petty Sessions charged with assaulting Elizabeth Miller at Mangotsfield on 27 June.

7 JULY

The Bench were told that Elizabeth was supposedly having an affair with a married man and as a result, she found herself surrounded by an angry mob of around 200 people, carrying effigies and playing 'rough music', beating on trays and saucepans. The crowd pelted Elizabeth with stones and she swore that she distinctly saw Guest throw two, which struck her head and back. The police were called to deal with the disturbance and Elizabeth was rescued by PS White and taken to the police station for her own protection. The mob remained outside hooting derisively for some time before they could be persuaded to disperse.

Guest called two witnesses in his defence. The first was Mrs Davis, who told the magistrates that, along with many other people, Guest threw clods of dirt but no stones. The second witness was Ann Porter, the wife of Elizabeth's alleged lover.

Mrs Porter told the court that Elizabeth confronted her and told her that she had slept with her husband more than once and would soon have him for good. Mrs Porter had also seen mud thrown but no stones.

The magistrates believed that, while there was some truth in Elizabeth's allegations, she had provoked the attack. They therefore treated Guest leniently, fining him 2s 6d or fourteen days' imprisonment.

8 JULY   1861 Coroner Mr J.B. Grindon held inquests at the Infirmary on the deaths of two children from St Philip's, who died as a result of accidents. While out playing, John French of Milk Street decided to climb a wall. As he reached the top, he slipped and although he tried to hang on to one of the coping stones, he pulled it from the wall. The stone, which weighed almost 60lbs, fell on top of him and he died from head injuries shortly after his admission to hospital. Elizabeth Morgan hurt her knee falling off a stool on 3 July. An abscess formed around the wound and she died on 7 July from inflammation of the lungs.

9 JULY   1860 William Pocock appeared at Bristol Police Court charged with assaulting Elizabeth Golding.

Mrs Golding, her husband Henry and their two daughters rented an apartment in Pocock's house on Guinea Street, as did three single men and another married couple. Seaman Henry Golding left home on 3 July and was expected back on the midday tide on 7 July.

On 5 July, Mrs Golding suddenly awoke, aware that there was someone in bed with her. Sleepily, she stretched out her hand, feeling that the man had whiskers under his chin and assuming that it was her husband.

'Where's your vessel, Henry?' she asked. When 'Henry' didn't reply, Mrs Golding put her hand out again and realised that the man was wearing a cap. She and 'Henry' leaped out of bed simultaneously, as Mrs Golding realised that her sleeping companion was not her husband but her landlord. 'Good God, Pocock, what do you do here?' she asked him, calling him 'a disgraceful villain' and pushing him hard against a table.

The hullabaloo aroused the whole house, including Mrs Pocock. In front of his wife, Pocock insisted that Elizabeth had been drinking and dreamed the whole affair. However, the next morning he spoke to Elizabeth privately, claiming to have been drunk himself and to have entered her room by mistake. He offered to explain his conduct to Henry Golding personally and begged Elizabeth not to take the matter any further.

Magistrates called Henry Golding and stood him next to William Pocock. The two men were almost identical in height and build and both had whiskers. Elizabeth called witnesses to prove that she had drunk only half a pint of cider that evening and was thus completely sober.

Pocock was committed to appear at the next Assizes, and his case was heard on 23 October 1860. He was found guilty and sentenced to twelve months' imprisonment.

1854 Elizabeth and Robert Ball appeared at the Council House charged with stealing potatoes from the garden of Mr Baynton of Bedminster.

Baynton said that he had no desire to see the children prosecuted, but simply wanted to bring them to the magistrates' attention. Elizabeth and Robert were two of four motherless and abandoned siblings, aged between eleven and seventeen years old. The four slept in a tiny room and rarely saw their father, who had left them to fend for themselves as best they could. When Baynton caught the two children helping themselves from his garden, they told him that they had eaten nothing for three days.

Magistrates thanked Baynton, placing the case in the hands of Mr Room, the relieving officer, so that he might trace the children's father and ensure that he was suitably punished.

10 JULY

1825 While working at Mr Bryant's Soda Water Manufactory, Mr Child suffered terrible facial burns from oil of vitriol and it was predicted that he would lose the sight of one eye as a result. The accident was particularly distressing, since Child had only recently returned to work after an accident one month earlier, in which fragments of glass from an exploding bottle of soda water caused the loss of the sight of his other eye.

11 JULY

1869 Seventy-four-year-old Edward Berry was charged at the Council House with indecently assaulting nine-year-old Ellen Ashton. It was his second appearance in court – one week earlier, when magistrates questioned Ellen, they found that she did not fully understand the concept of swearing an oath. They remanded Berry, so that Ellen might have some religious instruction.

After a week of coaching at the Ragged School, St James's Back, Ellen was able to convince magistrates that an assault had occurred. They found Berry guilty of 'the most disgraceful conduct' and sentenced him to six months' imprisonment with hard labour.

12 JULY

1845 An unnamed man from Herefordshire arrived in Bristol for a visit. While strolling through Clare Street, he was approached by a weeping young lady dressed in mourning, who told him that she was very much affected by his resemblance to her young lover, whose recent death had left her devastated.

Moved almost to tears by the woman's distress, the gentleman spent some time trying to comfort her. It was only when they parted company about

13 JULY

thirty minutes later that he realised that he had also parted company with his purse, containing two £10 notes and half a sovereign.

14 JULY **1880** Mr Dilger went to run an errand, leaving his wife alone at his jeweller's shop in St Phillip's. No sooner had Dilger left, than a man walked through the shop to the living quarters and seized Mrs Dilger by the throat. She begged him not to hurt her, telling him to take what he wanted from the shop but the man threw her onto a sofa, pulled out a knife and began slashing her. Mrs Dilger fought desperately and the intruder only managed to cut her hands as she tried to disarm him.

Eventually, he gave up and went back into the shop, where he began helping himself to the stock. Bravely, Mrs Dilger ran past him into the street, shouting 'Murder!' The man fled, stealing a horse and cart in an effort to make a quick getaway. However, the horse stumbled and the man was apprehended by passers-by.

William Gardiner appeared at the Bristol Assizes on 30 July charged with 'feloniously demanding money with menaces'. Deemed guilty, he was sentenced to five years' penal servitude. When the robbery occurred, Gardiner had only recently been released from prison after serving time for robbing another jeweller's shop. On his arrest, he expressed regret that he hadn't managed to kill Mrs Dilger.

15 JULY **1854** Farmer Henry Werrett of Coalpit Heath was infuriated by a fox that was taking his poultry in broad daylight and vowed to kill it. Accordingly, he loaded his gun and balanced on a manger to get a clear view of the animal.

Unfortunately, his foot slipped and as he fell to the ground, his gun went off, shooting him in the chest. 'I'm a dead man,' he exclaimed, before expiring almost instantly.

At the subsequent inquest, the jury returned a verdict of 'accidental death'. The coroner remarked that it was most fortunate that the gun hadn't claimed the lives of Werrett's wife, brother, son and daughter, who were all watching him at the time.

16 JULY **1886** Navvy William Jones appeared at Bristol Police Court charged with deserting his wife and six children, causing them to become chargeable to the Barton Regis Union.

The Bench heard that Jones ran off with a widow and her four children in November 1883 and was found living with her in Ilford, Essex. Jones was not only supporting her children but also two more from his new relationship. He had never seen the child that his wife gave birth to shortly after his departure, nor was he aware that another of his children had died and been buried by the parish.

Jones, who was also a drummer in the Salvation Army, promised to support his original family but only earned one guinea a week. When the magistrates learned that he didn't have £38 5s 2d – the cost so far of maintaining his first wife and children – they sentenced him to three months' imprisonment with hard labour.

1876 When Charles Connor called on Bedminster laundress Ann Redman to collect some washing, she refused to hand it over until she was paid. An argument ensued, in the course of which Ann was stabbed twice in the forehead.

There were numerous witnesses to the incident, all of whom gave totally different accounts at the Bristol Assizes, where Connor faced a charge of 'felonious wounding with intent to do grievous bodily harm'. The witnesses could not agree on whether Connor had the knife in his pocket or up his sleeve, or whether it was open or closed when drawn.

Defence counsel Mr Norris offered a guilty plea to the lesser offence of 'unlawfully wounding', which was accepted. Connor, who said that he was drunk at the time of the offence, was sentenced to twelve months' hard labour.

1876 Benjamin Smith of Avon Street came home drunk with a terrible craving for pickled onions. When his wife couldn't immediately supply any, he struck her across the throat before picking up a chair, with which he beat her senseless.

Brought before magistrates the following day, Smith had nothing to say in his own defence. Telling him that he was guilty of 'a most barbarous assault', the magistrates sentenced him to three months' imprisonment with hard labour, stipulating that he must keep the peace for a further three months after his release.

1842 Charles Williams and Emmanuel Brittan appeared at the Bristol Quarter Sessions charged with stealing a black silk handbag, containing money and a lawn handkerchief, from Mary Ann Roberts.

When the two men snatched the bag from Mary Ann as she walked near the Victoria Rooms on 14 July, they were unaware that their actions had been observed by two off-duty London policemen, who happened to be in Bristol to visit the annual agricultural show. The officers quickly arrested them and later appeared in court as witnesses. Each of the defendants was sentenced to six months' imprisonment with hard labour.

1878 Two cotton factory workers were playing billiards in a public house in Barton Hill, when an argument broke out about which of them could read and write the best. Alfred Theophilus Freeguard taunted Francis Ferris until Ferris lost his temper and punched his tormentor in the face, making his nose bleed.

Freeguard pulled out a knife and, before anyone could stop him, plunged it into Ferris's chest so hard that it penetrated almost all of the way though his body. Ferris was taken home, where he died soon afterwards.

Since Ferris struck the first blow, Freeguard was charged with manslaughter rather than 'wilful murder'. Tried at the Bristol Assizes on 3 August, he was found guilty and sentenced to twelve years' transportation.

1880 Mrs Tolkien of Carlton Place, Clifton, rang for ner servant Harriet Wybourn. When Harriet didn't respond, Mrs Tolkien went to see why not,

A view of Clifton from Ashton Meadows. (Author's collection)

finding the eighteen-year-old dead, kneeling over a wash tub, her face immersed in 10in of water.

An inquest held by Mr H.S. Wasbrough heard that Harriet was distraught after her relationship with her boyfriend ended. (She left a note to that effect, asking Mrs Tolkien to notify the young man of her death.)

Dr Spencer theorised that Harriet had fainted on first placing her face in the water, falling forward and drowning. The inquest jury returned a verdict of 'suicide while of unsound mind'.

22 JULY

1850 As the steamship *Red Rover* waited at the entrance to the Cumberland Lock in the Floating Harbour, it suddenly exploded, sending up a huge cloud of steam. As the steam slowly cleared, a scene of great carnage was revealed to horrified onlookers. The boat carried almost fifty passengers, who were blown skywards, along with fragments of the ship. Now they were in the water, most struggling and screaming, a few ominously still.

Numerous small boats were launched to go to their aid and vehicles were commandeered to transport them to the Infirmary. An inquest was opened the following day at the Commercial Hotel, Hotwells Road. By the time the proceedings terminated some days later, the dead were listed as William Brewer (41), Charles Keating (26), William Cooper (23), Isaac West, Robert Pavey, Henry Starr (21), Samuel Jefferies (28), Eliza Fulford (28) and her daughters Susan (8) and Mary Ann (6), Thomas Venn (2) and William Nicholas. Several more people were said to be in a hopeless condition.

The last named was the engineer aboard the ill-fated steam ship and witnesses at the inquest stated that, shortly before the explosion, he turned off the safety valve, causing a build-up of steam pressure. However, other witnesses were equally certain that the cause of the explosion was not excess pressure, but a lack of water in the boiler.

The *Red Rover* was quite an old, slow ship and some felt that it was not fit for use as a passenger ferry. The owner, Mr Anderson, was on board with his wife at the time of the explosion – both survived and Anderson was later to tell the inquest that the boiler had very recently been repaired, although the inquest jury questioned the quality of the repair work. By chance, the ship had been thoroughly inspected by an engineer on behalf of someone who was contemplating buying it and he told the inquest that it seemed in good order.

The inquest jury eventually recorded verdicts of 'accidental deaths' on all of the victims, adding that they believed Mr Anderson bore some responsibility for the tragedy. When coroner Mr J.B. Grindon asked if they wanted to return a verdict of manslaughter against Anderson, they unanimously said that they did not.

1857 At eleven o'clock at night, Durdham Downs was rocked by a huge explosion. People rushed outside to find that Burns's Firework Manufactory at the rear of Gallows Acre Lane had exploded, showering the area with fragments of the sheds. The police were quickly on the scene and evacuated neighbouring houses, marshalling the residents into a bucket chain in order to douse the flames.

23 JULY

Mr Burns, who was not insured, was later to estimate his losses at around £200. He was particularly upset to have lost the fireworks for a big display due to be held in Bath to celebrate a wedding, which would feature the names of the bride and groom in fireworks, surrounded by lover's knots and cupids. Mr Burns insisted that he had taken every possible safety precaution, even to the extent of banning matches from his premises.

By a miracle, the only fatality was one pet hen from a nearby garden.

Durdham Downs.
(Author's collection)

1857 Seventeen-year-old James Hole worked for carriers Pickford & Co. Normally he worked in the office, but due to the illness of another employee, he went out with driver John Price to take a load of sugar to Bristol railway station.

24 JULY

As they neared the bridge at the end of Bath Street, James, who was walking alongside the cart, complained of sore feet and climbed aboard. He perched on top of the sugar but had not been there for long when the load slipped, pitching him over the side of the cart. The wheel passed over his chest and the cart's axle crushed his lower body.

The accident was witnessed by a policeman who, together with a passer-by, procured a shutter and carried Hole to St Peter's Hospital. However, he was dead on arrival.

The inquest jury returned a verdict of 'accidental death', absolving Price of any blame for the tragedy.

25 JULY

1890 Clifton Station on the Port and Pier Railway was always busy on Friday evenings with workmen hurrying home. The train was usually too long for the platform and passengers in the last carriages often had to wait some time for those in front to disembark before the train was moved forward. In order to catch their buses, many workmen saved precious minutes by jumping off the train before it reached the platform. Unfortunately, when Jeremiah O'Brien did this he stumbled and fell beneath the wheels of the train just as it started to move.

O'Brien died from a fractured spine and at his inquest deputy coroner Mr H.G. Doggett condemned the widespread practice of leaving carriages before they had reached the platform. The stationmaster agreed, telling Doggett that it was strictly forbidden and that notices were regularly placed in the carriages, advising people of the dangers. However, no sooner were the notices put up, than they were torn down again. Doggett suggested that the railway authorities prosecute future offenders.

26 JULY

1876 James and Mary Newman of Baptist Mills appeared at the Guildhall charged with neglecting their seven children. One child, Alfred, had died from scarlet fever at the Workhouse and a second, Harriet, was at death's door. The magistrates adjourned the case for twenty-four hours, by which time five-year-old Harriet had died from typhoid fever, diarrhoea and general neglect.

Although James was a steady, hard-working man, Mary was a drunkard, who spent his wages on drink, leaving the children alone for hours on end while she went to the pub. Her house was likened to a cesspit and the children were starved and crawling with vermin – when Harriet was first removed from her mother's care, it took nearly two hours to wash her.

When the magistrates heard that Harriet had died, they shelved the charge of neglect and committed both parents to the Assizes on a charge of manslaughter, where both were acquitted. The medical evidence showed that Harriet had died from typhoid fever and as the drains in Baptist Mills were known to be in poor condition, the judge did not feel that there was sufficient evidence to prove the charge against her parents.

27 JULY

1876 As *The Flying Dutchman* passenger train neared Long Ashton, it suddenly left the tracks, somersaulting several times and hitting a bank before finally coming to rest. Driver William Dunscombe (45) and stoker James Randall (28) were killed instantly. Guard Thomas Watts jumped out of the train and survived with a broken arm and another crew member and fourteen passengers were injured. Their injuries ranged from scalds and broken bones to cuts and bruises and one passenger lost an eye.

The Flying Dutchman disaster on the Great Western Railway, 1876. (Author's collection)

At the time, *The Flying Dutchman* was the fastest train in the world, capable of speeds of up to sixty miles an hour. However, this was her third recent accident, with previous crashes at Paddington and Exeter.

Government Inspector Captain Tyler was appointed to investigate the incident and came to the conclusion that the line had fallen into decay, with defective rails and timbers and bad joints. He determined that the crash was caused by an irregularity in the level of the rails on a curve. Great Western Railway immediately employed 500 extra men to rectify the defects in the line, at a cost of £50,000.

1876 Fifty-year-old farmer Jonathan Gibbs of Dodds Farm, Pucklechurch had been very depressed of late and spent a week's holiday staying with his sister at Wapley. When Jonathan expressed a wish to see his wife, Frances, his nephew drove him back to Pucklechurch for a visit and, while the young man was attending to the horse, Gibbs attacked Frances, slashing her throat with a razor.

He then climbed back into the trap for the return journey to Wapley, but had not gone far when he suddenly jumped out and cut his own throat with a small pocket knife. His nephew went for assistance but by the time he returned his uncle had bled to death.

The inquest jury returned a verdict of 'suicide while temporarily insane' on Jonathan Gibbs. Frances fortunately survived her injuries.

28 JULY

1854 'Missy Hall', called a little voice and Johanna Hall looked to see who was hailing her. She recognised the two-year-old daughter of Ann and William Haines of Phoenix Street, who was being carried by a young girl. Johanna waved to the toddler then thought no more about her until she heard that she was missing from home.

29 JULY

Johanna vaguely recognised the girl as someone she had seen walking to and from the Great Western Cotton Factory and began to make enquiries to see if she could establish her identity. She found someone at Crew's Hole who had seen the girl with the child and knew her parents and, when she visited them, they said that their daughter, Mary Ann Smith, had run away four days earlier, having stolen £1 12s.

Still playing detective, Johanna located other people who had seen Mary Ann with the child and established that they were heading towards Wiltshire. She informed William Haines, who set off in pursuit, eventually finding a constable who had spoken to Mary Ann near Box. Haines and the policeman caught up with her just outside Chippenham and, although the toddler was very bruised and appeared to have been hit on the head, she was alive.

Mary Ann was charged with 'enticing away a child under the age of ten years with intent to deprive the father of its possession' and appeared at the Bristol Quarter Sessions on 25 October. She was found guilty and sentenced to two years' imprisonment, with hard labour.

30 JULY **1877** Norwegian seaman Ole Savrin Olsen was tried at the Gloucester Assizes for the manslaughter of his shipmate, Niels Berg.

In the company of a third sailor, Olsen and Berg were in Bristol on 24 May, spending their shore leave drinking and visiting prostitutes. At The White Hart Inn, on Lower Maudlin Street, they began arguing and were thrown out of the pub. They went from there to a house of ill-repute on Gravel Street, where the argument rumbled on for some time before Olsen ended it by pulling out his knife and stabbing Berg in his head and side. As Berg fell to the floor, Olsen took to his heels, with several prostitutes in hot pursuit.

Meanwhile, PC Brimble arrived at The White Hart, having been summoned by the landlord to assist in removing the fighting Norwegians from the pub. Learning that he was no longer needed, Brimble was returning to the Central Police Station when his attention was attracted by a cry at a yard in

Lewin's Mead. When Brimble went to investigate, he found Olsen cornered by a group of women, his hands still red with his shipmate's blood.

When Berg died at the Infirmary the next day, Olsen was charged with his manslaughter and found guilty. He was sentenced to seven years' penal servitude.

1878 While ship's carpenter Frederick Brown was at sea, his wife Caroline openly lived with Hugh Latimer Clements, taking Brown's pay. In March 1878, Clements moved out, leaving the way clear for Brown's return, but by his next shore leave on 28 July, Caroline was back with Clements and had a new baby, the Brown's own child having been farmed out to live with policeman's wife, Mrs Mounstevens (or Mountstevens).

31 JULY

Frederick announced that he wanted nothing more to do with his wife and moved to Mrs Mounstevens' house but on 30 July, Caroline visited him there and spent the night with him. The next evening, Caroline and Clements were at The Cannon Tavern, when Frederick came in. He offered Clements a drink, suggesting that afterwards they should go for a little walk together. However, as the two men drank, Clements accused Brown of sleeping with Caroline the previous night.

'Who has a better right to sleep with my own wife than myself?' asked Brown and he and Clements began scuffling.

Landlord Mr Kemp stepped in to break up the fight, escorting Clements some distance up the road. However, Clements followed Kemp back to the pub and the fight began anew, with Caroline urging her husband on. Then Caroline and Clements began fighting and Brown pulled them apart, saying that Clements could have her. Brown offered to officially sign her over, if Kemp would lend him a pen and paper, but Kemp refused to let them back into the pub, so the two men shook hands and walked off together. They got as far as St James's churchyard when Brown stabbed Clements in the chest. He died in hospital on 9 August, when Brown was charged with his 'wilful murder' and Caroline with being an accessory before the fact.

Lord Chief Justice Coleridge. (Author's collection)

Brown never denied stabbing Clements but claimed that he was cutting a plug of tobacco and momentarily lost his temper. At the Bristol Assizes, his defence counsel cited the many years of provocation Brown had received at the hands of his wife and her lover, adding that Clements started the fight and suggesting that Brown was defending Caroline.

There was no evidence against Caroline and the judge advised the jury to acquit her, even though she could conceivably be held morally responsible for Clements's death. The jury found Brown guilty of the lesser offence of manslaughter, specifically asking the judge to be lenient with him and, saying that he sympathised with Brown, Lord Chief Justice Coleridge sentenced him to six months' imprisonment with hard labour.

AUGUST

Bristol from Cabot Tower, 1905. (Author's collection)

1922 Fifty-five-year-old Morgan Evans was found dead in a house in Bristol, with his throat cut. His wife lay nearby with severe head injuries, believed to have been inflicted by an axe or a hammer.

Only the previous week, Morgan was discharged from the Bristol Quarter Sessions, where he was charged with maliciously wounding his wife. The jury heard that after drinking heavily, Morgan attempted to cut his wife's throat, inflicting a slight wound. He was found guilty of unlawfully wounding but was judged incapable of understanding his act. At the time, Morgan told police that his knife wasn't sharp enough to 'finish the job' – had he used the bloody razor found next to him after his death, the outcome might have been very different. As it was, his wife survived Morgan's penultimate act of violence.

1855 As Daniel Kennedy went about his work as a boiler maker, he was visited by his estranged wife, Elizabeth. The couple parted after enduring a tempestuous relationship since Elizabeth found out six years earlier that her husband had another wife. Even though Daniel had allegedly beaten and ill-used her, Elizabeth wasn't ready to end their marriage and asked him, 'Why don't you come home?'

'Because I don't choose to,' Daniel replied, at which Elizabeth took an eight-inch long stone out of her basket and threw it at him, hitting him on the back of his head. Daniel fell to the floor and Elizabeth walked off laughing.

At hospital, surgeon William Marrack found that Daniel had a fractured skull. Initially conscious, Daniel was told of the severity of his injury and that he was not likely to recover. Accordingly, on 6 August, he gave a deposition to magistrates in Elizabeth's presence.

'I know I did it,' admitted Elizabeth. 'He used me very bad,' she added.

When Daniel died on 14 August, Elizabeth was charged with 'wilful murder', appearing before Mr Justice Williams at the Gloucestershire Winter Assizes. The main issue for the jury was whether Elizabeth intended to kill or injure her husband or had just acted on impulse. Defence counsel Mr Sawyer insisted that her crime was not murder but manslaughter and the jury agreed, finding her guilty of the lesser offence. She was sentenced to two years' imprisonment.

1852 Twenty-two-year-old Charles Mayo was a fireman on a Great Western Railway train. As his driver neared the Bristol Terminus, he realised that the points needed to be switched before he could approach the station. Mayo saw that switchman John Ford was some distance away and jumped down from the train to do it himself. As he climbed back onto the train, which was now moving towards the terminus, he slipped and fell and the train passed over his legs.

Ford rushed to where Mayo lay on the tracks and saw that his legs were almost completely severed from his body, attached only by two small flaps of skin. In spite of this, Mayo was still fully conscious and, according to Ford, 'in excellent spirits'.

As they waited for a cart to transfer Mayo to hospital, he chatted easily to Ford, telling him that his clothes had caught on the handle of the points switch as he was remounting the train. Mayo was still fully conscious when he reached hospital, where surgeon Nathaniel Crisp amputated both of his legs.

Sadly, Mayo died at five o'clock the next morning, remaining perfectly sensible almost to the moment of his death.

At his inquest, the jury asked if it was normal practice for drivers or firemen to jump off engines to alter switches and were told that it was a frequent occurrence. Returning a verdict of 'accidental death', the jury condemned this practice and suggested that people should never attempt to get on or off a moving engine.

4 AUGUST   **1847** Thirty-year-old John Skinner of Clifton appeared at the Gloucestershire Assizes charged with the 'wilful murder' of his wife, Sarah, on 1 June.

Skinner frequently beat his wife and, when her brother, Mr Irving, visited on 31 May, she was badly bruised, but said that she had fallen off a ladder. Irving visited again the next day to find his sister sporting yet more bruises. The broken hearth brush found there confirmed that she had been beaten. When Irving began to ask questions, Skinner lost his temper and demanded he leave. Sarah clung to her brother, begging him not to go as her husband would kill her, but Skinner threatened Irving with a knife. As Irving left, he heard a tremendous crash and, when he got downstairs, Sarah lay dying on the pavement.

At Skinner's trial, although one witness believed that she had clearly seen John push Sarah out of the third-storey window, a man named Daniel Clanney swore that she had thrown herself out and John was nowhere near her at the time. After she fell, John calmly closed the window and went to bed.

To the astonishment of the court, the jury found Skinner 'not guilty'.

5 AUGUST   **1860** George Hayes Hinchcliffe, a coroner from Stafford, married at West Bromwich on 1 August then travelled to The Queen's Hotel, Clifton, for his honeymoon. Eventually, Mrs Hinchcliffe retired for the night, to be followed shortly afterwards by her husband. Within minutes, Hinchcliffe came downstairs and demanded another room. The hotel was full, so he went to The Sedan Chair Tavern on Broad Quay, where he found a bed for the night. Meanwhile, his distraught bride telegraphed her brother in West Bromwich, telling him that she was afraid of her husband and thought he had gone insane.

Hinchcliffe met his wife and her brother, Mr Fereday, at The Queen's Hotel for dinner on 2 August. Hinchcliffe behaved perfectly normally and readily agreed to go back to his wife. Yet he left the hotel again that night and went back to The Sedan Chair.

On Saturday 4 August, Hinchcliffe approached grocer Walter Price of Thomas Street and persuaded Price to rent him a bedroom. In the early hours of 5 August, the police were alarmed when Hinchcliffe shouted from his bedroom window that he had been robbed. When PS Foot approached, Hinchcliffe reassured him that he had now found what he thought he had lost. Foot asked him his name but Hinchcliffe refused to tell him and, knowing that a patient had recently escaped from a nearby asylum, Foot went to knock up Mr Price to find out the identity of his guest. When he returned, Hinchcliffe was hanging out of the upstairs window, clutching the sill with his fingertips. His tenuous hold soon gave way and he fell to the street below, breaking his leg and fracturing his skull and, although he was taken to the General Hospital, he was dead on arrival.

Coroner Mr J.B. Grindon held an inquest at the Ship Inn, Redcliff Hill. Hinchcliffe was a particularly sensitive and nervous man and his bride was also an exceedingly nervous woman. The only explanation that anyone could suggest for his suicide was that he suffered from a hernia and may have believed that it precluded him from having a normal relationship with his wife. However, this was pure conjecture and the inquest jury eventually returned a verdict that Hinchcliffe 'destroyed himself while labouring under temporary insanity.'

1873 Work on the construction of the Clifton Extension Railway was taking place day and night and, in the early hours of the morning, foreman John Parson heard an explosion on Whiteladies Road, Clifton. Not having heard warning shouts before the blast, Parson rushed to the scene to find two of his workmen seriously injured. Thomas Harwood and Thomas Maisey were taken to the Infirmary, where forty-four-year-old Harwood died soon after admission. Maisey was blinded by the explosion and it was feared that he would not recover his sight.

Deputy coroner Mr F.F. Cartwright held an inquest at the hospital later that day. Having heard that Harwood was an experienced blaster, who was known for being very careful, the coroner and his jury visited Maisey on the ward to hear his account of the explosion.

The upper part of Maisey's face and his chest were wrapped in wadding and oiled silk, while his lower face was stippled with gunpowder, which had been driven under his skin. Maisey related that he and Harwood were preparing holes in the rock for blasting the following morning. Having

6 AUGUST

Whiteladies Road, Clifton. (Author's collection)

finished one hole, they moved to the next, pouring gunpowder into the cavity and topping it up with rubble to prevent it from exploding too quickly once the fuse was lit.

As Harwood tamped down the rubble the charge exploded, blowing both men off their feet. The only explanation that Maisey could offer was that the tamper had struck a rock, creating a spark, which then ignited the gunpowder.

The inquest jury returned a verdict of 'accidental death'.

7 AUGUST   **1888** Three-year-old Frances Lena Betty spent the afternoon playing with a puppy in the grounds of Ethelbert House, Park Row. When she didn't appear for tea, a search was made of the grounds and the body of the puppy was found floating in a rainwater tank at the rear of the house. When the tank was examined more closely, Frances's body was found at the bottom of the 4ft-deep water.

The tank had been in its present position for twenty years and rubble had accumulated at the sides making it easily accessible for a curious child.

At an inquest held by coroner Mr H.S. Wasbrough, the jury returned a verdict of 'accidental death' and suggested that the tank should be covered and the rubble removed to prevent a repeat of the tragedy.

8 AUGUST   **1859** George Sheppard (or Shepherd) appeared at the Gloucestershire Assizes charged with the manslaughter of George Tilley.

Tilley worked at a timber yard at St Augustine's on the banks of the Avon and rowed to work every day in a flat-bottomed boat. On 23 May 1859, he rowed the foreman across the river and was returning to the yard when his boat was struck by the steam-tug, *Dido*, which was under Sheppard's command.

There were numerous witnesses to the incident, all of whom had apparently seen completely different things. Some maintained that Tilley was managing his rowing boat skilfully and that, had Sheppard given the order for his tug to reverse in time, the collision could easily have been avoided. Another witness insisted that the tug ran right over Tilley's boat. The chief witness for the defence was *Dido*'s engineer, who stated that Sheppard had given an order to reverse the boat in plenty of time and that no collision had taken place. The engineer further stated that he had seen Tilley jump from his boat and that, rather than being killed, Tilley killed himself. Whatever happened, Tilley was not pulled from the water for almost thirteen minutes, by which time he had drowned.

The key point for the jury to consider was whether or not Sheppard had been grossly negligent, hence causing Tilley's death. The jury decided that he had not and found him not guilty.

9 AUGUST   **1851** As Robert Moffat, Thomas Pike, William Smith, Philip Pring and William Webster were lowered down to the coal seam at Malago Vale Colliery, the rope supporting the cart in which they were travelling broke, plunging them to the bottom of the shaft. There was standing water at the pit bottom

and those men who didn't die from injuries caused by the fall were drowned. Indirectly, the tragedy claimed a sixth victim when Thomas Parsons went to the pit to try and discover the fate of his son. Although he was assured that his son wasn't involved, Parsons refused to believe it until he had seen the boy for himself and, while waiting at the pit head, suddenly collapsed and died.

At the subsequent inquest, doubts were raised about whether the rope used to lower the men was fit for the purpose and the proceedings culminated in the committal for manslaughter of mine foreman Henry Pillinger (or Pillager) and agent Moses Gildroy Stewart. They were tried at the Gloucestershire Assizes on 27 March 1852, where both were acquitted.

Just weeks later, a similar tragedy was narrowly avoided at the pit, after somebody deliberately cut one of the ropes.

1844 Ellen Brindle was notorious around Barton Hill for her fearsome temper and, while in a beer-house, she argued with Mary Ann Platt. After Mary Ann called her a rude name, Ellen struck Mary Ann, who retaliated by throwing a half-pint earthenware mug, hitting Ellen above her eye.

10 AUGUST

Ellen's husband John intervened and took Ellen home, but just two days later she drunkenly provoked a quarrel with him and he struck her on the side of the head, knocking her over. Ellen didn't seem too badly affected by either of the blows but, on the evening of 12 August, she was found asleep in a privy. She was taken home, where she died the following morning.

Coroner Mr W. Joyner Ellis opened an inquest at The Piebald Horse, Barton Hill, on 14 August, by which time a post-mortem examination had been conducted. Surgeon Mr Day gave his opinion that Ellen had died from apoplexy. Either of the blows might have precipitated the apoplexy but he could find no direct connection between the blows and Ellen's demise.

The inquest jury returned a verdict of 'death from natural causes', but the police were not satisfied. Both Mary Ann Platt and John Brindle had been in custody on suspicion of homicide since Ellen's death and the police wanted the case heard by magistrates.

Having heard all the evidence from the inquest, magistrate Reverend Mr Mirehouse stated that if either of the blows were proved to have accelerated Ellen's death, even by a minute, it would have been his duty to send the prisoners for trial, but the evidence failed to satisfy him that this was the case. He then discharged both prisoners.

1837 Seven-year-old Hannah Oswald was brought before magistrates at the Council House charged with having been found wandering near Rownham Ferry. The child was found at three o'clock in the morning and was in a state of near nudity.

11 AUGUST

She told the magistrates that her father abandoned her on the street three days earlier, forcing her to sleep outdoors and scavenge what food she could. The magistrates decided that she must not be left to starve and asked a policeman to take her to the Clifton Poor House. One magistrate, Mr McBayne, benevolently presented her with a halfpenny, so that she could buy some food.

Clifton Suspension Bridge from Rownham Ferry. (Author's collection)

12 AUGUST · **1878** Italian sailor Dario 'David' Scapuzzi married an English woman and settled in Bristol. For Mrs Scapuzzi's, absence certainly didn't make the heart grow fonder as, while her husband was at sea, she began an affair with twenty-eight-year-old bricklayer James Millett. When Scapuzzi returned from a two-year-voyage in June 1878, his wife welcomed him home, although she left him days later to live with Millett.

On 12 August Scapuzzi was standing outside The Spotted Horse in Bedminster, when his wife and her lover walked round the corner arm-in-arm. Millett was heard to say, 'I'll stab the *******.'

'Jim, don't you do it,' warned Mrs Scapuzzi. However, Scapuzzi heard Millett's remark and hit him before he could make good his threat. The two men scuffled for a while, both falling to the pavement, before Millett scrambled to his feet, pulled something from his pocket and hit Scapuzzi in the face. Scapuzzi immediately began shouting that he had been stabbed and at the hospital, he was found to have a puncture wound near his eye. Millett was arrested and charged with 'maliciously wounding, with intent to do grievous bodily harm'.

At his trial before Mr Justice Coleridge at the Bristol Assizes on 2 November 1878, Millett freely admitted hitting Scapuzzi but only after Scapuzzi hit him first. He denied using a weapon, adding that Scapuzzi had banged his face on a kerb stone.

After much deliberation, the jury found Millett guilty of the lesser offence of 'unlawful wounding without intent' and he was sentenced to nine months' hard labour.

13 AUGUST · **1915** A group of 130 children, along with twenty adult helpers, went for a pleasure cruise along the Avon on a steam boat. Everyone had a lovely day, but as the party was boarding the boat to return home there was a slight delay in setting off, which caused a build up of steam.

When the steam was let off, the noise caused a mass panic among the young passengers. In a frenzied state, twelve of them actually jumped overboard and fell between the boat and a steep bank, which was only 2ft away.

Two boys and two girls, aged between seven and ten years old, were drowned.

1842 *The Bristol Mercury* reported that William Smith and Henry Jenkins   **14 AUGUST**
had been found guilty 'on the clearest evidence, which is of course wholly unfit for publication', of an unnatural offence, committed in the parish of St Phillip and Jacob. The records of the Gloucestershire Assizes show that thirty-five-year-old Smith was charged with sodomy and sixteen-year-old Jenkins with aiding and abetting him.

The judge sentenced both men to death, for what he referred to as, 'a crime of a horrible and disgusting nature', although he later commuted their sentences to transportation for life, saying that they would 'pass the remainder of their lives in a state of dreadful slavery.'

1875 Robert Hopkins was buried at Brislington, having been hit by a train   **15 AUGUST**
on 12 August, while walking with his wife along the Great Western Railway line. Surgeon John Lodge of Keynsham was called to visit the injured man at his home on 13 August and, when Hopkins died the next day, Lodge wrote a death certificate confirming the cause of death as abdominal injuries, due to being hit by a train. Mrs Hopkins then buried her husband, before sending the death certificate to the registrar.

Unfortunately, as Hopkins had died a violent death, an inquest should have been held. On receipt of the death certificate, the registrar contacted coroner Robert Biggs, who, on the advice of two other coroners, insisted that Hopkins was exhumed so that the proper procedure could be followed.

Mrs Hopkins was forced to identify the exhumed body of her husband and the inquest jury had to view the body, before the coroner heard evidence

Brislington
Cemetery, 2007.
(© N. Sly)

from Mrs Hopkins and Mr Lodge about the circumstances of Hopkins' death. The jury returned a verdict of 'accidental death' and the deceased was quickly returned to his grave.

16 AUGUST   **1840** At two o'clock in the morning, Alfred Gough spotted a youth stealing apples from his father's garden. Gough attracted the attention of watchman James Pearce and the two men apprehended the youth and took him to St Philip's police station. When they arrived, they were told that the garden was just outside the city boundary, so they must take the boy to Hanham.

They got to Redfield, where they were overtaken by three men, who attempted to rescue the boy from Pearce's clutches. One man beat Pearce's head with a large stone, threatening to 'dash out his brains' if he didn't release his prisoner. When two passers-by came to Pearce's assistance, his attackers ran away but shortly afterwards, one returned and beat Gough and Pearce until they let the youth go.

Having been punched, beaten with a stone and had his head slammed against the ground several times, Pearce was stupefied, although he was able to identify his attackers. His condition gradually worsened, until he died on 10 September from 'extraversion of blood on the brain'.

James Porter (18) was arrested with John Thomas (45) and his sons William (16) and the apple thief, John (19). Although the jury at Pearce's inquest returned a verdict of 'wilful murder' against all four, they were actually tried for manslaughter at the Gloucestershire Assizes in April 1841. All were found guilty and sentenced to transportation for life.

17 AUGUST   **1842** Eight-year-old David Beynon decided to amuse himself by throwing a dog off the Bath Bridge into the tidal waters below. The dog managed to swim ashore but was unable to get up the steep banks to dry land. Beynon dashed down to the water's edge to rescue it but was running so fast that he was unable to stop and ran straight off the bank into the river. Although several bystanders tried to save him, he drowned.

At an inquest held by coroner Mr J.B. Grindon, the jury returned a verdict of 'accidental death'.

18 AUGUST   **1876** At 11 p.m. on 16 August, passers-by noticed that the hat factory on Castle Street was on fire. The fire quickly reached the second floor, where the owner and his family lived, but spectators only became aware that there were people inside the building when they heard screams coming from within.

Somebody fetched a ladder but it proved too short to reach the window in the building's gable end. Another ladder was tied to the first and Edward Davis climbed up and began to break the windows with his fists and feet. However, the ties on the ladder broke before anyone could be brought out of the burning building and the broken windows allowed in air, which fanned the flames and intensified the conflagration. The ladders were lashed together again and Davis, Mr Popham and Mr Salmon tried desperately to reach those inside. Although they could hear groans and cries for help, the

Castle Street, 1934. (Author's collection)

smoke was so thick that they were unable to find anybody. Mr Rubery went through a neighbouring building to the roof, from where he assisted two of the occupants to escape. Rubery could hear children screaming in the rooms below but was unable to get to them.

When the fire brigade arrived, their efforts were hampered by a lack of water and by a delay in getting the portable fire escape to the scene. The fire claimed the lives of hatter Thomas Skinner (56), his son Henry (5) and his daughter Kate (13). Mrs Ellen Tyler Skinner and another daughter, Annie, escaped, as did Mrs Skinner's nephew, Joseph Hewlett.

At the two-day inquest into the three deaths, which concluded on 18 August, aspersions were cast on the Water Works, fire brigade and police. The brigade received the alarm at 11.18 p.m. and, although they were at the scene in five minutes, the first water wasn't directed at the flames until 11.54 p.m. The water at the fire hydrant was turned off and the firemen had to wait for the arrival of a turnkey from the Water Works.

The jury recorded verdicts of death by suffocation on all three victims, stating that the fire was an accident. However, they believed that all three could have been saved had the proper appliances been available. The jury recommended that fire escapes were placed at various locations throughout the city and that the authorities should ensure that there was always an adequate water supply.

1872 As chambermaid Mary Cooley was dressing in the bedroom at the Queen's Hotel, which she shared with three other servants, the proprietor's son knocked at the door and demanded the key to the room.

19 AUGUST

The girls didn't feel that it was proper to allow a man into the room until they had been given a chance to tidy up and refused to hand it over. Minutes later, when Mary went downstairs to begin her work, proprietor William Bateman Reed insisted that she give him the key. Mary refused again, at which Reed took her by the shoulders and shook her violently, threatening to turn her out of the house, to shake her liver out and to tear every stitch of clothing from her back until he found the key.

Mary summoned Reed, who appeared at the Police Court charged with assaulting her and with using abusive language. Her story was corroborated by a waiter from the hotel and by a fellow servant, Fanny Porter, who agreed with Mary that it was most improper for a gentleman to go into a bedroom when the female occupants had just got up.

In his defence, Reed stated that he had asked Mary many times to let him have the key by seven o'clock that morning as there had been complaints about the room and he had arranged for a tradesman to go in and rectify them. With the tradesman waiting and no sign of the key, Reed asked his son to go and get it. He admitted that he had been angry, as he eventually had to send the tradesman home without completing the work, but denied assaulting Mary or swearing at her.

The magistrates believed Mary rather than Reed and asked him to retire with Mary and negotiate some form of compensation for his ill-treatment but Reed refused, agreeing to accept the decision of the Bench. It was decided that Mary should be awarded £1 in damages, plus her court costs, which Reed promptly paid.

20 AUGUST
1899 Eleven-year-old Edward Skinner got into difficulties while bathing at the New Cut. Although other swimmers went to his aid, he disappeared beneath the water.

One of those who tried to save Edward was fourteen-year-old Charles Richard Harwood Wurgan (or Worgan). Charles was soon floundering and, even though several bathers and bystanders went to his assistance, he too vanished under the water. The bodies of both boys were recovered days later.

At an inquest held by coroner Mr Doggett, the jury returned verdicts of 'accidental death' on Skinner and 'accidentally drowned' on Wurgan.

21 AUGUST
1872 Mr and Mrs Anger went out, leaving their seven-month-old daughter Emily Louise fast asleep, in the knowledge that the other occupants of their house would listen out for her. When they got back, Emily had been crying and thirty-one-year-old Thomas Harris was rocking her gently in an attempt to pacify her. Suddenly Mrs Hopes, another lodger, rushed into the room and accused Harris of attacking the baby. Harris fled to his own room and when the Angers examined their daughter more closely, it was evident that she had been raped. Mr Anger immediately turned Harris out of the house and he was pursued by an angry mob and handed into police custody. Meanwhile, a surgeon confirmed the Angers' worst fears and Harris was charged with the rape of a child under ten years old.

Tried at the Bristol Assizes on 1 April 1873, he was found guilty as charged and sentenced to fifteen years' penal servitude, in spite of his request to the judge to deal with him leniently, since it was his first offence.

22 AUGUST
1896 Collier Thomas Lewis lived with Cecilia Legg in Bedminster and, although they were not legally married, they had several children together.

On 22 August, Cecilia stormed out of their home after a quarrel and, when Lewis met her on the street later that evening, he showed his displeasure by punching her three times in the face.

Cecilia was convinced that, rather than just using his fist, Thomas had actually stabbed her. Neighbour Eliza Williams, who witnessed the attack, saw a knife in Thomas's hand and surgeon William Nevill confirmed that she had three cuts on her face, which he believed to be stab wounds. Yet when Lewis was arrested, he swore that he had no weapon but had only struck Cecilia with his hand.

Lewis was tried at the Bristol Assizes charged with wounding Cecilia Legg, with intent to do grievous bodily harm. Having listened to all the evidence, the jury found Lewis guilty of the lesser offence of 'unlawful wounding', on the grounds that they believed that the stab wounds on Cecilia's face were made by Lewis's thumbnail.

The verdict initially provoked a stunned silence and then nervous laughter. Mr Justice Wills called the surgeon back into the witness box to state that the wounds had been made by a knife and could not possibly have been caused by a thumbnail and the jury deliberated again briefly and returned exactly the same verdict, this time without qualifying their reasons for doing so.

Mr Justice Wills.
(Author's collection)

Cecilia was then recalled to the witness box. Her wounds were not serious and she assured the judge that she was not afraid of Lewis and intended to live with him again. At that, Wills told Lewis that he had treated his woman very badly but, since she was prepared to give him another chance, he was willing to do the same. Lewis was bound over to come for judgement if called upon to do so in future and effectively walked from the court a free man.

1872 Alfred Giles of Norton Fitzwarren, near Taunton, was hauling stone from a boat moored in the quay to a yard in St Philip's. As he was standing by his cart, waiting for it to be loaded, the horse suddenly turned round and Giles was jammed between the side of the cart and an iron post. He was taken to the General Hospital but died from his injuries within hours of his admission.

23 AUGUST

The jury at the subsequent inquest returned a verdict of 'accidental death'.

1857 Nine-year-old Emma Clark appeared at the Council House charged with stabbing a little girl named Buckingham. Fortunately, Miss Buckingham was not seriously injured, although surgeons testified that Emma's knife

24 AUGUST

missed her heart by only an eighth of an inch.

The stabbing occurred when Miss Buckingham and her two brothers were walking home from chapel. One of the little boys made a remark to Emma, who chased after them, but while the boys got away their sister stumbled and fell.

In Emma's defence, her counsel stated that she was cutting a pear at the time and just happened to have a knife in her hand. Emma seemed remarkably indifferent to her fate and seemed incapable of understanding that she had done anything wrong.

The magistrates said that, if Emma had 'any proper sense of her position', they would hand her over to her parents to deal with her as they saw fit. However, since she didn't, they adjourned the case for two days to give Emma a taste of life in the Bridewell.

When proceedings resumed, Emma's attitude was unchanged and, unable to decide if she was 'obstinate or stupid', the magistrates discharged her to her parents, on condition that she was severely punished.

25 AUGUST **1857** Francis Hopkinson appeared at the Council House charged with assaulting his wife, Mary Ann, to whom he had been married for less than four months.

Francis earned 12s a week as a soda bottler but rarely gave his wife any housekeeping money. Mary Ann told the magistrates that, having received nothing from her husband for two weeks, she stole 2s 6d out of his trouser pocket, for which he had beaten her.

Francis accused his wife of neglect, saying that he gave her everything that she could wish for but still frequently got home from work to find no fire lit, no meal cooked and no dry clothes for him to wear. Such was the state of affairs when he returned home on the night after she stole his money and, knowing that she had 2s 6d, he was angry. Francis alleged that Mary Ann hit him over the head with a poker when he complained and Mary Ann admitted that this was true, saying that Francis called her an offensive name.

Magistrates discharged Francis, advising the couple to settle their differences, which they agreed to do.

26 AUGUST **1858** Twenty-year-old Elizabeth, the oldest daughter of Isaac Pyne of Kingsland Road, The Dings, went into labour with a baby sired by her father. Elizabeth's mother, who had no idea that her daughter was even pregnant, was understandably furious at finding out that her husband had committed incest and, after sending her younger daughter Eliza in search of a midwife, Ann Pyne stormed out of the house, vowing never to return.

When neighbours realised that Elizabeth was no longer pregnant, they asked about the baby, which she tearfully admitted was dead and buried. The neighbours insisted on seeing it and Eliza, who had buried the infant at Crew's Hole, was sent to dig it up. Once it was washed, the neighbours noticed marks of violence and reported their concerns to the police, who immediately arrested Isaac Pyne. Isaac made a statement admitting, 'I am sorry for what I have done. I can now see my error and am penitent to it; all they have against me is for making away with the child. I would not have done so if trade had not been so bad.' Pyne went on to say that he sent Eliza to bury the child, fearful of the reaction of his neighbours to Elizabeth's disgrace. He added that he and Elizabeth were alone in the kitchen when the baby was born and that Eliza had been unable to find a midwife – he tried to go and find one himself, but Elizabeth clung to him so tightly that he was unable to get away.

An inquest was conducted by coroner Mr J.B. Grindon, who asked the jury to consider three questions – whose child was it, did it die by violence and, if so, who caused that violence? He reminded the jury that Elizabeth Pyne had deposed that she had been insensible with pain during her labour and could remember nothing at all until the evening after the baby's birth.

The jury returned a verdict of 'wilful murder' against Isaac Pyne, who was committed for trial at the Gloucester Assizes. In spite of his confession, the jury found that the evidence against him, although strong, was purely circumstantial and he was acquitted.

1837 William Wilfred Short quarrelled with his wife, Elizabeth, after learning that she had borrowed and spent 10s without telling him about it. Elizabeth, who had the couple's baby in her arms at the time, was severely beaten and later maintained that the child became ill on account of her being 'flurried'. 27 AUGUST

William refused to give her any money to pay for a surgeon to attend the baby so she went to her father's house, where the child later died. Elizabeth carried their dead child to her marital home but William refused to let her in, claiming that to do so would leave him responsible for the cost of the funeral.

With no money to pay for the burial, Elizabeth ordered a funeral coach anyway but, as they were travelling to the service, William stopped the coach and snatched the baby's body.

The couple were brought before magistrates at the Council House to try and resolve the matter. William maintained that he had no money to give his wife because his employer – her father – had sacked him. He insisted that he stopped the funeral for valid reasons. Contrary to what Elizabeth said, he was refused permission to see the child and, as the procession passed, another man was walking in his place as father of the deceased.

The magistrates said that they had never heard of a more disgraceful occurrence. Since Elizabeth was determined that she would never live with William again, they discharged him with an admonition.

1867 The sorry saga of an unnamed Bristol pickpocket was reported in newspapers countrywide. Tried for stealing a purse, he was acquitted on the grounds of insanity and ordered to be detained in a lunatic asylum during Her Majesty's Pleasure. 28 AUGUST

He so disliked the experience that he confessed to feigning madness and asked to be tried again. He got his wish and was found guilty at the Bristol Assizes, where he made a long, rambling plea to the court to be allowed to serve his sentence in a 'proper' prison, on the grounds that he had tried

Bristol and County Asylum, 1906. (Author's collection)

'Queen's Pleasure' and didn't want it again. The judge was only too happy to oblige, sending him to prison for six months with hard labour.

29 AUGUST **1857** Coroner Mr J.B. Grindon held an inquest at The Ship, Redcliff Hill, on the death of labourer Edward Robbs.

Robbs worked at a timber yard and, on 28 August, was relaxing during his dinner hour, lying down by a large pile of planks, some 20ft high. As a heavily laden wagon passed, the vibration caused the stack to fall and, although his workmates shouted a warning, Robbs was buried beneath the collapsed timber.

The inquest jury returned a verdict of 'accidental death' on twenty-two-year-old Robbs, who left a wife and three young children.

30 AUGUST **1736** Among the prisoners tried at the Guildhall were John 'Long Jack' Vernon, who was charged with robbery from a house in St Michael's Hill and Joshua Harding, charged with shoplifting.

Vernon refused to plead and was told that, if he didn't, he would be pressed to death – placed beneath a board to which weights were added until the condemned prisoner was crushed. Vernon still refused to plead and an order was made for his pressing. Terror caused Vernon to reconsider and he was eventually sentenced to death by the more conventional method of hanging, as was Harding. 'Damn it, I don't value my life as a halfpenny,' Vernon remarked on hearing the sentence.

Both men were executed at Gallows Acre on 3 September 1736. However, both survived their execution and, although Vernon died later that day, Harding was reprieved and subsequently transported for life.

31 AUGUST **1857** Coroner Mr J.B. Grindon opened and adjourned an inquest on the death of eleven-year-old William Baker, who had died that morning. When the proceedings concluded on 3 September, the jury heard that Baker was injured on 30 August, while rowing a small boat with friends on the Avon.

As the boat neared Redcliff Parade, a group of boys began to pelt the water around it with large stones, one of which accidentally hit Baker on the head. A post-mortem examination revealed that he had a large skull fracture.

The fatal stone was thrown by twelve-year-old Henry Wicketts, who tearfully told the inquest that he never intended the stone to go anywhere near the boat but just wanted to make a splash in the water nearby. The inquest jury returned a verdict that Baker was 'accidentally killed by Henry Wicketts' and the coroner discharged him with a caution.

SEPTEMBER

Whiteladies Road (*see* 11 and 12 September). (Author's collection)

1894 Coroner Mr H.S. Wasbrough held an inquest at Bedminster police station on the death of nineteen-year-old Edwin Doddrell. On 29 August, Edwin and his friend Henry William Keey (or Kesy) hired a boat to row around the harbour, as they had done many times before.

As they rowed towards Hotwells, Henry noticed the steam boat, *Lincolnshire*, apparently moored in the centre of the harbour, but, as the boys drew nearer he realised that *Lincolnshire* was moving very slowly towards them.

Henry remarked on this to Edwin, telling him to row harder so that they would miss the steamer. Instead of doing so, Edwin stood up in the boat and turned round to look. Henry shouted at him to sit down and row but Edwin lost one of his oars. Suddenly, the *Lincolnshire* collided with the rowing boat, tipping both boys into the water. Henry began to swim for shore, losing sight of Edwin.

The *Lincolnshire* lowered a boat to look for him and a group of boys in a rowing boat joined in the search, but to no avail. As it began to get dark, Henry climbed into the *Lincolnshire*'s boat and was taken to the water police, who found Edwin's body at half-past ten that night.

Bristol Harbour. (Author's collection)

At the inquest, the Captain of the *Lincolnshire*, William Rees, stated that he had seen something in front of his steamer and sounded his whistle. The rowing boat then steered straight across his bows and, although he immediately went into reverse, it was too late to avoid a collision.

The inquest jury returned a verdict of 'accidental death'.

1850 Caroline Rees of Merchant's Parade, Hotwells, and her husband's apprentice, Richard Gill, went to Abbot's Leigh on business, where Richard picked some mushrooms. They were given to servant Mary Jane Jones, who broiled them on the griddle, adding butter, salt and pepper.

Hours later, Mrs Rees woke her husband, complaining of violent vomiting. Mr Rees called surgeon James Witchell Crichton, who found her deathly cold, with a weak, thready pulse, suffering from sickness, diarrhoea and stomach pains. Crichton concluded that Caroline had eaten poisonous fungi but was hopeful that she had vomited most of them up, since her vomit was now a watery fluid, with no trace of any solids. Crichton administered antispasmodic medicine and tried to get Mrs Rees warm.

Meanwhile, her three sons, James, William and Henry, who had all eaten the mushrooms as well, had gone to school. Mary Jones was sent to fetch them and found that they too were ill, three-year-old James particularly so.

Caroline gradually grew weaker and Crichton called in another surgeon for a second opinion. Later that day, a third surgeon was consulted but to no avail. Caroline died on 4 September and James the next day.

Curiously, Richard Gill, who had eaten several raw mushrooms on the way home, as well as the cooked ones, felt unwell and was confined to his bed, but had no sickness and diarrhoea.

At the inquest on the deaths, Crichton stated that, although their symptoms were consistent with those of Asiatic cholera, he believed that Caroline and James Rees died from eating poisonous fungi. The jury returned a verdict that both were 'accidentally killed'.

3 SEPTEMBER 1872 When Mrs Moorhead of Cathay went to wake her eight-year-old son, William, she found him unconscious. William's father was a sailor and, on a recent trip to the West Indies, brought back a large bottle of rum, steeped with various local herbs. Mrs Moorhead used the mixture as a 'stomachic' and had poured herself a measure to treat stomach ache during the night of 2/3 September.

Unfortunately, she left the bottle in William's room and next morning, most of the rum had disappeared. He died from alcohol poisoning later that day at the General Hospital. At an inquest held by coroner Mr H.S. Wasbrough, the jury returned a verdict of 'death by misadventure'.

4 SEPTEMBER 1853 Seventeen-year-old Anne Blannin died at the Infirmary. On 5 November of the previous year, Ann had procured some fireworks to celebrate Guy Fawkes Night, which she tucked into the bodice of her dress for safekeeping. A chance spark ignited the fireworks and Ann was terribly burned on her neck and breasts, in spite of which she lingered in hospital for almost ten months before dying from her injuries.

At an inquest held by coroner Mr J.B. Grindon, the jury returned a verdict of 'accidental death'.

5 SEPTEMBER 1868 An old woman named Jane Richards appeared at the Council House charged with stealing a pair of trousers from a shop in College Place.

When searched at the police station, Jane was found to have £12 10s in gold and 11s 6d in silver on her person, as well as a few coppers and the stolen trousers. Since she appeared 'simple minded', shop owner Mr Hemings generously agreed not to press charges, although Jane was detained at the police station while enquiries were made about her mental health.

At her appearance before magistrates, Jane complained bitterly that she had been given nothing to eat since her arrest and one of the magistrates asked a female searcher, Mrs Dawes, to take her to a refreshment house. Mrs Dawes later returned to tell him that, as soon as Jane realised that she would have to pay for her own food, she refused to order any, since she felt that 2*d* was far too much to pay for tea and bread and butter.

1843 A fire broke out at The Old Castle Tavern on Castle Street. The premises 6 SEPTEMBER
were occupied by Thomas Worthington, his wife and son, their servant, Eliza Buck and his ten-year-old niece, Lydia Groves.

Worthington was bedridden due to 'a severe cerebral affection' and was, according to the contemporary newspapers, 'bordering on mental imbecility'. He was incapable of doing anything for himself.

Lydia helped Eliza feed Worthington some gruel at about ten o'clock at night then went back down to the bar. She complained of being tired and went upstairs, supposedly to bed. However instead of going to her own room, Lydia went into her uncle's and moved the candle from its normal place to a position closer to his bed. The flame set the bed curtains alight and Lydia tried to beat out the flames, badly burning her hands, arms, face and neck. When this proved impossible, she screamed for help.

Her aunt rushed upstairs with Eliza Buck and two young men from the bar. Mrs Worthington tried to rescue her husband but was prevented from doing so by the men, who shut the door so that the fire wouldn't spread. They then hustled the two women out of the house. The men went back inside to try and douse the flames with water but by that time the fire was raging out of control.

Worthington's charred body was eventually found in the tap room, two floors below his bedroom and Lydia also died from shock. At the inquest into the two deaths, the jury found that Worthington 'accidentally burned to death in his bed' and Lydia died an 'accidental death'. The coroner condemned the two unidentified men who left Mr Worthington to his fate, pointing out that it would have taken only seconds to carry him to safety. A box containing about seventy sovereigns and £60 in bank notes was also destroyed in the blaze.

1872 Brothers Samuel, Robert and John Abrahams burgled a house on 7 SEPTEMBER
Cumberland Road. They were caught red-handed, when PC Wedlake noticed that the house door was open and saw Samuel peeping out. After a desperate struggle, in which Wedlake was injured, all three were arrested and appeared at the Bristol Assizes in April 1873. John pleaded guilty, taking all responsibility for the burglary but the jury found the three brothers equally culpable and, since they all had previous convictions, each was sentenced to seven years' penal servitude.

As they were being escorted to the cells after receiving their sentences, the brothers began struggling with the warders. PC Giles was hit in the face and Sergeant Minett was kicked in the abdomen.

Samuel, described as 'a repulsive-looking fellow', was judged to have been the ringleader and, since it was he who kicked Minett, he was taken back to court and charged with assault with intent to do bodily harm. Mr Justice

Grove sentenced him to a further thirteen years, making a grand total of twenty years' penal servitude.

8 SEPTEMBER   1854 Fifteen-year-old Thomas Morgan had recently started working for railway contractor Mr Hennet, where two of his workmates made his life a misery with constant jealous arguments.

On 8 September, thirteen-year-old Thomas Roberts and twelve-year-old Thomas Davidge challenged Morgan to a fight. Morgan tried to walk away, saying that he wouldn't fight younger boys but Davidge and Roberts were insistent and, since Morgan was both older and taller, it was agreed that he would fight both at once.

At lunchtime, the boys squared up in the yard at Temple Meads but the fight was quickly over when Roberts was hit on the head, immediately falling face down to the ground and rolling onto his back. Morgan and Derridge went for help but Roberts was already dead from an extraversion of blood to the brain.

Morgan was arrested and taken into custody pending the findings of the inquest. Having heard testimony from Davidge and other witnesses, coroner Mr J.B. Grindon told the jury that, in his opinion, there was no possible verdict other than manslaughter against Morgan, since a human life had been sacrificed at his hands. Stubbornly, the jury returned a verdict of 'accidentally killed whilst boxing', reasoning that Morgan had done everything in his power to avoid fighting.

9 SEPTEMBER   1872 Ann Harvey and William Elliott had lived together as man and wife for many years and had several children together. The couple shared a fondness for alcohol and were drinking in The Stag and Hounds on Old Market Street, when they began quarrelling and Ann threw her drink in William's face.

She ran out of the pub, calling for William to come outside and, when he didn't follow her, she went back in, finding him standing in the hallway.

Old Market Street. (Author's collection)

She hit him twice on the head, at which William knocked her down and kicked her.

Ann was taken to hospital in a cab, where assistant surgeon Mr H.M. Chute found that she had a cut on her lower abdomen, which was bleeding heavily. She died from blood loss three days later and Elliott was charged with her manslaughter.

At his trial in April 1873, Mr Chute testified that all of Ann's organs were in a bad state, especially her lungs. Although she had died from excessive haemorrhage, had her general health been better, she would probably have survived.

Mr Justice Grove commented that this was yet another sad result of 'a drop of drink', although since both Elliott and Ann had consumed vast quantities of ale, gin and rum before her death, that was something of an understatement. The jury found Elliott guilty and he was sentenced to six months' imprisonment with hard labour.

1858 William Henry Twitchings, aged five and a half, was out playing when he came across Thomas Clark, sitting on a doorstep with a little girl named Eliza Thomas. William tried to pull Eliza away and Clark punched him hard in the side. **10 SEPTEMBER**

William ran home crying to his mother and, when he was still complaining of pain some hours later, he was taken to the Infirmary, where doctors diagnosed a rupture. He was admitted to the hospital and, when his condition hadn't improved by 16 September, it was decided to operate. Sadly, William didn't survive the anaesthetic and died on the operating table.

At the inquest held the following day, the coroner found himself with something of a dilemma. Although the blow by Thomas Clark had almost certainly caused William's death, the coroner didn't feel that he could charge a ten-year-old child with manslaughter. Eventually, the jury returned a verdict of 'accidental death' and a police constable was despatched to speak to Clark's parents and warn them that, if they didn't punish him, the case might yet be taken up by the police.

1872 As Amelia Howell was walking across Durdham Downs towards Clifton, a young man leaped out of the bushes and said, 'Come along with me, my pretty one. I have something to show you.' Exactly what the young man intended to show his victim is probably best left to the imagination but, being a respectable young woman, Amelia fought to defend her virtue. Fortunately, her attacker was interrupted by a man approaching on horseback. The assailant stood up, bowed to Amelia and walked off leaving her battered and bruised, her clothes in tatters. **11 SEPTEMBER**

The horseman was groom Edwin Peats and, having established that Amelia had been attacked, he wasted no time in pursuing her attacker. When he caught him, the young man happily gave his name and address, which turned out to be false. However, by coincidence, Robert Brown, a relative of Miss Howell's, spotted the youth on Whiteladies Road some days later and, thinking that he bore a strong resemblance to her description of

Durdham
Downs. (Author's
collection)

her assailant, asked his name. Once again, the youth gave the same false name, 'Seymour'.

'Seymour' was actually fifteen-year-old Robert Shuttleworth Meyer and, when taken to his home by Brown, Miss Howell immediately identified him. Her identification was confirmed by Peats and also by another witness, who had seen Peats pursuing the young man.

Meyer appeared at the Bristol Quarter Sessions charged with assault with criminal intent, inflicting grievous bodily harm, causing actual bodily harm and common assault. His defence was threefold – firstly he was a young man of impeccable character, secondly he suffered from St Vitus's Dance and would not have been physically capable of assaulting Miss Howell and thirdly, he was at home with his mother and sisters at the time of the attack. Each strand of the defence was supported by several apparently reliable witnesses but the prosecution managed to raise doubts about the supposed time of the offence, thus invalidating Meyer's alibi. The jury ultimately found him guilty of common assault.

He was sentenced to one month's imprisonment and, in deference to his alleged ill-health, there was no hard labour.

12 SEPTEMBER   1896 Dentist Walter Perry of Whiteladies Road couldn't understand why his practice was getting through so many artificial teeth. When he did his stocktaking and found himself 2,000 teeth short, Perry remarked to his apprentice William Lewin that he would have to take steps to find out where they had gone.

On 3 September, as Perry was leaving his workshop, he brushed against Lewin's coat, which was hanging on the door. The coat rattled and, when Perry put his hand in the pocket, he found a small tin containing dental gold and platinum. Perry wasted no time in contacting the police, who arrested Lewin.

Seventeen-year-old Lewin confessed that he had been stealing from the dental surgery for some time and selling what he stole to Mr Earl, a dealer in old gold and silver and 'buyer of dental alloy, scraps and fillings'.

Lewin appeared at Bristol Police Court on 12 September, where he was sentenced to two months' imprisonment with hard labour. The magistrates also censured Mr Earl, suggesting that he should have known better than to buy such items from so young a man.

1895 Three workmen employed by builder Samuel Govett were demolishing an old lavatory at Messrs Cresswell Ltd, a wine and spirit merchants on Bridge Parade. After two days' work, all that remained was to drain the cesspit. **13 SEPTEMBER**

A pump took care of the liquid waste but left a large quantity of sludge, which had to be cleared by hand. The men tested the air with lighted candles and, when it seemed to be clean, took it in turns to be lowered into the pit, to bucket out the slurry.

The air smelled bad to Frederick Hooper and, twenty minutes after descending, his eyes were smarting. He reported this to the foreman, Samuel Baker, who pulled him to the surface and sent Alfred Summers down in his place. Within minutes, Summers was in trouble and, seeing him fall into the slurry, Baker went down to help him. Hearing Hooper's frantic shouts, William Mellhuish of Cresswell's fetched the police. Several officers arrived within minutes, but Summers and Baker were both dead when dragged from the cesspit.

At the inquest on their deaths, held by coroner Mr H.G. Doggett at Bedminster police station, public analysts testified to finding the cesspit filled with 'sulphuretted hydrogen' [*sic*]. Normally, 'carbonic acid gas' [*sic*] was given off by decomposing human effluent but, in this case, the pit had been contaminated by waste chemicals from a nearby photographer's shop. Whereas a lighted candle would be a satisfactory test for carbonic acid, it would not detect the sulphuretted hydrogen, which killed the two labourers.

1853 Shortly after seven o'clock in the morning, a fire broke out on the female lunatics' ward of St Peter's Hospital. The nurse in charge of the locked ward was still asleep but was roused from her bed and rushed half-dressed to the ward with the keys. **14 SEPTEMBER**

A room at St Peter's Hospital, 1904. (Author's collection)

When the doors were opened, inmate Caroline Gwillam was found to be on fire. Her burning clothes were ripped from her body and she was placed in the care of the house surgeon but died from extensive burns the following morning. Conscious almost to death, she told people that she wanted to burn down the hospital with all its inhabitants. To that end, she took some Lucifer matches, which were hidden in a copper kettle in the day room fireplace, and lit the gas in the ward bathroom, before deliberately setting fire to her own clothing.

At a later inquest, the coroner's jury found that Caroline – an inmate of the asylum for twenty-nine years – committed suicide while insane.

15 SEPTEMBER   **1856** Ann Clark, described in the contemporary newspapers as 'a wretched-looking object', appeared at the Council House charged with stealing a purse containing 18s.

The complainant was a foreigner named Michelangelo Nicolai, who struggled to explain in English that he met Ann in a pub and, hearing that she had nowhere to live, invited her to sleep in a chair at his lodgings. Ann stayed for five or six days, leaving at the same time as Nicolai's purse and its contents.

Magistrates told Nicolai that no jury would ever convict Ann on such flimsy evidence and discharged her, advising Nicolai to be more careful in future about taking strange women home to his bedroom.

16 SEPTEMBER   **1890** Coroner Dr E.M. Grace held an inquest on the death of fourteen-year-old Frederick Ward of St Michael's, who drowned two days earlier while bathing in the Avon at Sneyd Park.

Frederick went to bathe with a group of boys and stayed in the water longer than the others. As his friends were dressing, they heard Frederick shouting for help. Walter Holloway ran back into the river and seized Frederick's hand but, feeling himself being dragged out of his depth by the current, he was forced to let go.

The boys' shouts brought nearby resident Edwin Tanner and his son to the scene and they continued to drag the river until well after dark but were unable to find any trace of Frederick. It was only when the tide went out the following morning that they saw that there was a hole in the river bed, which was so deep that the receding tide had left Frederick's body in the hole rather than carrying it out to sea. Had Frederick been able to move just a few feet in the water, he would have been able to stand up.

The inquest jury returned a verdict of 'accidental death by drowning'.

17 SEPTEMBER   **1949** Less than one year into a seven-year sentence for a crime of violence, former RAF Officer Jack Hobbs was transferred to an open prison at Leyhill, Gloucestershire and, on 17 September, he walked out unchallenged and went on the run.

He was recaptured in a spinney at Charfield two days later, after a manhunt involving hundreds of police officers and dogs. During his brief spell of freedom, he broke into the Kingswood home of Mr Reginald Downs, attacking Downs, his wife Winifred and their sixteen-year-old daughter, Margaret, with a heavy metal bar. Downs, who suffered severe head injuries, was detained in the Bristol Royal Infirmary.

Hobbs appeared at the Gloucester Assizes on 13 December charged with three counts of attempted murder and one of burglary. Mr Justice Finnemore was extremely critical of the decision to transfer Hobbs to the 'prison without bars', given his record of violence. Described by his defence counsel as 'a homicidal maniac', Hobbs insisted that he could remember absolutely nothing that happened between 1944 and 1949.

He was found not guilty of attempted murder but guilty of three counts of 'wounding with intent to do grievous bodily harm' and sentenced to ten years' imprisonment, to run concurrently with his previous sentence, which was imposed in June 1948. The following year, the Home Office awarded the Downs family compensation totalling £1,550 for their injuries.

1896 At two o'clock in the morning two boatmen on the river below the Clifton Suspension Bridge heard a loud thudding sound, followed by a scream and a splash. Rowing to the spot where the noises originated, the boatmen found two little girls in the river, one face down and unconscious and the other floating on her back, crying. They were pulled out and rushed to the Infirmary.   **18 SEPTEMBER**

The younger child, who was barely injured in spite of having fallen more than 250ft from the bridge, told doctors that her name was Elsie Brown and that she was four years old. The other girl was her sister, Ruby, who was twelve and, according to Elsie, their father had thrown them off the bridge. Ruby was much more seriously injured than her sister, with damage to her neck and spine but, once she regained consciousness, she confirmed her sister's incredible story.

The police found Mr Brown wandering distractedly along Bridge Valley Road. They established that he ran a grocer's shop in Birmingham. However, the shop was failing and, under financial pressure, Charles Brown began to show signs of mental derangement. Against medical advice, his wife refused to have him committed to an asylum and, on the previous day, he had taken the girls out and not returned home. Instead he had travelled to Bristol, where he threw both of his daughters off the bridge.

Magistrates committed Brown for trial at the next Bristol Assizes, where he was found guilty but insane and ordered to be detained during Her Majesty's Pleasure.

1872 The weaving shed of the Great Western Cotton Works covered nearly an acre of ground and housed more than 800 looms. More than 500, mainly female, employees worked in the shed. Machinery in the adjacent sheds was powered by a revolving shaft, some 180ft in length, which weighed several tons. The shaft crossed the weaving shed, fixed to a solid ceiling beam by heavy iron bearings. The beam itself was supported by cast-iron columns.   **19 SEPTEMBER**

Shortly after two o'clock, one end of the beam broke away from its fastenings. As it swung slowly round, more bearings and columns were

A cotton-weaving shed. (Author's collection)

broken and within seconds, the shaft and beam crashed onto the looms below, completely crushing them.

More than seventy girls were working directly below the beam but miraculously only ten were injured. Five were well enough to be sent home but the remaining five were sent to the Infirmary, where Clara Robins (15) died from her injuries. An inquest on her death held by coroner Mr H.S. Wasbrough recorded a verdict of 'accidental death'.

Martha Vernon (19) escaped the first fall, but a piece of iron fell onto her head as she was trying to pull a little girl out of the debris. Martha later died from a fractured skull.

20 SEPTEMBER 1897 Andrew Garrod appeared at the Police Court charged with causing the death of his brother, William, by administering an overdose of morphine.

William, a sailor, returned from sea determined to enjoy his shore leave by consuming as much alcohol as possible. Unfortunately, his excesses caused him to snore loudly and for days, the entire Garrod household was unable to sleep a wink.

Eventually, the family asked Andrew, who worked for a veterinary surgeon, to obtain a sleeping draught for William, which they placed in his glass of beer. William fell into a deep sleep but, noticing that his brother's breathing was becoming increasingly laboured, Andrew checked the dose and found that he had accidentally given his brother sufficient morphine to kill nine men. A surgeon was summoned but twenty-eight-year-old William never woke from his slumbers.

The magistrates committed Andrew for trial at the Bristol Assizes and he appeared before Mr Justice Hawkins on 27 November. His demeanour in court reduced many of the personnel and spectators to tears and, recognising William's death as a tragic accident, Hawkins discharged Andrew without penalty.

1859 Sawyer Henry Lovell was working near the New Cut when he happened to glance up from his work to see a man in the water, close to the opposite bank. The man's arm was held aloft and, assuming that he was in difficulty, Lovell hastened to the other side of the river. When he arrived, he realised that the man was dead and called the police.

PC Perrott recovered the body, which was mutilated beyond recognition. However, when they searched the man's pockets, Perrot found a portrait of a young girl, whom he recognised. She told Perrott that the deceased was Richard Winess Chidzoy of Whitehouse Street, adding that she and Richard were keeping company until they quarrelled two weeks earlier.

The body was so badly disfigured that Perrott believed that Chidzoy's throat had been cut and, in addition, one of his trouser pockets was open at the bottom, suggesting that he might have been robbed. Thus coroner Mr J.B. Grindon thought it necessary to order a post-mortem examination.

Surgeon Mr Joseph Mortimer Granville found no marks of violence on Chidzoy's body and was confident that he had died from drowning. The hole in his trouser pocket seemed to have been caused by general wear and tear and his facial mutilation was unquestionably the work of rats, which had eaten most of the right-hand side of Chidzoy's face, as well as his nose and chin.

Nobody could imagine how Chidzoy ended up in the New Cut. He had spent the previous evening out with a friend and, according to several witnesses, was perfectly sober when he left for home at about half-past ten that night. Although he had recently broken up with his girlfriend, he did not seem unduly upset and was certainly not depressed or suicidal.

Unable to solve the mystery, the jury returned a verdict of 'found drowned'.

1896 Norwegian sailor Christopher Johnson appeared at the Police Court charged with being drunk and disorderly, with damaging a Great Western Railway carriage and with exposing himself to danger by climbing onto the footboard of the Taunton to Bristol train, while it was travelling at full speed.

Johnson could recall little after boarding the train at Plymouth, when he remembered taking some whisky on board with him. He had no recollection of starting a fight with another passenger or of smashing his way out of the train through the door windows, cutting himself badly in the process. He definitely had no memory of Mrs Edith Hall of Trowbridge and another passenger, who clung onto him through the windows as he balanced precariously on the footboard, with the train travelling at fifty miles an hour. He didn't recall other passengers pulling the communication cord, nor did he remember guards William Crocker and Robert Greely, who hauled him back onto the train and placed him in a compartment with other men for his own safety until they reached Bristol, where he was arrested.

Magistrates sentenced Johnson to one month's hard labour for his drunkenness and ordered him to pay 30s for damaging the train. He was also fined 10s for breaching railway by-laws. The magistrates closed with a lecture on the dangers of taking liquor on a train and, although the guards themselves were not blamed, the GWR was censured for putting Johnson in a carriage with a group of drunken sailors and for having their communications cords located outside the trains, which was thought to put female travellers at risk.

23 SEPTEMBER   **1925** Flying Officers G.W. Thorpe of Sheffield and P.A. Cox of Upton-on-Severn died at Filton Aerodrome when the wings of the planes they were piloting touched in mid air. The undercarriages of the two planes locked together and, spinning out of control, they plummeted to the ground. Both men were trapped by the tangled wreckage and Thorpe died almost as soon as he was extricated. Cox expired en route to hospital.

Both men were capable pilots and their aeroplanes were mechanically sound. Eyewitnesses seemed to think that the pilots were trying to overtake each other when the crash occurred and, at an inquest held at the aerodrome on the death of Thorpe, the coroner could only theorise that one or both men made an error of judgement. A verdict of 'accidental death' was recorded.

24 SEPTEMBER   **1866** There was anarchy aboard *Sandusky*, a New York ship docked in the Cumberland Basin, as the crew refused to obey the orders of the first mate. While the mate and captain were ashore at the Council House, complaining about the insubordination of the crew, a fight broke out between the ship's cook, Alexander Richardson and cabin boy, Manuel Libano, when the former tried to remove a chair from a cabin.

Richardson was shot in left the arm and, when the wound wouldn't stop bleeding, he was taken to the Infirmary. Magistrates were sent to take his deposition, but Richardson was so weak through loss of blood that this proved impossible and he died shortly afterwards.

Libano appeared at the Gloucestershire Assizes on 2 April 1866 charged with the manslaughter of his shipmate and, found guilty, was sentenced to seven years' penal servitude.

25 SEPTEMBER   **1896** Several people appeared at the Police Court charged with using bad language. John Horlor pleaded guilty and was fined 5s or seven days imprisonment in default. Charlotte Reynolds, who was described as 'a married woman', denied a like offence, but was found guilty as charged and awarded the same penalty. Margaret Colston, Kate Rudge and Philip Gill were also each fined 5s for 'expressing their feelings in somewhat strong terms.'

26 SEPTEMBER   **1824** As Misses O'Connor and Wrentmore and Mrs Ann Roche walked through Tyndall's Park, a man snatched Miss O'Connor's reticule. The chain strap broke and the reticule fell to the ground. There was a brief struggle as both Miss O'Connor and her assailant tried to pick it up, but the man finally won and ran off with the purse, along with three men who were obviously his accomplices.

The daylight robbery was witnessed by several people and a number of men set off in pursuit of the thieves, who were quickly apprehended and handed over to the police. Eventually, James Rutherford, John Jenkins, James

Lesley and William Hale appeared at the Bristol Quarter Sessions charged with robbery.

They were well known to the police as a desperate gang of thieves and all four were sentenced to be transported for the term of their natural lives. (Even though only Rutherford actually committed the robbery, the Bench found that there was 'a community of purpose' – his companions were guilty of aiding and abetting and so equally culpable.) When the Town Clerk informed them of their sentence, Rutherford asked if he might say something. Given permission, he stated that the witnesses had all perjured themselves and should have their ears cut off. Taken from the court to the cells, Rutherford delivered a parting comment, saying that he sincerely hoped that the Town Clerk's arse would stick to the Bench until their sentence expired.

All four set sail aboard the convict ship *Medina* for Van Dieman's Land on 25 April 1825.

1886 An inquest returned verdicts of 'accidental death' on the ten victims of an explosion at Dean Lane Colliery in Bedminster on 10 September. The colliery was known as a safe one, where the men were permitted to work with naked lights rather than safety lamps. The jury ruled that the ventilation was adequate, attributing the cause of the tragedy to a sudden unexpected pocket of gas. **27 SEPTEMBER**

George Hyman, Robert Tovey, John Broke, William Garland, James Mallard, Richard Davies, James Marsh, Samuel Moxham, Samuel Jones and Mr Latham perished in the tragedy, some mere boys, others leaving wives and children. The mine managers resolved to use safety lamps in future.

1886 Coroner Mr Wasbrough held an inquest on the death of nineteen-year-old Joseph Turner. **28 SEPTEMBER**

Turner stood to inherit a considerable fortune on his twenty-first birthday, but was a wild young man who drank heavily. In early October, he should have married Annie Perry, with whom he was already living in a house of ill-repute in Lewin's Mead. However, on the night of 27 September, after a quarrel with Annie, he walked into her room and asked her, 'Are you ready to die?'

Before Annie could answer, he shot her, once in the shoulder and once in the left breast. As she fell to the floor, he placed the barrel of his pistol in his mouth and pulled the trigger, dying instantly.

After hearing that jealousy was the supposed motive for the attempt on Annie's life, the inquest jury returned a verdict of 'suicide while temporarily insane'. At the time of the inquest, Annie was said to be 'in a precarious state' in the Infirmary, but she is believed to have survived her injuries.

1850 Reverend H.G. Walsh of St John's, Clifton, penned a letter to magistrates on behalf of one of his parishioners. Nathaniel Blackmore had a wife and four children and on 23 September, his youngest child died. **29 SEPTEMBER**

Walsh wrote that Nathaniel had twice applied to the relieving officer at Clifton for financial assistance to bury the infant, but had been turned down.

He had also appeared before the Board of Guardians at Stapleton with the same result. Meanwhile, the baby's body was slowly decomposing and presenting a health hazard to the family and their neighbours.

Nathaniel earned 10s a week, out of which he paid 2s 6d in rent. He pleaded that he had spent 12s 6d on a coffin and simply could not afford the cost of internment. The magistrates sympathised but regretted that they had no power to help, saying that they had subsidised burials from borough funds for the Clifton guardians in the past, but were not prepared to keep doing so. They could only suggest that Nathaniel made yet another application to the guardians.

30 SEPTEMBER 1874 The wife of the manager of the Volunteer Club, Queen's Road, could smell gas. She mentioned the smell to her husband and, with billiard marker George Henry Fudge, Mr Woodrow went over the entire club, sniffing carefully. They could find no evidence of any leakage until they went into the Officer's Room. Even there, the smell was so faint that it was barely noticeable and, having searched the room from top to bottom, Woodrow and Fudge could find no evidence of a leak.

Eventually, Woodrow sat down at a table and lit a cigar. Fudge continued to prowl around the room, standing on a table to examine the gasoliers – a branched hanging for gaslights. When Fudge asked Woodrow for his matches, the manager handed them over without question.

Fudge struck a match and placed it by the gasoliers. There was a sudden blue flash, immediately followed by an enormous explosion and both Woodrow and Fudge were badly burned. Fudge died from his injuries on 12 October, at which time Woodrow was still confined to his bed and coroner Mr Cartwright had to hold part of the inquest on Fudge in Woodrow's bedroom, to allow him to give evidence.

By then, gasman John Clark had examined the gasoliers and found a small hole in one of the inner tubes, from where he believed the gas was escaping. He added that, had the gasoliers been properly maintained, the leak would not have occurred.

The inquest jury returned a verdict of 'accidental death' on twenty-year-old Fudge.

OCTOBER

Merchant Venturers Technical College. (Author's collection)

1 OCTOBER   **1898** Twelve-year-old Harry Sims appeared at the Police Court charged with cruelty to a sheep.

The Bench was told that Harry and a group of other boys were chasing a flock of sheep around a field at Fishponds. When they finally managed to catch one, Harry sat on its back and tried to ride it like a horse. Even when the sheep collapsed with exhaustion, Harry continued kicking it and hitting it on its head to drive it on.

Magistrates remanded him to the Bristol Union.

2 OCTOBER   **1890** Ten-year-old Henry Haydon was sitting with his father, William, on a truck on Wine Street, when he saw some friends on the other side of the road. His father gave him permission to go and talk to them and watched as the boy crossed the busy street. The next thing he saw was Henry lying on the ground under an omnibus.

Henry died as a result of his injuries and at the subsequent inquest both William Haydon and witness Alfred Edwards told the coroner that they believed that he had been deliberately pushed under the bus.

Haydon said that he was too distressed at the time of the accident to be absolutely certain but Edwards was positive that he had seen a hand reach out to Henry before he fell. The coroner felt that nobody would be cruel enough to deliberately push a child under a bus and that if there was a hand, it was more likely to have been trying to protect Henry than to throw him down. He considered it more probable that Henry had run against someone and fallen backwards, saying that he had heard six similar cases in the last month. The jury agreed, finding a verdict of 'accidental death' and exonerating driver Thomas Perrin from all blame.

Wine Street. (Author's collection)

3 OCTOBER   **1934** Coroner Mr W.G. Burrough held an inquest on the death of eighteen-year-old Maurice Peter Widgwood Gillum. 'Peter' was expected to return to Winchester College on 21 September, after spending a holiday in Buckinghamshire with his guardian, Lieutenant-Colonel Molloy. Molloy travelled with the boy as far as Baker Street Station, where he left him to continue his journey back to school. However Maurice never arrived and,

Winchester College Chapel. (Author's collection)

in spite of police appeals for his whereabouts, seemed to have vanished into thin air.

On 30 September, boys playing in Leigh Woods found Gillum's body lying in bushes beneath the buttress of the Clifton Suspension Bridge. He lay on his left side, with his head against a tree trunk. His pockets contained £2 3s 2½d, a letter, which had been torn to pieces and a return toll ticket for the Suspension Bridge, along with a cloakroom ticket from Temple Meads Station which, when redeemed, was found to be for the boy's coat and bag.

There were no signs of a struggle having taken place in the area and it was first thought that Gillum may have jumped from the bridge, but a post-mortem examination conducted by Dr W.J. Parramore showed no marks of violence and no broken bones. Parramore determined that Gillum had died from toxaemia (blood poisoning) as a result of pneumonia, which may have originated from exposure. (Parramore complained bitterly at the inquest about the lack of facilities afforded to him for his examination of the body, informing the coroner that he had performed the post-mortem in an open field.)

The inquest heard evidence from Molloy, who related that Peter was keen to return to school, having just received news that he had passed his School Certificate. As far as Molloy was aware, Peter had no enemies and had never threatened suicide, neither was there any family history of insanity. The only thing he could suggest was that Peter had spent much of the summer holidays reading high-brow literature and religious books and Molloy suggested that he might have 'overloaded his brain'.

The inquest jury returned a verdict of 'death from natural causes', adding that they could find nothing to indicate why Peter had been in Leigh Woods. They also strongly recommended the erection of a mortuary in the district.

1904 Harry E. Thomas, the treasurer of Bristol University College, received an anonymous donation of a £1,000 Bank of England note. The gift was acknowledged in the local and national newspapers and, on 11 October, Thomas received a letter signed 'William Peploe Hartford'. Claiming to be the

4 OCTOBER

anonymous benefactor, Hartford wrote that he had accidentally sent £1,000 when he meant to send £100 and asked for the balance of £900 to be returned.

The bank authorities knew the identity of the donor and it wasn't Hartford. As he had put his address at the top of the letter, he was soon traced.

Joseph Fitch claimed that he had simply written a letter for Hartford and did not know where he lived. He was subsequently found guilty of attempted fraud at the Bristol Quarter Sessions and sentenced to four months' imprisonment.

5 OCTOBER

1872 Elizabeth Cann was clearly dying, but her father refused to call a doctor.

She and her illegitimate daughter lived with John Cann in Easton, although Elizabeth was supposedly married to a gentleman called Lot Hayward, who was banned from visiting her, as John Cann disliked him intensely. Now, Elizabeth was pregnant and, for six weeks, had suffered from 'a derangement of the urinary organs'.

Her friend Mary Thomas took her to a chemist, who prescribed medicine but recommended that she consulted a doctor urgently. However, John Cann saw no need and put his daughter to bed, where she simply wasted away.

Although Mary Thomas and Elizabeth's brother John protested, Elizabeth was kept short of food and, since there was no fireplace in her room, was freezing cold. Both Mary and John junior visited Elizabeth on 5 October and implored John to call a doctor, but he refused. John junior even offered to pay, although his father could easily have afforded to engage a surgeon.

Elizabeth died on the evening of 6 October and a post-mortem examination was carried out by surgeon Mr D.E. Bennett. He confirmed that Elizabeth would have survived had she been treated by a doctor for the 'disarrangement of certain internal organs'. Bennett also noted that Elizabeth was dirty and malnourished. However, he put the cause of her death as inflammation of the heart and lungs, as a consequence of her illness.

John Cann was committed for his daughter's manslaughter on the coroner's warrant, even though magistrates declined to send him for trial. He appeared at the Gloucestershire Assizes on 1 April 1873 and, although prosecuting counsel Mr Griffiths had 'abundant evidence' to support the fact that the defendant's negligence in not sending for a doctor had caused his daughter's death, the judge pointed out that Elizabeth was a grown woman, who could easily have contacted a surgeon herself. Besides which, she had actually died from complications arising from her original illness, which nobody could have foreseen.

The case was further weakened by the fact that Mrs Thomas's evidence differed from that which she gave at the inquest and eventually Mr Justice Honeyman ordered the jury to return a verdict of not guilty.

1876 At the cooperage attached to Messrs Finzel's sugar refinery, forty workmen were stacking a consignment of the spruce staves used to make barrels. The staves were stacked in 4ft square piles, each between 40ft and 50ft high. A number of stacks had been completed, when the end stack suddenly toppled over, taking several others with it.

6 OCTOBER

By a stroke of good fortune, the Infirmary had very recently reopened, having been closed for twelve months for refurbishment. Thus, there were plenty of beds available for the twenty-nine workmen who were rushed there.

The worst injuries were to those who had been at ground level at the time of the collapse. The men working at height were able to slow their falls by grabbing at sections of the falling stacks. They landed on top of the pile of timber, rather than being buried beneath hundreds of tons of wood.

Perhaps not surprisingly, reports of the disaster in the contemporary newspapers show some discrepancies, but as far as can be ascertained Albert Nash (19), Henry Quick (53) and John Hemmings (25) died and it was feared that several more men would not recover from their injuries.

Bristol Royal Infirmary. (Author's collection)

7 OCTOBER   **1875** An explosion of fire damp at the South Liberty Pit at Bedminster claimed the lives of four miners and injured several others. James Willing, William Payne, John Smith and William Parker perished, all but Parker leaving widows and children.

The area was regularly inspected for fire damp and had been pronounced safe shortly before the incident, although small pockets of gas had previously been detected near the roof of the vein. At the inquest, the jury were told that the ventilation was barely adequate, but mine manager Mr Cowcill reminded them that they had inspected the scene of the explosion themselves and had not complained of a lack of air. Although the miners were provided with safety lamps, there was a suggestion that one of the deceased might have taken a naked light underground.

Coroner Mr H.S. Wasbrough remarked that the rarity of fire damp in this particular pit may have made the miners and management less attuned to the dangers. His jury were asked to decide whether the deaths were accidental or a result of any negligence by the management. The jury plumped for the former option, recording verdicts of 'accidental death' on all four men, even though just one week earlier another explosion at the pit had claimed the life of miner William Mitchell.

8 OCTOBER   **1885** Frederick Pearce heard his twenty-one-month-old son crying outside the family home in Montagne Hill. He found Francis Sidney standing in the yard adjacent to the house and noticed a small wound on his head. The Pearces kept a few chickens and Francis's older brother had accidentally left the yard gate open. Francis wandered in and was pecked by the cockerel.

Mr Pearce took Francis to the Infirmary, where the minor injury was dressed and he was sent home. When the wound refused to heal, Pearce consulted Dr Norton, who sent Francis to the Children's Hospital. He died there on 16 November and a post-mortem examination showed that he had an abscess on his brain beneath the wound on his head.

At an inquest held by coroner Mr H.S. Wasborough, the jury returned a verdict of 'died from the peck of a cock'.

9 OCTOBER   **1906** A fire broke out in the top floor chemistry laboratory of the Merchant Venturers Technical College, adjoining College Green. Although the fire

brigade were quickly on the scene, the fire moved downwards from storey to storey and, since it was evident that the blaze was raging out of control, the firemen focused on saving adjoining historic buildings such as the Lord Mayor's Chapel and the Red Maids' School.

The College, which was erected in 1885, was completely gutted by the fire, which caused damage estimated at £80,000. Fortunately, the buildings were fully insured and there were no fatalities.

1854 Surgeon Mr Grainger was called to the home of the Karr family to visit servant Jane Perry. Jane could offer no explanation for her symptoms, telling Grainger that she had felt unwell for the past few days.

10 OCTOBER

Grainger found that she had recently given birth, a fact which she strenuously denied. The surgeon stepped out of the room for a moment to talk to Mr Karr and, as he left, he heard Jane locking the bedroom door. Grainger demanded admittance and, on searching the room, found the body of a newborn baby boy under her pillow.

Grainger and his colleague, Mr Hore, made a post-mortem examination and noted that the child had a severe wound on his throat, which could have caused his death. However, the surgeons were unable to establish whether he had been born alive and believed that the wound was inflicted during delivery.

Jane was charged with the 'wilful murder' of her son, appearing at the Gloucester Assizes on 31 March 1855. Having heard the evidence, the judge told the jury that it was impossible for them to find a verdict of 'wilful murder'. However, he was uncertain whether the circumstances warranted a conviction for 'concealment of birth' and proposed to consult with other judges, making his decision at the next Assizes.

On 4 August, Jane was again brought to court to receive a six-month prison sentence for concealment. Since she had been incarcerated since her arrest, the judge determined that the sentence should run from 31 March.

1847 As Miss Ann Loosemore walked between Upper Knowle and Bedminster she realised that she was being followed. Suddenly, a man hit

11 OCTOBER

her over the head with his walking stick and demanded her money as she was knocked to the ground.

Ann handed over 1s 6d, but her attacker was not satisfied and, when she told him that was all the money she had, he hit her again. As she lay on the ground, blood flowing from her head, the man searched her clothes, tearing off her dress pocket and even pawing her bosom to ensure she had nothing hidden there. He then ran away, telling Ann that his accomplice was watching and would kill her if she tried to follow him.

Later that evening, James Venn handed himself in to the police and confessed to having hit and robbed Miss Loosemore. Venn, who had recently returned from a period of transportation for a previous offence, was afraid that he might have killed her and couldn't live with his guilt.

Venn appeared before magistrates the following morning. Told that he was likely to be hanged if found guilty, he replied that it was no more than he deserved. He was tried for highway robbery at the Gloucester Assizes in March 1848 and sentenced to be transported for a further fourteen years, boarding the convict ship *Eliza* bound for Van Dieman's Land on 12 December 1849.

12 OCTOBER **1839** Coroner Mr J.B. Grindon held an inquest at The New Globe Inn, Christmas Street, on the death of five-year-old Edward Conner. Edward's parents rented a house at Lewin's Mead and, unbeknown to them, a cistern overflowed in the cellar, flooding it to a depth of 5ft.

Edward fell into the water and although he was rescued within minutes, he was beyond medical assistance. In returning a verdict of 'accidental death', the jury recommended that the cellar should be drained.

13 OCTOBER **1891** The thirteen-year-old boy who went by the impressive name of General George Washington Jones had only worked as messenger boy for Brain & Sons for three weeks and was anxious to do well. Consequently, when he was sent on an errand at just before six o'clock in the evening, he knew he would have to hurry, since the premises he was to visit closed in a few minutes.

As Jones left Brains's premises, two tramcars were travelling in opposite directions along Victoria Road. The boy gambled at being able to dodge between them and dashed across the road. Sadly, he was run over by one of the trams. The wheel passed over his chest before driver Edward Henry Bowles could stop.

The jury at the subsequent inquest returned a verdict of 'accidental death', exonerating the drivers of both trams from any blame but commenting on the foolhardiness of his employers in sending the boy out with so little time to complete his errand.

14 OCTOBER **1849** Byron Blythe of Orchard Street had cholera and, in spite of treatment by surgeons Dr Green, Dr Wallis and Mr Kelson, died in the early hours of 13 October. Green issued a death certificate giving the cause of death as 'malignant cholera' and Byron was placed in his coffin, surrounded by sawdust and the lid screwed down.

Green called on the family on 14 October and, as the carpenter was still there, Green asked for a final look at the body. To his amazement, when the coffin lid was unscrewed, Blythe was still warm.

Green halted the funeral and called in his colleagues. They visited the house at nine o'clock and midday on 14 October and, finding the body still warm on their second visit, began to have doubts about whether Blythe was dead or simply in a cataleptic state. They injected his veins with warm salt water and, when that produced no effect, subjected the body to 'powerful galvanic shocks'. They noticed that Blythe's body changed colour, his hands became suppler and he began to foam at the mouth, although he showed no other signs of life.

The question of whether or not Blythe was dead was not resolved until 17 October, when his body began to decompose. Until then, his corpse had remained uncharacteristically warm, although the finest medical skills in Bristol were unable to restore what contemporary newspapers referred to as 'the vital spark'.

1898 Two policemen came across a disturbance on Pennywell Road. To PC Gasson, the cause of the disturbance seemed to be Isaac Roach, who was drunkenly offering to fight anyone who would take him on. The policemen advised Roach to go home quietly and, when he wouldn't, tried to arrest him. Roach punched and kicked the officers, who blew their whistles for assistance before drawing their truncheons. The resulting melee drew a huge crowd of people, some of whom tried to assist the police, others who took Roach's part. Among the latter were Roach's mother and sister, who tried to prevent his arrest.

Roach, his mother and his sister, Mary Ann Taylor, were brought to Bristol Police Court, Isaac charged with being drunk and disorderly and assaulting the police and the women charged with attempting to rescue him and also with assault.

15 OCTOBER

Pennywell Road. (© N. Sly)

All three defendants downplayed the incident. Mrs Roach denied that Isaac was drunk, saying that he was innocently talking to a man outside his house when the police appeared from nowhere and arrested him. According to Mrs Roach, both she and Isaac asked the police to 'let him go quietly', but the officers brutally attacked him with their truncheons.

Isaac insisted that he was sober and didn't know why he had been arrested, telling the magistrates that he had never been in trouble before. When reminded that he had recently spent six weeks in prison with hard labour for assaulting a police officer, he laughingly maintained that it was 'just a drop of drink'.

Magistrates sentenced him to one month's imprisonment and his mother and sister were bound over in their own recognisances to keep the peace.

16 OCTOBER   **1877** Thirteen-year-old Margaret Ahern appeared at the Council House charged with being beyond the control of her parents.

Mrs and Mrs Ahern, a respectable couple, told the magistrates that their daughter was in service at Clifton until she suddenly left on 29 September, telling her employer that she was going to visit her sister in London. When Margaret didn't arrive, her parents began a frantic search, eventually tracing her to a brothel on Upper Wells Street, where she was making a very good living.

The Aherns wanted their daughter dealt with under the Industrial Schools Act of 1861, which allowed parents who believed their child to be beyond their control to ask magistrates to send him or her to a strict school, combining education and the learning of a trade.

The magistrates agreed that this was the best course of action in Margaret's case and remanded her to Barton Regis Workhouse for one week while the necessary arrangements were made.

As Margaret was taken from the court, she turned to the magistrates and threatened, 'I'll do it again when I get out.'

17 OCTOBER   **1839** Coroner Mr J.B. Grindon held an inquest at The Bell Inn on Prewett Street on the death of five-year-old Jane Franklyn.

Jane's father and brother made some rockets, which they intended to let off on Guy Fawkes Night and left them on the hob in the parlour of their house to dry. As Jane's mother was cooking some meat, she stirred the fire to produce more heat and a spark ignited the rockets, which whizzed around the room.

Jane along with her mother, father and uncle were all severely burned and Jane died in hospital the next day. The inquest jury returned a verdict of 'accidental death'.

18 OCTOBER   **1912** As waggoner Arthur William Cheacker drove a horse-drawn lorry at Almondsbury, a racing car suddenly shot by them at speed, making a frightful din. The horses bolted in terror and fifty-year-old Cheacker fell under the wheels of the lorry, sustaining fatal injuries.

The car driver was quickly traced and appeared before magistrates, who committed him to trial for manslaughter. At the Gloucestershire Assizes, aviator William Barnard Rhodes Moorhouse from Northamptonshire admitted driving at excessive speed, but denied that this had caused the horses to shy. He added that he knew nothing of the accident until he reached Gloucester.

The jury found Moorhouse guilty of 'criminal negligence', stating that this was the cause of the fatal accident. However, they were unwilling to convict Moorhouse of manslaughter and added a strong recommendation for mercy to their verdict. Mr Justice Channell imposed a fine of £20 plus costs.

1892 William Clements called on his sweetheart in Temple Backs but she was out. He asked the girl's sister, twelve-year-old Jane Davis, to help him look for her and the couple got as far as Water Lane when Davis suddenly lunged at Jane and sexually assaulted her. Unbeknown to Clements, he was being observed by a police officer, who saw him indecently exposing himself and arrested him.

When Clements was charged with indecency towards Jane, the policeman told magistrates that, although he had seen Davis exposing himself, he had not witnessed any assault on the little girl. However, he admitted that the child's clothing was disarranged. Mr Tonkin, who acted for the prisoner, actually called Jane's mother as a defence witness and Mrs Davis stated that Clements was a frequent visitor to her home but had never committed any impropriety towards her daughter.

The magistrates dismissed the charge of 'indecent conduct', although they found Clements guilty of 'indecent exposure' and sentenced him to six weeks' imprisonment.

1864 Coroner Mr J.B. Grindon held an inquest on the death of a baby girl, one of a set of illegitimate twins born to Mary Ann Andrews at Clifton.

Mary Ann's mother, also called Mary Ann, told the inquest that she and her family were suffering extreme poverty and had sold all their furniture to

Clifton Promenade from Durdham Downs. (Author's collection)

buy food. On the night before the baby's death, she tried to get medical help for the infant but was refused because she couldn't afford to pay.

In recording a verdict of 'death by natural causes', the coroner remarked that, while he had seen many cases of destitution, this was the worst he had ever come across. Several jurors were moved to donate their fees to Mrs Andrews, so that she might buy food for herself and her family.

Soon afterwards, the *Bristol Mercury* received a letter from James Duffett of the Estate and House Agency Offices. On behalf of Mrs Andrews's landlord, he wrote that she was £12 in arrears with her rent and had indeed sold all the furniture. As this belonged to the landlord, he was now £100 out of pocket. Duffett added that Mrs Andrews had demanded £10 to vacate the house and return the key. Although he had agreed to this he had been unable to gain possession of the property.

21 OCTOBER **1898** Coroner Mr H.G. Doggett held an inquest at the General Hospital on the death of thirty-seven-year-old haulier, Thomas Brayley.

On 11 October, Brayley was delivering a load to Pill, in the company of another carter, Joseph Henry Healey. On the return journey, Brayley scraped his ankle and Healey put him on the back of one of his horses and led the two carts home.

Brayley refused to go to the hospital, although his wife insisted on calling a doctor the next day, who also advised him to go to the hospital to have the ankle examined. Brayley was adamant that it was just a minor wound but, one week later, he was so ill that he had no choice in the matter. He died thirty-six hours later.

Surgeon Robert Palling told the inquest that Brayley had a foul, suppurating wound on the inside of his left ankle and, although everything possible was done to save his life, he experienced tetanic convulsions and died. Palling attributed his death to lockjaw, saying that the bacilli had undoubtedly entered the wound as it rubbed against the horse's side on the ride home.

The inquest jury returned a verdict of 'accidental death'.

22 OCTOBER **1894** Ann Davis was brought before magistrates charged with neglecting her three children.

Ann's husband, James, had been taken to the Workhouse, having 'gone wrong in his mind'. John Ottley, the Inspector for the Society for the Prevention of Cruelty to Children, told the Bench that when he visited the house on Leek Lane where Ann rented a room, he found her three children, aged six years, four years and eighteen months, in a deplorable state. None of the children could walk and the legs of the two oldest were twisted like corkscrews. All three were caked in excrement.

Ottley tried to get Ann to enter the Workhouse, where her children would be properly cared for, but she refused. She did promise faithfully that she would take Ottley's advice and the case was adjourned for a month.

One month later, Ann was back in court, claiming to have lost the order for admission to the Workhouse. She was sentenced to one month's imprisonment with hard labour and the children were sent to the Workhouse without her.

1882 Heavy storms of rain, hail and snow caused what were at the time   23 OCTOBER
the worst floods in living memory. Miles of land between Bristol and Nailsea were flooded and a flood defence wall, which had only recently been built at Baptist Mills at a cost of £7,000, was completely washed away. Hundreds of houses were flooded and the occupants were forced to flee upstairs.

The floods claimed at least one life, that of a baker who was trying to deliver bread to besieged houses on Mina Road. He drowned when his horse and cart were swept away by the force of the water. A second man was fortunate to escape after rising flood water forced him to take refuge in a tree, from where he was later rescued by boat.

1874 Six-year-old Archie John Hamilton Walters left home to attend the   24 OCTOBER
Wesleyan School on the morning of 23 October. He should have returned for lunch, but when he didn't arrive his mother went to look for him and found that he hadn't been to school. Mrs Walters reported him missing and extensive searches were made.

The next morning, a message reached Mrs Walters that there were two lost children at the police station in Horfield. She sent her daughter to see if one of them was Archie and the girl was sent from the police station to a farm, where Archie lay dead.

An inquest was held on 28 October at The Royal Oak, Horfield, by coroner Mr Scott. There it emerged that farmer John Roslyn and his two brothers had found two children in one of their fields on the morning of 24 October – Archie and three-year-old Ernest Price, who had also been missing from home since the previous day.

Archie was naked, apart from his shirt, socks and boots and Ernest, who wore no shoes, was wrapped in Archie's clothes. While Ernest was just very cold, Archie was unconscious. The brothers rushed them back to the farmhouse where, having sent for the police and a surgeon, they tried to warm the boys with hot drinks in front of the fire. However, Archie died soon afterwards. Surgeon William Lacy confirmed that his death was due to congestion of the lungs and brain from exposure.

Ernest was brought to inquest but was able to give very little useful information. All he could remember was that Archie had stolen his hoop and he followed him, hoping to get it back. Archie apparently tried to get Ernest to undress in the field but Ernest wouldn't, so Archie took off his own clothes to keep him warm. Ernest recalled losing his shoes and asking a man to help look for them, but couldn't remember if any other children had gone to Horfield with him and Archie.

Witness John York saw both boys on the afternoon of 23 October, when Archie, who was leading Ernest by the hand, refused to tell him his name and address and insisted that they weren't lost and knew their way home.

Unable to unravel the mystery of Archie's death, the inquest jury returned a verdict of 'died from cold through exposure'. In June 1900, it was reported that a stained-glass window had been installed in Horfield Chapel as a memorial to 'the boy hero from Horfield', who had sacrificed his clothes and ultimately his life to keep his little companion warm.

25 OCTOBER   **1845** Miners at Upper Soundwell Colliery, Kingswood, finished their shift and prepared to be hauled to the surface. Five were in the cage when it stopped at an upper cutting to pick up more men and, just after George Britten boarded, the supporting rope suddenly snapped, plunging the cage almost 80ft to the pit bottom.

There was no spare rope at the colliery, so a messenger was sent to a neighbouring pit to borrow one. As soon as it arrived, the men were brought to the surface, where a crowd of anxious people assembled, all fearing the worst.

Britten was alive, calmly smoking his pipe, although one of his arms hung by a thread of flesh and was later amputated. William Bassett (aged between 60 and 70) and Benjamin Wiltshire (33) died within minutes, while Thomas Bird (40), William Harris (60) and John Porter (30) were already dead, their bodies terribly mangled. Most of the men left wives and large families.

By sheer good fortune, Benjamin Wiltshire's brother, George, was standing directly behind George Britten, waiting to enter the cage. He had a sack across his shoulders to protect himself from dripping water and somebody gave the sack a playful tug just as he was about to climb aboard. He turned to remonstrate with his tormentor at the exact moment that the rope broke.

It emerged at the inquest on the five deaths that the rope had broken two weeks earlier, while hauling up a load of coal and had been repaired. It was in a terrible condition and in some places two of the four strands were completely worn through.

The miners complained numerous times to the overseer that the rope was dangerous and were told that, if they didn't wish to use it, they could descend at another part of the pit. However, even though they were worried about the safety of the rope, most of the colliers continued to use it. Some stated that they couldn't afford not to work, while others were more concerned that descending at another location meant a twelve-minute underground walk to the coal face.

In recording a verdict of 'accidental death' on the five miners, the jury heavily censured pit owner Mr J. Whittick and foreman Charles Stone for their total disregard for the safety of the men.

26 OCTOBER   **1843** A patrolling policeman found Martha Lane lying drunk in a gutter, her skirts pulled over her head and her screaming baby lying across her chest. Her husband Richard, also befuddled with drink, stood nearby.

Brought before magistrates charged with drunkenness, Richard placed the blame squarely on the Conservative Party, who had held 'a feed' at St Michael's Hill. He and his wife were such enthusiastic supporters of the Blues that they had imbibed rather too much of the free beer on offer.

Magistrates noted 'the filthy dress and debauched appearance' of the couple which, according to the *Bristol Mercury*, 'clearly indicated their characters'. They were fined 5s each.

1931 When businessman Henry Bowden returned to his home after work in Alexandria Park, Fishponds, he found his thirty-five-year-old wife, Nellie, and the couple's two children dead on the floor, their throats cut. A bloodstained razor lay by Nellie's side and an inquest later determined that she had killed Margaret Eileen (12) and Kenneth James (7) before committing suicide, while the balance of her mind was disturbed. The tragedy was apparently precipitated by a joke about politics made by Mr Bowden at breakfast.

1872 Edwin Chick lived in Providence Place, Little Avon Street. Although not officially married, he and Elizabeth Rood, his 'wife' of eighteen years, had several children together, the oldest of whom was fourteen-year-old Susanna Rood (aka Chick).

When Elizabeth found Edwin and Susanna in a compromising position in the kitchen, she reported Edwin to the authorities and, when questioned by the police, Susanna and Edwin told completely different stories.

Susanna insisted that her father had raped her at least three times, threatening to hurt her if she didn't comply with his demands or if she told her mother. Edwin, on the other hand, insisted that Susanna was not his daughter and furthermore was a willing sexual partner who demanded money from him after they had intercourse.

When Susanna was examined by Mr P. Thornton, the assistant house surgeon at Bristol General Hospital, he found that although she was no longer a virgin, she showed no signs of having been violently assaulted. At Edwin's trial for rape in April 1873, the judge gave Edwin the benefit of the doubt and discharged him.

1831 The arrival of Recorder Sir Charles Wetherall began three days of rioting in Bristol. Wetherall was a prominent opponent of the Reform Bill, which aimed to give people in cities like Bristol a greater representation in the House of Commons – at the time, out of a population of 104,000, only 6,000 Bristol people had the right to vote.

Over three days, hundreds of properties were burned to the ground, including the Mansion House, Custom House and the Bishop's Palace. Queen's Square was destroyed and the Gaol was breached. Around 170 prisoners were released and the gallows and treadmill were burned and thrown into the New Cut.

Order was eventually restored by troops from Gloucester, who opened fire on the rioters or slashed them with their sabres. An estimated 130 people lost their lives and many more were injured.

Those involved in the rioting were tried and five were sentenced to death. Christopher Davis, William Clarke, Joseph Kayes and Thomas Gregory were executed on 27 January 1832, while the fifth condemned man, Richard Vines, was declared mentally unsound and his sentence was commuted to one of transportation for life.

1896 Servant Matilda Crabb gave birth to a baby girl on 17 October. Although unmarried, she assured her landlady Ellen Cottrell that the baby's father would provide for her and, indeed, she seemed to have everything she needed and her rent was always paid promptly.

On 30 October, farmer James Burrow Baker visited Matilda at her lodgings in Bedminster and soon afterwards, he left in a cab with Matilda and the baby.

Cabman John James was ordered to drive to Temple Meads station, where the couple deposited their luggage and, having left the station, James was asked to stop the cab. Baker told James that he needn't get out and, after a few minutes, asked him to continue driving to the General Hospital, where Baker left a large, black portmanteau. James then drove the couple to a refreshment house on Deanery Road, where he left them.

At the General Hospital, house surgeon Martin Randell found the portmanteau, which contained a baby girl. The infant was wrapped in a shawl although the top of her head was uncovered and, it being quite a cold night, Randell believed that exposure to the cold was likely to cause her suffering. He reported his find to the police and the baby was taken to St Peter's Children's Hospital, where she was given a clean bill of health.

She was quickly traced to Matilda and Baker, who were arrested, Matilda at Weston-Super-Mare and Baker at his father's home in Ilchester. Both were charged with 'abandoning and exposing a child under fourteen years of age in a way likely to cause unnecessary suffering.' While Matilda made no comment when charged, Baker freely admitted abandoning his daughter, saying that he believed that it was the best thing for both mother and child and that he fully intended to make a large donation to the hospital.

Crabb and Baker appeared at the Bristol Assizes, where both were found guilty as charged, although the jury recommended mercy for Matilda since Baker took full responsibility for the offence, insisting that Matilda had acted under his influence. Mr Justice Wills took that into consideration, sentencing Baker to six months' imprisonment with hard labour and binding Matilda over in the sum of £10 to receive justice if called upon to do so in the future.

31 OCTOBER **1857** John Poole appeared at the Council House charged with cruelly killing a cat and with assaulting a police officer.

Two police constables told magistrates that they had seen Poole pick up a cat by its tail, whirl it around over his head several times and then throw it as high as he could. The cat landed on the pavement and died before it could be taken to a veterinary surgeon.

On seeing the constables, Poole and his colleagues ran off with the officers in pursuit. They caught Poole who resisted arrest, punching one of the policemen in the eye.

'You must be a very cruel fellow to treat a poor animal so,' remarked magistrate Mr Coates, at which Poole excused his behaviour, saying that he had drunk a drop of beer.

'A man when he is tipsy often betrays his real disposition,' replied Coates.

'That is not my disposition. I was never here before,' argued Poole.

Magistrates fined him £1 plus costs and, when he couldn't afford to pay, sentenced him to three weeks' imprisonment with hard labour.

NOVEMBER

College Green and Bristol Cathedral. (Author's collection)

1 NOVEMBER **1866** As the steam tug *Black Eagle* towed a Norwegian barge at Hotwells, her boiler suddenly exploded, showering homes on St Vincent's Parade with debris. Although the damage to property was extensive, there were no lives lost on shore but the five- man crew of the *Black Eagle* perished in the disaster.

The bodies of William Huish, Daniel Woodman, George Ledger and James Livings were recovered and, at the time of Huish's inquest, the body of the fifth crew member was still missing. (It was also rumoured that a woman and child had been on board at the time of the explosion.) The sole survivor of the disaster was a small black and tan terrier, who swam to the Somerset bank of the Avon.

It was the second boiler explosion on the boat, the previous one near Cardiff in 1859 resulting in the deaths of eight crew members. Thus the boiler was relatively new and, although many theories were advanced, the cause of the explosion was never conclusively determined.

2 NOVEMBER **1872** One-year-old Arthur John Woodey was grizzling, so as his father was eating his dinner, he cut a small piece of meat fat and handed it to the girl who was nursing the baby, who placed it in Arthur's mouth. Almost immediately, the baby turned blue and struggled to breathe. The meat had lodged in Arthur's throat and choked him to death within minutes.

At the subsequent inquest held by coroner Mr W. Gaisford at Crew's Hole, the jury returned a verdict of 'accidentally suffocated'. Arthur's father admitted that he had not considered how so young a child, with so few teeth, would be able to eat a piece of fat.

3 NOVEMBER **1896** For more than thirty years, Harriett Boardman led a dog's life at the hands of her brutal husband, Thomas. A violent drunkard, he assaulted her again and again until, after a particularly vicious attack, Harriett obtained a separation order in April 1893 and Thomas was ordered to pay 8*s* per week maintenance for her and their two children.

Harriett's misery didn't end there. She was frequently forced to summon Thomas for non-payment, usually when the arrears amounted to £10 or more. Not only that but he continued to assault her, serving a two-month prison sentence in October 1894.

By 1896, Harriett and her daughter, Louisa, were living on Harleston Street and, on 3 November, Thomas paid them a visit, demanding some pictures that he believed she had stolen when she left him. Anxious to get rid of him, Harriett took the pictures off their nails but was too frightened to give them to Thomas, fearing that he would attack her if she got close enough to hand them over. Seeing her coming downstairs without the pictures, Thomas suddenly sprang at his wife and seized her by the neck. Aware that she was bleeding, Harriet screamed 'Murder!' at the top of her voice and two neighbours rushed to assist her.

Seeing them, Thomas held out his cut-throat razor and threatened to 'do for them too', before running way.

The police were called and Inspector Durbin managed to stop the bleeding, taking Harriett to the Infirmary. Surgeon Thomas Carwadine found three

Parkhurst Prison, Isle of Wight. (Author's collection)

slash wounds in her throat which, had they been a fraction deeper, would certainly have proved fatal. As it was, Harriett was weak through loss of blood and took several weeks to recover.

Seventy-one-year-old Thomas was tried for attempted murder at the next Bristol Assizes. The chief witnesses were Harriett, who appeared swathed in bandages and the couple's two grown-up children, Louisa and Thomas, both of whom related their father's years of drunkenness and ill-treatment towards their mother. The jury found Boardman guilty and he was sentenced to life imprisonment. He spent part of his sentence in Parkhurst Prison on the Isle of Wight then transferred to Broadmoor Criminal Lunatic Asylum, where he is believed to have died in 1907, aged eighty-one.

4 NOVEMBER

1872 Forty-nine-year-old Robert Thomas had an insatiable appetite for alcohol and his job as an ostler at The Lamb Inn, West Street, gave him plenty of opportunity to indulge. While climbing a ladder in the yard to light a lamp, he toppled off and broke his leg in two places, as well as dislocating his ankle.

Thomas was taken to the Infirmary, where the bones were set. For two days, he appeared to be recovering but was then seized by a violent attack of *delirium tremens*, during which he displaced the set bones.

With Thomas still subject to uncontrollable spasms, it was decided to administer chloroform in order to reset his leg. Unfortunately, Thomas died within minutes and, although doctors tried artificial respiration and a number of other restorative measures, they were unable to resuscitate him. A post-mortem examination revealed that he had died from a heart condition, whilst under the influence of chloroform.

5 NOVEMBER

1874 As children celebrated Guy Fawkes Night, one group of boys on Merchant Street managed to get hold of a pistol, which was given to eleven-year-old Alfred Adams to fire.

Alfred intended to fire into the air but closed his eyes and turned his head away as he pulled the trigger, causing his aim to drop. Eleven-year-old Sarah

Ann Hooper was bending down nearby and, when the pistol was fired, she immediately cried out 'Oh, mother!' and staggered a few steps before collapsing. She was rushed to hospital, where surgeon Mr J.E. Shaw found that she had a laceration on her forehead, beneath which was a depressed fracture of her skull. Sadly, Sarah died soon afterwards.

PC Fletcher identified the boys involved and Alfred was arrested and charged with causing Sarah Hooper's death by discharging fireworks in the street. As no inquest had been held, magistrates remanded Adams until coroner Mr H.S. Wasbrough had sat on Sarah's death.

There was some confusion as to what exactly had happened. At the precise moment the pistol was discharged, a cannon was fired very close to where Sarah was standing – just moments earlier, her friend had warned her not to bend down in case she got hit, since the cannon's muzzle was pointing directly at her. A number of metal rivets and similar pieces of scrap metal were picked up close to where Sarah fell and it was suggested that the boys had loaded them into the revolver and that one fractured Sarah's skull.

The four boys involved swore that there was nothing but gunpowder in the pistol, which they had bought earlier for 1s 6d. The coroner reasoned that so cheap a gun would be incapable of causing much damage, adding that the scene of the shooting was directly outside a blacksmith's shop, where scraps of metal were likely to be thrown onto the street. Furthermore, several people insisted that Sarah screamed before the pistol retort was heard.

The coroner believed that the expulsion of gas from the cannon caused a small stone or a piece of the metal to fly up and hit Sarah's head and the jury concurred, returning a verdict of 'accidental death' on the grounds that there was insufficient evidence to show where the fatal shot came from. Alfred was discharged and no further charges were brought in connection with Sarah's death.

6 NOVEMBER   1861 An inquest was held by coroner Mr J.B. Grindon at the Cat and Wheel Tavern, Castle Green, on the death of two-year-old Frederick William Fisher of Castle Mill Street. On 5 November, Frederick was slightly feverish from teething and his mother Maria gave him a cooling powder, after which the little boy went straight to sleep.

Soon afterwards, Maria noticed that Frederick was twitching. She called her husband to look at the child, but by the time he arrived Frederick was sleeping peacefully again. However, a few minutes later, he began to convulse violently, his tiny hands clenched into fists. Walter Fisher stripped off his son's clothes and plunged him into warm water, where he continued to fit.

A neighbour reassured Maria and Walter, saying that her child had suffered from teething convulsions but had fully recovered. She asked if the Fishers had given the baby any medicine and Maria went to fetch the packet to show her. Only then did she realise that she had accidentally given Frederick rat poison.

A doctor was summoned and arrived within minutes. Walter and Maria showed Mr Joseph Mortimer Granville the empty packet of 'Marsden's poison for killing rats and vermin', telling him that Frederick was given the powder approximately two hours earlier and had been fitting for about an hour. Granville again immersed Frederick in warm water and tried to administer an emetic, but the child's jaws were firmly locked and the doctor was unable to prise them apart to introduce any medicine. Although he called in two colleagues, they were unable to save the little boy.

The teething powder and rat poison were wrapped in almost identical white paper envelopes but the rat poison, which contained strychnine, also had a blue outer wrapping, which was clearly inscribed 'Poison' in large letters. The two powders were stored in a cupboard and the poison had somehow fallen out of its outer wrapping.

The inquest jury found that Frederick was accidentally poisoned by strychnine, administered by mistake instead of soothing medicine. They remarked that they thought that it was very careless of Mrs Fisher to administer any medicine to a child without carefully checking it first.

1851 At the Infirmary, coroner Mr J.B. Grindon concluded the inquest on   7 NOVEMBER
William Escott, a victim of a steam boat explosion at Conham on 5 November.

The inquest heard that Escott's wife visited him in hospital before his death, when he told her that the *Lady Emily* had too much steam and that he had repeatedly told the engineer not to put so much steam on.

In returning a verdict that 'the deceased lost his life through the bursting of a steam boiler', the jury stated that, had the engineer survived, they would have charged him with manslaughter.

The contemporary newspapers report that four men died in the explosion – William Escott, William Hopkins, William Griffiths and William Bailey. (Some newspapers also report a fifth death, naming the victim as William Haggett.)

1844 Bedminster shoemaker Mr Perdue was charged at the Council House   8 NOVEMBER
with having cruelly beaten his apprentice, John Torrington. The case was brought by Perdue's neighbours, who were most distressed at the treatment meted out to the boy by his master.

John, who was apprenticed from the Poor House, was asked to bare his back, which was covered with wheals and bruises. He alleged that Perdue beat him regularly, the last occasion being yesterday, when he was thrashed with a strap because his face was dirty.

Perdue told the magistrates that he was at his wits end trying to manage the boy, who was 'very trying'. The magistrates gave Torrington a severe ticking off, telling him that, if he didn't behave better, he would be liable for criminal charges. Perdue was let off with a 5s fine.

1857 James Freestone appeared before magistrates charged with having   9 NOVEMBER
been found drunk on Thomas Street.

After Sergeant Franklin described Freestone's arrest, Freestone admitted being insensible but insisted that he was not drunk. He told the magistrates that he had been to Cathay on business and, while returning, was suddenly attacked by somebody who thrust a handkerchief over his nose and tried to force him to swallow something.

Freestone believed that he was drugged with chloroform and dragged to a nearby house, where his watch, chain and wallet were stolen. He recalled nothing apart from the police trying to arouse him and then arresting him for being drunk and incapable, ignoring his complaints about being robbed and refusing to look at the wet marks on his shirt, which quickly evaporated.

The magistrates asked about the area where Freestone was found and, finding that it was heavily populated with brothels, decided that they believed his story. They dismissed the charge of drunkenness against him and ordered the police to investigate the alleged robbery immediately.

10 NOVEMBER   **1812** As was customary with suicides, the body of John Allen was buried in an unmarked grave at a crossroads near Bristol.

For more than fourteen years, Allen was employed by wholesale shoemaker Mr Rogers of Ellbroad Street (now the site of the Broadmead Shopping Centre). Rogers suspected that he was being robbed and, when a customer called to collect a large order, Rogers waited until Allen had served him before checking the order himself. As he suspected, the customer had many more shoes than he was entitled to and Rogers accused both Allen and his customer of theft.

Both men ran off but Allen returned two days later. When Rogers told him that he was pressing charges, Allen initially expressed surprise and disbelief, denying any wrongdoing. Eventually, he admitted his guilt and both he and his wife knelt before Rogers and begged his pardon.

Convinced that he still hadn't been told the whole truth, Rogers locked Allen in a room in his home to give him some time to decide what to do next. When he went back a few hours later, Rogers surprised Allen in the act of cutting his own throat.

He grappled with Allen for the knife and Allen tried to stab him, along with another employee who rushed to assist Rogers after hearing his cries for help. Weak through loss of blood, Allen was eventually overpowered before he could inflict any more injuries.

After an inquest jury returned a verdict of *felo de se*, Allen's body was taken from the house for its ignominious internment.

11 NOVEMBER   **1891** A ferocious gale blew down a large chimney stack at the Feeder Road Saw Mills and Timber Company in St Philip's Marsh. The stack crashed through the roof, burying the men in rubble during their dinner hour, as they congregated in a boiler house, sheltering from the wind.

Of the nineteen workers, only William Ford and George Cantle sustained any injuries, Ford a broken arm and Cantle severe bruising. However, there was also one fatality, as fifty-six-year-old Benjamin Smith was crushed by falling masonry.

Ironically, Smith, who had worked at the saw mill for eight years, invariably went home for his dinner, usually returning two or three minutes before he was due to start work again. On this occasion, for the first time ever, he arrived back ten minutes early. He had only just entered the boiler house and remarked about the rough weather, when the stack fell.

1876 Fourteen-year-old John William Harris, a labourer at the Netham   12 NOVEMBER
Chemical Works at Crew's Hole, was sent to fetch some water. When he
didn't return, his colleagues went to search for him, finding him lying on the
ground dead. A post-mortem examination showed that the boy had died due
to the inhalation of noxious gases.

Harris's route to the nearest water supply took him by some large vats in
which chemicals were stored. It was shown that, just by walking past the
tanks, Harris had breathed in sufficient 'poisonous exhalations' to kill him.

At an inquest held at the Lamb Inn, Crew's Hole, later that evening by
coroner Dr E.M. Grace, the jury returned a verdict of 'accidental death',
apportioning no blame to the Chemical Works.

1909 As Winston Churchill arrived in Bristol to speak at a meeting he was   13 NOVEMBER
attacked by a suffragette wielding a whip. There had been suffragist disturbances
throughout Bristol on the previous day and the police were expecting trouble.
Hence Churchill and his wife were
surrounded by a core of detectives
and a cordon of police kept the
crowds at a safe distance. Even so,
Miss Theresa Garnett managed to
strike Churchill on the cheek with
a whip, shouting, 'Take that, you
brute.'

Miss Garnett was only one of
a number of women charged
that weekend. Effie Lawes, Helen
Pickford, Mary Allen and Vera
Wentworth were all arrested for
breaking windows by throwing
stones. Although they were fined,
all chose to serve prison terms
rather than pay. Miss Wentworth
and Miss Allen immediately
went on hunger strike and were
eventually force fed, while Miss
Garnett set fire to her cell and was
sent to the punishment block.

Winston Churchill.
(Author's
collection)

1875 Thomas Buller, John 'Jack' Richards and Henry Click from Bedminster   14 NOVEMBER
worked together as pit sawyers and, having finished work, called in at The
Forester's Arms on the Feeder Road for a quick drink. As they left the pub
half an hour later, Richards accidentally brushed past a young woman and
her husband took exception, insisting that Richards had insulted his wife.

'Ted, he did not insult me. He did not touch me,' Ann Clapp said soothingly,
but her husband Edward refused to listen and slapped Richards' face hard.
Richards did not retaliate until Clapp struck him again, when the two men
began tussling.

Richards fell to the ground and Thomas Buller went to help him up, saying, 'Come on, Jack, don't have any more bother.' Clapp immediately punched Buller in the face, knocking him over. The back of Buller's head hit the kerb hard and, although his friends rushed him to hospital, he died on the way from concussion of the brain.

The magistrates and inquest jury both reached the same verdict – that of manslaughter against Edward Clapp, who was committed for trial at the next Assizes. The death of Thomas Buller occurred on what should have been the happiest day of Clapp's life, since he had married his wife only that morning.

Nineteen-year-old Edward Clapp was tried at Gloucester on 1 April 1876 and discharged on his own recognisance to keep the peace and to appear for judgement if called upon to do so in future.

15 NOVEMBER   1854 Nine-year-old William Irwin made his third appearance at the Council House charged with stealing biscuits.

William first appeared on 13 November, when magistrates heard that witnesses had seen him taking the biscuits. He was described by the police as 'a hardened little thief', who had evaded punishment so far because few of his victims were willing to appear against him in view of his youth. William had even trained his little brother – a mere toddler – to help him steal.

Magistrates sent for William's parents and his mother came to court. A respectably dressed woman, she stated that her husband was in Staffordshire and that she had four other children. When her husband was in work, he sent her 10s a week but she had received nothing from him for the past five weeks.

Magistrates suggested sending William to a Reformatory School and asked his mother how much she could afford to pay towards his maintenance. She agreed on 2s a week and William was remanded in custody, while the possibility of sending him to Miss Carpenter's school was investigated.

On his second court appearance, William's father appeared and magistrates found that he had never been in Staffordshire and that Mrs Irwin had lied to them. William was remanded again and by 15 November the magistrates had discovered that his mother was addicted to drink and actively encouraged her children to go out stealing to support her habit. Rather than punishing his parents, the magistrates sent William to prison for one month with hard labour, also ordering him to be whipped.

16 NOVEMBER   1876 Coroner Mr Wasbrough held an inquest at the Infirmary on the death of forty-nine-year-old Richard Smith.

Two days earlier, Smith visited the cooperage on Jacob Street owned by Mr Dash in search of work. While climbing the steps leading to the workshops, he tripped and fell, immediately losing consciousness. He was taken to the Infirmary but died from his injuries the following day, when a post-mortem examination revealed that he had a large skull fracture.

After hearing from Robert Edbrook and John Rawlings, who had seen Smith fall, the jury returned a verdict of 'accidental death'.

1869 Inspector Bell of the Bristol Board of Health visited the home of Thomas and Elizabeth Mann on Thatched Cottage Lane. He found the house dirty, squalid and very sparsely furnished and, in one of the bedrooms, the couple's eighteen-month-old son lay in a box, filthy and emaciated, weighing only 13lbs.

Bell went in search of Elizabeth and found her hiding in a neighbour's house. She told Bell that she had applied for parish relief for medical help for her son, but had been turned down as her husband was in regular employment and earned more than enough money to pay for the services of a surgeon.

The couple were charged with 'wilful neglect' at the Council House. Thomas told magistrates that he left home early every morning and returned late at night, leaving the care of his four children entirely to his wife. Every week he handed over 18s to Elizabeth, who then drank the money. She showed 'not an atom of affection' for her husband and children, living a drunken and dissolute life and neglecting her home and family, beating her husband whenever he denied her the money for drink.

The magistrates determined that Elizabeth Mann was quite capable of working to support herself. They arranged a separation for the couple, ordering Thomas to take the three other children, aged three, five and seven years. He was to pay 2s 6d to support his wife and 3s 6d to St Peter's Hospital for the treatment of his youngest son. Elizabeth Mann was warned not to annoy her husband.

1872 Tailor John Kellher kicked his wife and hit her on the head with a poker. Three days later, he appeared at the Council House charged with assault.

With her three-week-old baby in her arms, Mrs Kellher told the Bench that her husband had come home drunk every night for the past five weeks. As well as kicking her and attacking her with the poker, he had even beaten her as she went into labour.

It was not the first time that Kellher had appeared before magistrates on a similar charge. Asked to explain himself, Kellher insisted, 'It was just a bit of a squabble,' adding that he hoped the magistrates would overlook it this time. The magistrates told him that he was a disgrace to the name of man and that his conduct towards his wife was brutal in the extreme, before sentencing him to three months' imprisonment with hard labour.

1898 Six spectators climbed a tree at the St George's Athletic Football Ground to get a better view of the game. As the final whistle blew, the fans in the tree began applauding. Just then, one of the men's hats blew off and, as he tried to grab it, he fell out of the tree, landing on the ground with a sickening thud.

Dr James Young MD examined the body of thirty-two-year-old Charles William Hayden from Clifton, who broke his neck in the fall and died instantly. A verdict of 'accidental death' was recorded at the subsequent inquest.

20 NOVEMBER   **1929** When a man saw Thomas John fall from top to bottom of the Avon Gorge, he rushed straight to the nearest telephone without pausing to check if John was alive or dead.

However, rather than calling for the police or an ambulance, the man dialled a national daily newspaper to try and claim the cash prize offered for the best news story of the week.

'His actions passed the limits of all decency,' the coroner commented on the conduct of the unnamed man, before recording a verdict of 'suicide while of unsound mind' on forty-three-year-old John.

21 NOVEMBER   **1895** Magistrates assembled at the Police Court to hear a case against William Francis Jackson, who was charged by the Medical Defence Union with pretending to be a doctor of medicine and a surgeon.

Since the summer of 1895, nineteen-year-old Jackson had displayed a brass plate on the door of his residence, proclaiming to be Dr Jackson, Bachelor of Medicine and Member of the Royal College of Surgeons. He had expensive notepaper printed, bearing the same claims on the letterhead and bragged about the rich and influential people he had treated and cured. His deception came to an end when splint manufacturer George William White called at his premises on 3 August, hoping for an order.

Although White got his business, no payment was ever received and, when White made further investigations, he discovered that Jackson was not qualified.

Since Jackson failed to attend the hearing, the proceedings were adjourned and a warrant was issued for his arrest. It took until September 1896 for Jackson to finally make an appearance before magistrates, when his solicitor Mr Robinson stated that Jackson had studied medicine 'to some extent' and had become convinced that he could cure sickness as well as anybody else.

An apparently penitent Jackson told the magistrates that he was extremely sorry and promised not to offend again. He was fined £5 and costs.

22 NOVEMBER   **1872** George Gordon appeared at the Council House charged with assaulting his wife, Elizabeth.

Both George and Elizabeth were swathed in bandages. Elizabeth told the magistrates that George had broken a jug over her head but George explained that, while he and his wife were 'having a few words', Elizabeth had thrown water over him, before plunging a knife into his hand between his thumb and forefinger.

The magistrates told the couple that they were both as bad as each other and dismissed the case on the grounds that Elizabeth was as much to blame as her husband.

23 NOVEMBER   **1852** The son of the proprietor of a Bristol timber yard was given a bear as a pet, which was kept in his father's yard. The task of looking after it fell to one of the boy's father's employees, Mr Fitzgerald.

As Fitzgerald was feeding the fully-grown bear it suddenly turned on him, plunging its teeth into his arm and shaking him like a terrier with a rat. The bear's teeth penetrated the flesh of Fitzgerald's upper arm and it was with some difficulty that he managed to free himself from the animal's strong jaws before collapsing in agony. He was rushed to Bristol Infirmary and the bear was subsequently shot.

Christmas Steps. (Author's collection)

1877 Fifteen-year-old John Jones of Christmas Steps appeared at the Council House charged with maliciously causing the death of a horse worth £60, the property of the Bristol Tramways Company, by thrusting a porcupine quill into its side.

24 NOVEMBER

Jones had recently been sacked by the Company and was given a porcupine quill by a boy named Albert Hazell, whose brother had just returned from Africa. Asked to urge the horse on, Jones pricked it on the flank with the quill, which broke, leaving about three inches embedded in the animal's intestines.

The magistrates called it 'a wicked, wanton offence' but decided that Jones had no malicious intent when he pricked the horse. He was sentenced to twenty-one days' imprisonment with hard labour.

1876 Albertina Wetherridge was enjoying a quiet drink with her sister and nephew in The Albert Tavern, St Philip's, when William Windows entered the bar. He sat next to Albertina and propositioned her and, when Albertina's companions protested, he went berserk. Having assaulted Albertina's nephew and pulled off her sister's bonnet, Windows seized Albertina by the shoulders and pushed her into a corner. Then, leaning forward as if to kiss her, he bit her chin right off, spitting it into the sawdust on the pub floor. Albertina promptly fainted. She was taken to hospital and her chin stitched, although the missing chunk of flesh wasn't found until some time later.

25 NOVEMBER

Windows was committed for trial at the next Bristol Assizes charged with feloniously and maliciously wounding Albertina with intent to maim and disfigure her. His defence counsel Mr Norris told the court that Windows, a master mariner, was a man of excellent character, although an accident some years earlier left him extremely susceptible to the effects of alcohol. On 25 November, he yielded to temptation and took a drink.

The jury saw this as a mitigating circumstance and found Windows guilty of the lesser offence of unlawful wounding. He was sentenced to twelve months' hard labour.

26 NOVEMBER **1946** George Alexander Maher appeared at the Bristol Assizes, accused of murdering his sixty-two-year-old wife, Alice. Judged unfit to plead, George was ordered to be detained in custody during the King's Pleasure and was sent to Broadmoor Criminal Lunatic Asylum, where he is believed to have died early the following year.

At the time of the murder, George was eighty-two years old.

Broadmoor Asylum, 1906. (Author's collection)

27 NOVEMBER **1893** Abraham George Brown of Durdham Downs called at Mr Troake's chemist's shop for Epsom salts. Assistant Arthur McCardle told him that they were on special offer – normally 1*d* a packet, Brown could have two for 1½*d*.

Brown's wife, Lydia, heated some water to dissolve the salts. Brown opened the first packet and commented that they seemed a bit 'coarse'. Lydia opened the second, noticing that the contents looked very different. 'This is what I call salts,' she told her husband but Brown had already drunk the solution. Within minutes, he rushed outside to vomit. Lydia showed her neighbour the two packets and was advised to take them back to Mr Troake.

Troake tasted the salts and said that what remained in the first packet tasted like oxalic acid. Lydia asked him for something for her husband and Troake gave her some powders but by the time Lydia got home, her husband was unconscious and neighbours had called the police and a doctor. PC William Dascombe was the first to arrive. He called a cab to take Brown to the hospital, but Brown was dead on arrival.

Surgeon Walter James Hill conducted a post-mortem examination and found that Brown had died from poisoning by oxalic acid. To confirm his diagnosis, he sent the stomach contents to analyst Mr F.W. Stoddart, who detected 21.8 grains of oxalic acid. While this was not normally a fatal dose, Stoddart believed that Brown had ingested much more, which he then vomited up.

Coroner Mr H.G. Doggett held an inquest on Brown's death, calling on Robert James Troake and McCardle to explain how the 'Purified Epsom Salts' could have become contaminated.

The Epsom salts were purchased in bulk and then placed in individual packets. Whereas Troake bought a quarter cwt of Epsom salts at a time, he never carried more than two pounds of oxalic acid, which was kept in a lidded tin. McCardle, who was very short-sighted, packed the Epsom salts and sometimes made up packets of oxalic acid, but only under Troake's direct supervision. For the two chemicals to be mixed, McCardle would have to take the oxalic acid out of the tin. There had been no complaints about any other packets of Epsom salts.

Chemist George Washington Isaacs examined Troake's entire stock of Epsom salts and oxalic acid and confirmed that the oxalic acid sold to Brown differed in appearance from that stocked by Troake, the crystals being larger and duller, as if they were dusty.

The inquest jury were certain that Brown died from poisoning by oxalic acid, sold to him by mistake by Mr Troake, but could not explain how the mistake might have occurred.

1842 Ann Shaw was arrested for begging in Lower Knowle. When her case came before magistrates, Ann told them that she was so destitute that she had been forced to pawn her shoes in order to buy bread. Since she couldn't work without shoes, she was only trying to beg enough money to redeem them so that she could look for a job. **28 NOVEMBER**

The magistrates found her guilty of being a common tramp and suggested that, if she was really so distressed, she should have gone to the Union for assistance. She was sentenced to three days' imprisonment.

1842 William Bebbington appeared at the Council House charged with deserting his wife and leaving her chargeable to the Clifton parish. **29 NOVEMBER**

Mary Bebbington told the Bench that her husband turned her out of the house so that he could live there with another woman. When she tried to go back indoors, he beat her dreadfully and threatened to cut her throat.

William denied everything but magistrate Mr Newman didn't believe him. 'I've no notion of men getting tired of their wives and turning them into the streets,' said Newman, sentencing Bebbington to one month's imprisonment and telling him that, if he refused to maintain his wife on his release, he would get a further three months.

On hearing the sentence, Mary begged the magistrates not to send William to jail, saying that she was willing to forgive him everything and imploring the Bench to leave his punishment to the Almighty. Exasperated, Newman agreed that, if Bebbington would make arrangements with the parish overseer for the maintenance of his wife, he would let him off.

30 NOVEMBER   **1843** Coroner Mr J.B. Grindon supervised an exhumation at St George's Church, Brandon Hill.

The deceased was thirty-six-year-old rope maker John Mountjoy, who died on 15 August from inflammation of the bowels. However, after his death, Mountjoy's sister-in-law communicated with the coroner, alleging that he had been poisoned.

The body was too decomposed to draw any visual conclusions, but samples were taken for analyst Mr Herapath. Although these ultimately revealed no trace of any poison, the remains of a small brass pin were found in Mountjoy's intestines.

At the subsequent inquest, the jury returned a verdict saying he had 'died from inflammation of the bowels', finally scotching the rumours that Mountjoy's wife had prematurely ended their unhappy marriage.

DECEMBER

Bristol from the Bath Road, 1829. (Author's collection)

1 DECEMBER **1866** Hawker Eliza Gingell was drinking in The Stag and Hounds on Old Market Street with her husband when Mr Llewellyn tried to light his pipe at the fire. Eliza objected to Llewellyn standing in front of her and hit him two or three times in the face.

Llewellyn sat down again but Eliza still wasn't happy, shouting that he was sitting in her husband's seat and, if he didn't get up, she would 'jab his eye out'. Llewellyn's companion, Mr Harper, took exception and told Eliza that, if she struck Llewellyn again, he would strike her. Eliza's husband promptly sprang to his wife's defence, pulling out his knife and threatening to 'rip up' Harper.

Pork butcher Joseph West tried to persuade Gingell to put his knife away but Gingell was having none of it. He and Harper began to scuffle and their fight spilled out of the bar into a passage. Llewellyn and West followed and, before long, Gingell dropped the knife, which was immediately snatched up by his wife. Before anyone could disarm her, she lashed out at West, stabbing him in the eye.

West was taken to the Infirmary, where he remained for ten days. He had a puncture wound in his eyeball and, although the wound healed, West lost the sight of one eye.

Eliza Gingell appeared at the Bristol Quarter Sessions in January 1867 charged with unlawfully and maliciously assaulting and stabbing Joseph West. The jury found her guilty but recommended mercy on the grounds that her husband initially drew the knife. She was sentenced to nine months' imprisonment with hard labour.

2 DECEMBER **1854** Richard Abrahams was brought up before magistrates on remand charged with 'assault with intent to do grievous bodily harm'.

He and Mark Vowles regularly played dominoes together, until one accused the other of cheating. The quarrel eventually blew over and seemed to have been forgotten by both men until 25 November, when Abrahams visited The Turk's Head in Bedminster and found Vowles playing dominoes with somebody else.

Soon, allegations of cheating were flying around and the argument resumed anew, culminating when Abrahams struck Vowles two sharp blows on the head with a hammer. Vowles was hospitalised for six weeks as a result of the incident and Abrahams was charged with 'illegal wounding', appearing at the Gloucestershire Assizes on 31 March 1855.

Found guilty as charged, he was sentenced to seven years' penal servitude.

3 DECEMBER **1896** Joseph Thomas McCoy of City Road was tried at the Bristol Assizes for what became known as 'the talking parrot frauds'. McCoy regularly advertised in newspapers: 'For sale – a splendid African gray parrot, by gentleman going abroad. Great bargain. Excellent talker. A sacrifice at £2, drawing room cage included. No dealers need apply.' McCoy sold several birds, most of which died and none of which ever talked.

At his trial before Mr Justice Wills, the court was told that McCoy had practised his systematic frauds for the past two years, working in Bristol,

Nottingham, Edinburgh, Dublin, Leeds and Walsall, during which time he had received at least £217 for the sale of birds. When the jury found him guilty as charged, Wills sentenced him to twelve months' hard labour, advising him to come out of prison a more honest man.

1891 Dock labourer Thomas Newland was busy at Kilby and Coleman's **4 DECEMBER** warehouse on Cheese Lane, unloading sacks of barley from a barge. The sacks were taken from the hold two at a time and lifted with a hoist. Thomas and another labourer, Charles Hazell, were responsible for guiding the sacks onto the second floor stage and unhitching them, before they were trucked away by other labourers.

As two sacks were landed, they began to overbalance. Newland grabbed one and tried to stop it falling, but the sack toppled from the stage onto the barge below with Newland still hanging on to it. Both of Newland's thighs were broken and, although he was taken to the Infirmary, he died four days later from shock and exhaustion.

At the inquest on his death held by coroner Mr H.G. Doggett, Hazell commented that he would let fifty sacks fall rather than hold onto one. The coroner agreed, saying that Newland was 'too manful'.

1877 Twenty-five-year-old Agnes Lee left her job as a domestic servant to **5 DECEMBER** live with George Webber, a married man who had deserted his wife and seven children. The couple took an apartment in Bedminster, where they lived as man and wife, together with Agnes's eleven-month-old daughter, Florence Charlotte.

Mrs Webber found out where her husband was living and turned up at their door. Only Agnes and Florence were at home and, after an animated conversation between the two women, Agnes left with the baby. Although Agnes begged her not to, Mrs Webber followed her, believing that Agnes was going to George and wanting to discover his whereabouts.

Eventually, Mrs Webber lost sight of Agnes and the baby as they headed towards the Port and Pier terminus and, although she later found Agnes's shawl on the banks of the Avon, Agnes herself seemed to have vanished into the darkness.

Florence's body was pulled from the water that evening and her mother's was found at midday on 6 December. An inquest was held at the General Draper Hotel, Hotwells, by coroner Mr Wasbrough and his jury returned a verdict that, 'Florence Lee was drowned when her mother, Agnes Lee, threw herself into the river with said baby in her arms in a sudden fit of frenzy and despair.' The jury were keen to implicate George Webber but, after much consideration, the coroner would not allow them to, since Webber was not immediately connected to the deaths. Nevertheless, Wasbrough censured Webber, calling his conduct 'cruel and reprehensible' and saying that he was morally responsible for the deaths.

1853 Coroner Mr J.B. Grindon held an inquest at The Ship and Castle, Marsh **6 DECEMBER** Street, on the death of six-month-old John Thomas Barry. About two weeks earlier, the child's mother was awakened by her son's screams. When she lit a candle and went to attend to him, she found that he had been bitten on his cheek by a rat, just under his right eye. The bite became infected and the baby died. The inquest jury returned a verdict that 'the deceased died from injuries occasioned by the bite of a rat.'

7 DECEMBER   **1874** Plasterer Henry Walters died in hospital following an accident on 27 November.

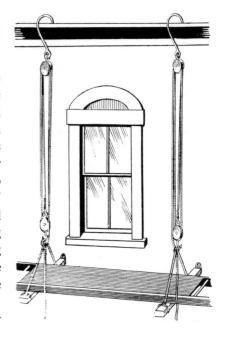

A swing scaffold. (Florida Center for Instructional Technology)

Thirty-two-year-old Henry was working on the exterior of a house on Temple Street and had constructed a swing scaffold which enabled him to raise and lower himself by means of ropes and pulleys. Working near the roof, he was driving a nail into some woodwork when the force of the hammer blow caused the scaffold on which he was standing to swing outwards away from the wall, leaving Henry suspended horizontally. Unable to support himself, he plummeted to the ground, sustaining multiple injuries.

At the subsequent inquest, the jury returned a verdict of 'accidental death'.

8 DECEMBER   **1872** One of the worst gales in living memory raged around Bristol and, at about half-past ten at night, the roof blew off a house on Trenchard Street, burying the four occupants in rubble.

Although all four were still alive when they were rescued, Thomas James Nicholas died from his injuries shortly afterwards. Thomas was suffering from consumption and, at the time of the accident, was being nursed by Mrs Charlotte Moody, who was also killed. Thomas's parents, Thomas and Mary Nicholas, survived with only minor injuries.

9 DECEMBER   **1881** Chemist Thomas Henry Stinchcombe shared his home in Bedminster with his wife and seven-year-old son, Frederick. Stinchcombe's brother, William, lodged at the house, sharing a bedroom with Frederick, who was deaf and dumb.

On 9 December, Thomas and his wife woke to a roomful of smoke and Thomas discovered that the dresser downstairs was smouldering, although at that stage there were no flames visible. Grabbing a bucket, he ran to the kitchen tap but the water pressure was so low that little more than a dribble emerged. Unable to get enough water to douse the fire, he roused his wife and the couple ran outside in their nightclothes. By that time, the fire was visible from the street and the police and fire brigade had been summoned by passers-by.

In the confusion, nobody thought about little Frederick. A few days earlier, he had lit the fire in the grate before his parents got up, so William had strict instructions to lock him in the bedroom when he left for work. Mrs Stinchcombe was taken to a nearby hotel and Thomas was later to say that he believed that Frederick went with her. When he found out that this was not the case, Thomas went back into the house but was unable to find Frederick and, when the flames were eventually extinguished, his charred remains were found by the back door.

When coroner Mr R. Briggs held an inquest on Frederick's death, he expressed disbelief that Stinchcombe had not managed to put out such a small fire, describing his actions as displaying 'a want of promptitude and energy' and adding that his search for his son was delayed and very superficial. Briggs also wondered how the rumour that Frederick was safe arose.

Mr Swann, a representative of the Water Works Company, was questioned about the lack of water pressure and maintained that the pressure was as great as the pipes would permit and should have been more than sufficient to extinguish a small blaze.

The jury returned a verdict that Frederick was accidentally burned to death, there being no evidence to show how the fire originated. They added a rider saying that, in their opinion, Thomas Stinchcombe had 'made nothing like an effort' either to subdue the fire or to search for his child.

10 DECEMBER

1812 As a coachman broke the ice on a pond in Stokes Croft so that his horses might have a drink, his attention was drawn to a number of crows circling over a nearby hedge. He went for a closer look and was faced with the bodies of three small children.

The bodies were of a newborn baby boy and girl, one of which had a length of tape wrapped around its neck. The third body was apparently that of a slightly older child, although it had been so mutilated by birds and animals that it was impossible to even determine its sex.

At an inquest held at The Swan public house, the jury returned a verdict of 'wilful murder by person or persons unknown' on all three children. Their identities – or those of their killer(s) – were never established.

11 DECEMBER

1842 Chimney sweep Robert Folks appeared at the Council House charged with assaulting Ann Guddlestone.

As Ann walked along Redcliff Street with a female companion, Folks approached and asked them to join him for refreshments in a nearby pub. The ladies accepted, but the more ale Folks drank, the bolder he grew, until he finally made an indecent proposal to Ann and tried to kiss her. When Ann indignantly turned him down, he picked up his sweep's brush and began to beat her with it.

Folks tried to tell magistrates that Ann had made advances towards him with such enthusiasm that he was obliged to use the brush in self-defence. Not surprisingly, the magistrates found Ann's account more believable and fined Folks 5s plus costs.

12 DECEMBER **1894** Surgeon Thomas Greaves Walker was called to Bedminster to visit a sick child but when he arrived, twelve-month old Mary Jane Gully had just died. Noticing bruising on the baby's face and a burn on her body, Walker made a post-mortem examination and found no signs of any organic disease, although Mary Jane appeared to have suffered from convulsions. He believed that she had died from 'cerebral apoplexy', but she was also very underweight. However, he was unable to say how far neglect had contributed to her death, as he had seen perfectly healthy children die in a similar manner from the irritations of teething.

Mary Jane was the step-daughter of Samuel Hancock, her mother being his second wife. The Hancocks explained that the bruising resulted from a fall and the burn occurred while the child was being washed. They also stated that Mary Jane had been fed regularly, although admitted to feeding her almost exclusively on bread and milk.

Unable to prove conclusively that neglect was a contributory factor in Mary Jane's death, after much deliberation, the inquest jury eventually returned a verdict of 'death from cerebral apoplexy', although they asked the coroner to severely censure her parents. The coroner was only too happy to oblige.

13 DECEMBER **1888** Herbalist Elizabeth Bannatyne (aka Davis) appeared at the Bristol Assizes charged with performing an unlawful operation, while Kate Evans was charged with being an accessory before the fact. Thirty-eight-year-old Elizabeth pleaded guilty, leaving the court to decide on the fate of her alleged accomplice, who pleaded not guilty.

The court heard that on 3 September, Ellen Porter and her sister, Martha James, went to Evans's house at Totterdown to have their fortunes told. Evans read in the cards that Mrs Porter was pregnant and told her, 'There is someone in my front room as will get you out of it.'

Ellen asked the price and was told £1. It was agreed that she would pay 10s down and 10s after the procedure, for which an appointment was made the following day. Nobody was prepared to elaborate on what went on between Elizabeth Bannatyne and Ellen Porter on 4 September, but two days later Bannatyne visited Ellen at home in St Paul's and was arrested on leaving. Searched at the police station, she was found to have 'certain instruments' and was charged with having performed an abortion on Ellen on either 4 or 6 September.

The jury found Kate Evans guilty of being an accessory before the fact and, before he passed sentence on the two women, the judge was informed that the two had allegedly committed a similar offence in Cardiff, which was being held in abeyance pending the outcome of the Bristol prosecution. Mr Justice Stephen sentenced Bannatyne to seven years' imprisonment and Evans to five.

14 DECEMBER **1868** Emma Saunders appeared at the Council House charged with stealing more than £5 from Walter Graver at a house on Church Street, Temple.

Magistrates heard that Graver was on his way to take up employment in the North and had taken lodgings at The Patriot on Temple Street to break his journey. After consuming several pints of ale, Graver agreed to go for a walk with a young man, who promised to introduce him to his sister, who would 'take good care of him'.

The 'sister', Emma Saunders, took Graver to a private house where she plied him with yet more ale. Some time later, Graver found himself lying on the street with a policeman bending over him and, when he checked his pockets, he found that all of his money had gone.

Since Graver could remember absolutely nothing prior to being woken by the constable, the magistrates determined that he was unable to provide sufficient evidence to prove the charge against Emma. Telling Graver that he had paid the penalty for drunkenness, they discharged her with a caution.

The Temple Church. (Author's collection)

1942 Police Sergeant Walter Hill was lecturing on firearms to a group of police cadets in the recreation room of the police station. At the conclusion of the lecture, one of the cadets asked a question on firing and Hill answered, using a gun to demonstrate. To his horror, the gun fired, fatally wounding nineteen-year-old Special Constable John Ansford Ratcliffe.

'I pulled the trigger three times, not realising it was loaded,' Hill later told coroner Mr A.E. Barker at the inquest in Bristol. 'Nobody was more surprised than I when it went off,' he continued.

15 DECEMBER

1826 Just before midnight on 15 December, hatter and hosier Mr Oxley of Wine Street awoke to find his bed on fire. He tried to beat out the flames with his hands, burning himself dreadfully in the process, then tried to wake his wife. Unable to rouse her, he ran downstairs and out into the street, shouting for help.

Still inside the house were Mrs Oxley, her six-week-old baby, two servants and four more children aged between four and nine years old. Mr Oxley tried to go back inside, but the moment he opened the door the draught stirred the flames and the house became a fireball.

A servant appeared at an upstairs window carrying a child and was told that a ladder was on its way. However, such was the intensity of the fire that the maid threw the child out of the window before jumping herself. People

16 DECEMBER

rushed forward to catch them but managed only to break their falls – both survived with minor injuries. Another maid climbed out of a back window into a neighbour's house carrying a second child, but Sophia Oxley and three of her children – Sophia, William and Ann – perished in the flames.

At the inquest into the four deaths, it was surmised that Mrs Oxley had woken to breast feed her baby and fallen asleep while doing so, the bedclothes accidentally making contact with her candle. The jury returned a verdict of 'accidentally burned' on all four victims.

17 DECEMBER   **1891** An inquest sat on the death of fifteen-year-old Kate Elizabeth Adams of Barton Hill. On 15 December, Kate, her fourteen-year-old sister Ellen (Nellie) and their older brother, Charles, were getting ready for work. Their mother, who was ill in bed, had packed Charles's breakfast and dinner for work but he decided to take an extra slice of bread and butter.

Nellie chided him for his greed, pointing out that there wasn't much bread left. The siblings began a good-natured argument and Charles flicked his sister in the face with a pair of stockings. Nellie picked up some scissors and threatened to throw them at him and, as Charles stooped to put on his boots, Kate screamed and slumped to the floor, bleeding from her neck.

Charles carried her upstairs to their mother. 'Oh, mother, I shall die,' Kate moaned. Meanwhile, Nellie ran into the street in hysterics and, when George Cox approached her to see what the matter was she told him, 'I threw the scissors at my sister.'

The police and a doctor were summoned, although the latter could do little more for Kate than pronounce life extinct. Nellie insisted, 'I did it. I did it,' and was arrested. She appeared before magistrates at Lawford's Gate, where she was committed to the Gloucestershire Assizes charged with her sister's manslaughter.

At her trial on 3 March 1892, Nellie initially pleaded guilty but was advised to change her plea to not guilty. The prosecution then addressed the jury on the difficulty of differentiating between death by misadventure and manslaughter, adding that, in this case, it could be argued that Kate's death was purely accidental. Accordingly, the prosecution did not intend to offer any evidence. The judge instructed the jury to acquit Nellie and she was discharged.

18 DECEMBER   **1855** Silversmith Mr Warry shared his home in St Augustine's Parade with his elderly housekeeper, Mary Brown. Just before midnight on 17 December, Warry retired to his bedroom above the shop and Miss Brown to her room on the second floor. About fifteen minutes later, Warry was woken by his dog barking and, when he went to see what was upsetting it, he found the building on fire.

Unable to get downstairs, he rang the bell to alert Miss Brown of the danger. She was also trapped in her room and shouted that she was going to jump out of the window, but Warry urged her to wait. He managed to climb out of his own bedroom window onto an adjacent roof and hollered 'Fire' as loudly as he could. Within minutes, his shouts brought several people to the scene, including PC William Henry Smith. A ladder was fetched, but proved too short to reach the second floor window.

A man in sailor's uniform shinned up onto the roof, dragging the ladder behind him and climbed to the window where Miss Brown was desperately waiting to be rescued. With almost superhuman strength, the sailor heaved the rather portly woman onto his back and began to descend the ladder. For a moment, it looked as though the sailor had saved the day, until Miss Brown loosened her hold around his neck and fell to the street below, landing on PC Smith and severely injuring him.

Miss Brown and Smith were taken to the Infirmary, where Smith was treated for injuries to his side and leg, eventually making a full recovery. Miss Brown was not so fortunate and died few days later.

At the inquest held by coroner Mr H. Wasbrough, nobody could offer any explanation for the fire, nor could they suggest why Mary Brown let go of her rescuer, apart from theorising that she may have become confused by the smoke or been unable to bear her own body weight. The inquest jury returned a verdict that she died from compound fractures of both legs, accidentally caused by falling from a ladder. The heroic sailor was never identified.

1839 William Harlow was arrested for stealing a pair of stockings and a handkerchief from a shop on Mary-Le-Port Street. However, the shop owner took pity on the sixteen-year-old thief with a wooden leg and refused to prosecute, leaving the police no alternative but to release him.

19 DECEMBER

Mary-Le-Port Street, 1905. (Author's collection)

The following evening, Harlow was seen by a policeman trying the doors of a premises on Broad Street. The constable followed him along Small Street and into The Exchange, where he was seen trying yet more doors before attempting to break into a tobacconist's shop. When arrested, he was carrying a chisel, file and bradawls.

At the Council House on 21 December, Harlow was described as 'a most incorrigible boy'. He was once apprenticed to a Mr Bussey but, determined not to work, he wounded his own leg then tied a penny to the wound. The resulting infection led to the amputation of his leg and, when Bussey kindly kept him on, Harlow made a similar attempt on the other leg. When this was discovered, Harlow placed some sugar of lead in the tea kettle, which was fortunately noticed before the Bussey family were all poisoned.

Magistrates were baffled at how best to reclaim such a boy, but started by sentencing him to three months' imprisonment with hard labour.

20 DECEMBER **1881** Just before six o'clock in the evening, the chimney of a house on Narrow Plain, St Philip's blew down. The weight of the masonry caused the roof to fall in, which in turn caused the internal floors to give way, plummeting all fifteen occupants into the cellar, where they were buried in rubble.

Hearing the tremendous crash, neighbours rushed to try and help. Realising the dangerous condition of the house, some of the men barred the door to prevent the crowd from entering. Only six men were allowed into the cellar to begin digging and gradually, survivors were helped out of the house and sheltered in The Spread Eagle pub.

Amazingly, there were only two fatalities – siblings John and Annie Bryan, aged five and three years respectively. Neither child had any injuries but both were suffocated by dust.

Coroner Mr H.S. Wasbrough held an inquest, at which the jury returned verdicts of 'accidental death'. It was announced that a public subscription had been opened to help the families who had lost all they possessed in the disaster and Wasbrough immediately donated £2.

21 DECEMBER **1909** Charles E. Gulliver appeared at the Police Court charged with the manslaughter of his friend, Joseph Charles Hatton.

At a party at Gulliver's home, Hatton was acting in an 'ungentlemanly manner' towards Mrs Gulliver. The host took offence and the two fought, tumbling downstairs in the process. Fortunately, neither appeared to have been hurt by the fall, after which Gulliver insisted that Hatton leave his house immediately.

Thirty-four-year-old Hatton didn't arrive home for four hours and, the next morning, was found dead in bed, leading to a charge of manslaughter against his friend.

Gulliver told magistrates that he never thought for one moment that he had injured Hatton. He had acted in the heat of passion, intending to give Hatton 'a good thrashing', which he believed he was entitled to do under the circumstances. His defence counsel stated that his client was only doing what any Englishman would, in turning out of his house a man who had insulted his wife. If a man was not allowed to protect his wife's honour, it would be a disgrace.

The magistrates could find no evidence that Gulliver had used excessive violence in dealing with Hatton and discharged him without penalty.

22 DECEMBER **1879** Frederick William Fowler was working with his brother, Charles, at a quarry. When Frederick decided to go home, Charles asked him to take his muzzle-loaded gun with him, warning him several times not to 'mess with it' as it was loaded.

Sixteen-year-old Frederick got to the house he shared with his brother and Annie Edwards in Mangotsfield. He began playing with the gun and it went off. The shot passed through Annie's mouth and exited through the back of her neck, killing her instantly.

Fowler ran to the local police house and told PC Phayre that Annie had accidentally shot herself, having moved the gun, which was leaning against the table. His explanation was accepted, but shortly before the inquest the following day Fowler burst into tears and told Phayre, 'Policeman, it is a bad job for me.' He confessed that he had shot Annie, the gun having gone off while he was fiddling with the trigger.

Fowler was charged with Annie's manslaughter and appeared at the Bristol Assizes on 12 February 1880. By that time, the gun had been tested and found to have an exceptionally light trigger. On hearing this, Judge Baron Pollock stopped the case and instructed the jury to acquit Fowler.

Note: The contemporary newspapers variously describe Annie Edwards as Charles's wife, partner, paramour and landlady. Since Charles was only seventeen years old, the latter seems most likely.

1883 Priscilla Jenkins lived at Penn Street, St Paul's, as did William and Sarah Priddes and Mrs Murphy. Hearing a commotion outside their house, Priscilla saw Mrs Murphy, an epileptic, lying in the street in the throes of a fit. She was being supported by William Priddes and Priscilla rushed to help him. **23 DECEMBER**

With the assistance of another neighbour, Priscilla and William carried Mrs Murphy upstairs to her room. Later that day, Sarah Priddes noticed her husband rubbing his arm and asked if he had hurt it. William said that he had just scratched himself, but on Christmas Day he asked Sarah for some hot water to bathe his arm.

Sarah bathed it for him and, noticing that it looked slightly swollen, put a poultice on it. During that night, William suffered a fit. Although Sarah begged him to go to the Infirmary, he refused and by the next morning his arm was so badly swollen and inflamed that she took him there in spite of his protests.

Forty-seven-year-old William died that evening and surgeon Mr Penny found that he had blood poisoning, arising from a human bite on his upper arm.

Coroner Mr H.S. Wasbrough held an inquest, at which Priscilla Jenkins recalled seeing William suddenly start as he was carrying Mrs Murphy upstairs, as if she had bitten or scratched him. The jury returned a verdict that 'death was due to blood poisoning resulting from an accidental bite inflicted by a woman whilst in a fit.'

1888 Unbeknown to his parents, fourteen-year-old George Parsons Pritchard bought a revolver. Along with James Pomeroy Milford, he locked them both in the loft of a brewery, with the intention of firing a few practice shots. **24 DECEMBER**

The boys fixed up a cigarette box for a target and were about to start shooting when George's companion heard noises in the street outside and suggested that they wait until the coast was clear. As George amused himself by looking into one of the revolver's chambers, it suddenly went off, shooting him through one eye and killing him instantly.

Coroner Mr Wasbrough held an inquest and the jury returned a verdict of 'accidental death', adding a rider condemning the shopkeeper who sold the gun to Pritchard. Wasbrough agreed, saying that it seemed reprehensible that a schoolboy should be able to go into a shop and purchase a deadly weapon without any questions being asked.

25 DECEMBER   **1882** Thirty-eight-year-old George Drewett was suddenly taken ill, dying within hours. The former manager of a tannery in Bedminster had a new job in Plymouth and returned to Bristol to arrange for his family to join him there. A post-mortem examination showed that he died from acute meningitis.

On 5 March, Drewett had tried to commit suicide by shooting himself in the head and the bullet was so deeply embedded in his brain that it was impossible to remove. Even so, he apparently made a complete recovery and showed no ill effects from the shooting. Charged with 'attempted suicide', he assured magistrates that he no longer had any wish to kill himself and was discharged.

Doctors thought it unlikely that the shooting was in any way connected to the meningitis that ultimately killed Drewett.

26 DECEMBER   **1876** William Collings was very drunk when went to The Pilgrim Inn on Pennywell Road and landlord William Pennington refused to serve him. Mrs Pennington persuaded Collings to leave the premises but Collings promptly put his fist through the plate glass door.

Pennington rushed outside, finding Collings about to smash the second door. What happened next is a matter of conjecture, but the fracas terminated in Collings being taken to the Infirmary, where he died from a fractured skull.

The inquest on Collings's death recorded a verdict of manslaughter against William Pennington, who was brought before a special sitting of magistrates at the Council House on 19 January 1877. The magistrates heard from several witnesses, some of whom testified to seeing Pennington punch Collings in the face, knocking him down. Others stated that Pennington had merely pushed Collings away from the door which, due to his drunken state, had caused Collings to fall over.

Surgeon James Greig Smith told the magistrates that the fracture was too severe to have been caused by an ordinary fall, but might have resulted from the deceased being pushed or knocked down. Pennington admitted to pushing Collings but swore that he hadn't hit him.

Magistrates expressed the opinion that no jury would convict Pennington of manslaughter but told him that he would have to appear at the Assizes on the coroner's warrant. They were proved wrong, since Pennington was found guilty. This astonished Mr Justice Hawkins, who promptly discharged him on his own recognisance to keep the peace.

27 DECEMBER   **1921** Rosina Ackerman separated from her husband and moved back to her mother's house on Catherine Street, Barton Hill, with a new boyfriend, Francis 'Frank' Hepper. None of Rosina's family approved of the relationship and Hepper was told in no uncertain terms that he was not a welcome guest and must move out.

In the early hours of the morning, Rosina and Hepper retired to bed, apparently reconciled after quarrelling earlier that day. Suddenly, Rosina's family were awakened by the sound of shots and thirty-five-year-old Rosina staggered out of the room she shared with Frank into her brother's room, where she died in his arms from gunshot wounds to her head. Hepper was later found dead on the floor of their bedroom.

The murder and suicide took place in the presence of Rosina's eight-year-old son.

1869 Coroner Mr H.S. Wasbrough opened an inquest at The Griffin Inn on   28 DECEMBER
the deaths of eighteen people, who were crushed or suffocated at the new
Theatre Royal on 27 December.

Although the theatre doors didn't open until seven o'clock in the evening,
people formed long queues outside to see the Christmas pantomime,
Robinson Crusoe. Some arrived as early as four o'clock in the afternoon and
by six o'clock, the steep, narrow gangway leading to the pit and gallery
was crammed with hundreds of people.

As the doors opened and the crowd stampeded into the theatre, a
woman fell over in the doorway. Several people tripped over her, while
those behind continued to push for entrance. Unaware that there was
an obstruction ahead, people scrambled over the fallen people in their
desperation to secure seats for the performance. Eventually, the police
resorted to shouting 'Fire!' to try and clear the crowds.

By the time anyone could reach them, twenty-three theatregoers were
unconscious and fourteen at the very bottom of the pile were dead. Fearful of
the consequences of cancelling the performance, the theatre manager had the six
women, four men and four children carried to the refreshment room, while the
remaining injured people were rushed to the Infirmary, where a further four died.

The inquest jury recorded verdicts of 'accidental death' on Mary Helen
Sherwood (16), Thomas Marchant (19), Eliza Lucas (18), Patrick Donovan
(15), Alfred Kew (18), Thomas Pearson (21), Samuel Hill (12), John Davis
(14), Henry Charles Vining, George Potter (11), Ellen Jones (15), Sarah Ann
Bilby (18), Elizabeth Hall (52), Catherine Brewer (16), Joseph Smith (15) ,
Charles Pring (18), William Samuel Alden (21) and Charles Talbot.

1832 Coroner Mr J.B. Grindon held an inquest at The Dolphin tavern on   29 DECEMBER
Marlborough Street on the mysterious death of 'Nelly Pool'.

On 22 December, William Hale went to milk his cows near Keynsham
and found an old woman lying face down under the hedge, covered in
blood. Four large stones and a clasp knife lay on the ground nearby, but
Hale could see no signs of blood on any of them. He spoke to the woman
several times before she responded, saying only that she was 'very bad'.
The kindly farmer went to fetch some tea and bread and butter and she
took it gratefully but vomited after the first few mouthfuls.

Surgeon George Keddell found that the woman's head was completely
staved in, like a broken eggshell. Although he saw no hope of saving her
life, he arranged for her to be transported to the Infirmary, where chief
surgeon Richard Smith found two skull fractures. Like Keddell, Smith
believed that the woman's condition was hopeless.

Injured though she was, she could still talk. In her strong Irish accent
she said that she was Nelly Pool and had been in Bristol only nine weeks,
having left her husband in Ireland. She insisted that she had been robbed
of three half-sovereigns and three shillings and, when asked who ill-used

her, she gave the name 'Jem Brooks'. She was unable to offer any more information on Brooks, apart from saying that he was 'always very bad'.

Smith summoned Irish nurse Eliza Daniel to Nelly's bedside but Nelly revealed little more in her native tongue, although she mentioned a Mr Jones near 'Kilbrook' who had been very kind to her and told Eliza that she had worked in the fields picking weeds. Since she was convinced that she would survive her injuries, there was little point in taking a deposition, but a couple of days later she lapsed into a coma and died.

In spite of extensive enquiries, police found no further information about Nelly Pool, 'Jem Brooks' or Mr Jones. Thus her murder – if it was indeed a murder – remains unsolved.

30 DECEMBER   1889 Coroner Mr H.G. Doggett held an inquest on the death of seventeen-month-old Margaret Cooper.

At six o'clock on Christmas Eve, Margaret's father, William, left their lodgings on Trenchard Street to go to work. His wife was also out working, although he was expecting her to return very shortly, hence he left Margaret and her three-year-old sister Ada Florence in bed.

Mrs Cooper's return from work was delayed and, when she got in she found the room full of smoke and her daughters lying badly burned on the floor. Although the girls were taken to the Infirmary, both sadly died.

The inquest jury heard that, although burned on her legs and arms, Margaret had actually died from bronchitis, an existing illness worsened by smoke inhalation. Ada survived for another week, before dying from 'exhaustion' as a result of her burns.

The juries at the two inquests returned verdicts of 'death from bronchitis intensified by burns', on Margaret and 'accidental death' on Ada. At both inquests, some members of the jury wanted charges of neglect to be brought against William Cooper. However, the coroner was under the impression that the parents had suffered enough.

Tragically, the Coopers' landlord and landlady were in the room below and saw no signs of anything unusual. Robert and Mary Powell stated that they would have gladly watched the children in their parents' absence, had they been asked.

31 DECEMBER   1846 An inquest was held at The Woolpack, Eugene Street, on the death of thirty-four-year-old Mary Old.

Mary lived with chain maker James Smith and their two-year-old daughter and had been ill for many months. Smith earned 16s a week, but spent most of his wages on alcohol. In order to feed her child, Mary frequently went without.

As Mary grew weaker, her concerned neighbours applied to the relieving officer on her behalf. He visited and offered to take her into the Poor House but Smith was against the idea and, although the relieving officer twice sent people to collect her, Smith refused to let her go, telling her that she would soon be better. The relieving officer then sent arrowroot and brandy for Mary, but it was too late to save her and she died from starvation. The inquest jury returned a verdict of 'died for want of sustenance' and, since they did not directly implicate Smith in Mary's death, he faced no charges.

INDEX